THE ROUGH GUIDE

GREEK
PHRASEBOOK

D0012420

Compiled by
LEXUS

**ROUGH
GUIDES**

www.roughguides.com

Credits

Greek Phrasebook

Text: Compiled by Lexus with
Costas Panayotakis
Lexus series editor: Sally Davies
Layout: Pradeep Thapliyal
Pictures: Rhiannon Furbear

Rough Guides Reference

Director: Andrew Lockett
Editors: Kate Berens, Tom Cabot,
Tracy Hopkins, Matthew Milton,
Joe Staines

Publishing information

First edition published in 1995.
This updated edition published September 2011 by
Rough Guides Ltd, 80 Strand, London, WC2R 0RL
Email: mail@roughguides.com

Distributed by the Penguin Group:
Penguin Books Ltd, 80 Strand, London, WC2R 0RL
Penguin Group (USA), 375 Hudson Street, NY 10014, USA
Penguin Group (Australia), 250 Camberwell Road, Camberwell,
Victoria 3124, Australia
Penguin Group (New Zealand), Cnr Rosedale and Airborne Roads,
Albany, Auckland, New Zealand

Rough Guides is represented in Canada by Tourmaline Editions Inc.,
662 King Street West, Suite 304, Toronto, Ontario, M5V 1M7

Printed in Singapore by Toppan Security Printing Pte. Ltd.

The publishers and author have done their best to ensure the accuracy and
currency of all information in *The Rough Guide Greek Phrasebook*; however,
they can accept no responsibility for any loss or inconvenience sustained by
any reader as a result of its information or advice.

240 pages

A catalogue record for this book is available from the British Library.

978-1-84836-741-8

1 3 5 7 9 8 6 4 2

CONTENTS

How to use this book

The **Rough Guide Greek Phrasebook** is a highly practical introduction to the contemporary language. It gets straight to the point in every situation you might encounter: in bars and shops, on trains and buses, in hotels and banks, on holiday or on business. Laid out in clear A–Z style with easy-to-find, colour-coded sections, it uses key words to take you directly to the phrase you need – so if you want some help booking a room, just look up "room" in the dictionary section.

The phrasebook starts off with **Basics**, where we list some essential phrases, including words for numbers, dates and telling the time, and give guidance on pronunciation, along with a short section on the different regional accents you might come across. Then, to get you started in two-way communication, the **Scenarios** section offers dialogues in key situations such as renting a car, asking directions or booking a taxi, and includes words and phrases for when something goes wrong, from getting a flat tyre or asking to move apartments to more serious emergencies. You can listen to these and download them for free from www.roughguides.com/phrasebooks for use on your computer, MP3 player or smartphone.

Forming the main part of the guide is a double dictionary, first **English–Greek**, which gives you the essential words you'll need written in an easy-to-read form in the Roman alphabet. Then, in the **Greek–English** dictionary, we've given not just the phrases you'll likely to hear (starting with a selection of slang and colloquialisms) but also many of the signs, labels and instructions you'll come across in print or in public places, all of which are accompanied by

a phonetic transliteration in the Roman alphabet. Scattered throughout the sections are travel tips direct from the authors of the Rough Guides guidebook series.

Finally, there's an extensive **Menu reader**. Consisting of separate food and drink sections, each starting with a list of essential terms, it's indispensable whether you're eating out, stopping for a quick drink or looking around a local food market.

Καλό ταξίδι!
kalo taxithi!
Have a good trip!

BASICS

Pronunciation

In this phrasebook, Greek words have been transliterated into romanized form (see the alphabet opposite) so that they can be read as though they were English, bearing in mind the notes on pronunciation given below:

a	as in cat
e	as in get
eh	represents e at end of a word; should always be pronounced as in get
g	as in goat
i	as in ski
kh	like the ch in the Scottish way of saying loch
o	as in hot
th	as in then
TH	as in theme

Letters given in bold type indicate the part of the word to be stressed. When two vowels (such as 'ea') are next to each other in the pronunciation, both should be pronounced, as for example in the word amfiTHeatro (**amphitheatre**).

Notes

In Greek, there are five words for **'the'**: o o, η i and το to for singular nouns, and οι i and τα ta for plural nouns. For example, **'the street'** ο δρόμος o thromos; **'the mountains'** τα βουνά ta voona. The correct Greek word for 'the' has been given throughout the dictionary sections, so you don't need to worry about which one to use.

One abbreviation is used in this book: *adj* for adjective.

The Greek alphabet

Set out below are the Greek alphabet, the names of the Greek letters and the system of transliteration used in this book:

A, α	alfa	a as in cat
B, β	vita	v as in vet
Γ, γ	gama	y as in yes, except before consonants and before a or o, when it's a throaty version of the g in gap
Δ, δ	thelta	th as in then
E, ε	epsilon	e as in get
Z, ζ	zita	z
H, η	ita	i as in ski
Θ, θ	thita	as the th in theme (represented by TH)
I, ι	yota	i as in bit
K, κ	kapa	k
Λ, λ	lamtha	l
M, μ	mi	m
N, ν	ni	n
Ξ, ξ	ksi	x
O, o	omikron	o as in hot
Π, π	pi	p
P, ρ	ro	r
Σ, σ, ς	sigma	s (the third version of this letter is only used at the end of a word in lower case)
T, τ	taf	t
Υ, υ	ipsilon	long i, indistinguishable from ita
Φ, φ	fi	f
X, χ	khi	h as in hat or harsh ch in the Scottish word loch (represented by kh)
Ψ, ψ	psi	ps as in lips
Ω, ω	omega	o as in hot, indistinguishable from omikron

Combinations and diphthongs

AI, αι	e as in get
AΥ, αυ	av or af depending on following consonant
EI, ει	long i, exactly like ita
OI, οι	long i, exactly like ita
EΥ, ευ	ev or ef depending on following consonant
OΥ, ου	oo as in moon
ΓΓ, γγ	ng as in angle
ΓΚ, γκ	g as in goat at the beginning of a word; ng in the middle
ΜΠ, μπ	b as in bar and sometimes mb as in embassy in the middle of a word
ΝΤ, ντ	d at the beginning of a word and sometimes nd as in end in the middle
ΤΣ, τσ	ts as in hits

Basic phrases

yes ναί neh

no όχι okhi

OK εντάξει endaxi

hello χαίρετε khereteh

good morning
καλημέρα kalimera

good evening
καλησπέρα kalispera

good night
καληνύχτα kalinikhta

goodbye αντίο andio

hi γειά ya

see you γειά, θα τα πούμε
ya, THα ta poomeh

please παρακαλώ parakalo

thank you ευχαριστώ
efkharisto

yes, please ναί, παρακαλώ
neh, parakalo

no thank you όχι, ευχαριστώ
okhi, efkharisto

excuse me, please (to attract
attention, to get past someone)
συγγνώμη, παρακαλώ
signomi, parakalo

sorry! συγγνώμη! signomi!

pardon? (sorry?, what did you say?)
ορίστε? oristeh?

what did you say?
πώς είπατε; pos ipateh?

I don't understand
δεν καταλαβαίνω
then katalaveno

do you speak English?
μιλάτε Αγγλικά;
milateh Anglika?

I don't speak Greek
δεν μιλάω Ελληνικά
then milao Elinika

please speak more slowly
παρακαλώ, μιλάτε πιό αργά;
parakalo, milateh pio arga?

could you repeat that? το
ξαναλέτε αυτό, σας παρακαλώ;
to xanaleteh afto, sas parakalo?

please write it down
μου το γράφετε, παρακαλώ;
moo to grafeteh, parakalo?

I would like...
θα ήθελα... THα iTHela...

can I have...?
μπορώ να έχω...;
boro na ekho...?

how much is it?
πόσο κάνει; poso kani?

cheers! εις υγείαν! is iyian!

where is/are the...?
πού είναι...; poo ineh...?

Dates

To say the date, take the ordinary number, then the form of the month shown below:

today is the 27th of February
σήμερα είναι εικοσιεφτά Φεβρουαρίου simera ineh ikosi-efta Fevroo-arioo

Exceptions are 'the first', 'the third' and 'the fourth' as well as 'the thirteenth, fourteenth, twenty-first, twenty-third, twenty-fourth and thirty-first'.

tomorrow is the 1st of July
αύριο είναι πρώτη Ιουλίου avrio ineh proti looli-oo

You can also say:

tomorrow is the 1st of July
αύριο είναι μία Ιουλίου avrio ineh mia looli-oo

yesterday was the 3rd/4th of December χθες ήταν τρεις/ τέσσερις Δεκεμβρίου khThes itan tris /teseris Thekemvrioo

the 13th/14th of December δεκατρείς/δεκατέσσερις Δεκεμβρίου thekatris/ thekateseris Thekemvrioo

the 23rd/31st of July είκοσι τρεις/τριάντα μία Ιουλίου ikosi tris/trianda mia looli-oo

Another form for 'the first' is:

1st of April Πρωταπριλιά Protaprilia

1st of May Πρωτομαγιά Protomaya

Instead of saying 'nineteen ninety-five' you literally say 'one thousand, nine hundred, ninety five':

χίλια ενιακόσια ενενήντα πέντε khilia eniakosia eneninda pendeh

Days

Monday i Theftera
Tuesday i Triti
Wednesday i Tetarti
Thursday i Pempti
Friday i Paraskevi
Saturday to Savato
Sunday i Kiriaki

Months

January o I-anooarios
February o Fevrooarios
March o Martios
April o Aprilios
May o Ma-ios
June o I-oonios
July o I-oolios
August o AvGoostos
September o Septemvrios
October o Oktovrios
November o No-emvrios
December o Thekemvrios

Time

what time is it? τί ώρα είναι;
ti ora ineh?

one o'clock μία η ώρα mia i ora

two o'clock δύο η ώρα thio i ora

it's one o'clock είναι μία η ώρα
ineh mia i ora

it's two o'clock είναι δύο η ώρα
ineh thio i ora

it's ten o'clock είναι δέκα η ώρα
ineh theka i ora

five past one μία και πέντε
mia keh pendeh

ten past two δύο και δέκα
thio keh theka

quarter past one μία και
τέταρτο mia keh tetarto

quarter past two δύο και
τέταρτο thio keh tetarto

twenty past ten δέκα και είκοσι
theka keh ikosi

half past ten δέκα και μισή
theka keh misi

twenty to ten δέκα παρά είκοσι
theka para ikosi

quarter to two δύο παρά
τέταρτο thio para tetarto

at half past four στις τέσσερις
και μισή stis teseris keh misi

at eight o'clock στις οκτώ
stis okto

14.00 δεκατέσσερις theka-teseris

17.30 δεκαεφτά και τριάντα
theka-efta keh trianda

2am δύο η ώρα το βράδυ
thio i ora to vrathi

2pm δύο η ώρα το μεσημέρι
thio i ora to mesimeri

6am έξι η ώρα το πρωί
exi i ora to pro-i

6pm έξι η ώρα το απόγευμα
exi i ora to apoyevma

noon το μεσημέρι to mesimeri

midnight τα μεσάνυχτα
ta mesanikhta

an hour μία ώρα mia ora

a minute ένα λεπτό ena lepto

one minute ένα λεπτό ena lepto

two minutes δύο λεπτά thio lepta

a second το δευτερόλεπτο
to thefterolepto

a quarter of an hour
ένα τέταρτο ena tetarto

half an hour μισή ώρα misi ora

three quarters of an hour
τρία τέταρτα της ώρας
tria tetarta tis oras

Numbers

0 μηδέν mithen

1 ένα ena

2 δύο thio

3 τρία tria

4 τέσσερα tesera

5 πέντε pendeh

6 έξι exi

7 επτά epta

8 οχτώ okhto
9 εννιά enia
10 δέκα theka
11 έντεκα endeka
12 δώδεκα thotheka
13 δεκατρία theka-tria
14 δεκατέσσερα theka-tesera
15 δεκαπέντε theka-pendeh
16 δεκαέξι theka-exi
17 δεκαεπτά theka-epta
18 δεκαοχτώ theka-okhto
19 δεκαεννιά theka-enia
20 είκοσι ikosi
21 είκοσι ένα ikosi ena
22 εικοσι δύο ikosi thio
30 τριάντα trianda
31 τριαντα ένα trianda ena
40 σαράντα saranda
50 πενήντα peninda
60 εξήντα exinda
70 εβδομήντα evthominda
80 ογδόντα ogthonda
90 ενενήντα eneninda
100 εκατό ekato
110 εκατό δέκα ekato theka
200 διακόσια thiakosia

300 τριακόσια triakosia
1,000 χίλια khilia
2,000 δύο χιλιάδες thio khiliathes
5,000 πέντε χιλιάδες
pendeh khiliathes
10,000 δέκα χιλιάδες
theka khiliathes
20,000 είκοσι χιλιάδες
ikosi khiliathes
50,000 πενήντα χιλιάδες
peninda khiliathes
100,000 εκατό χιλιάδες
ekato khiliathes
1,000,000 ένα εκατομμύριο
ena ekatomirio

Ordinals

1st πρώτος protos
2nd δεύτερος thefteros
3rd τρίτος tritos
4th τέταρτος tetartos
5th πέμπτος pemptos
6th έκτος ektos
7th έβδομος evthomos
8th όγδοος ogtho-os
9th ένατος enatos
10th δέκατος thekatos

Regional accents

Greek is the language you will hear spoken wherever you travel throughout Greece. Only a small number of schools in Thrace teach both the Greek and Turkish languages, since Turkish is spoken by the Muslim minority of Turks, Pomaks and Romanies here.

Modern Greek has an abundance of instantly identifiable local accents, most notably in Northern Greece (around Macedonia and Thrace), Crete and the Peloponnese; and in the Ionian islands you will hear a marked Italianate sing-song intonation.

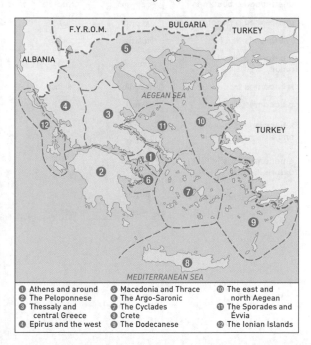

❶ Athens and around	❺ Macedonia and Thrace	❿ The east and
❷ The Peloponnese	❻ The Argo-Saronic	north Aegean
❸ Thessaly and	❼ The Cyclades	⓫ The Sporades and
central Greece	❽ Crete	Évvia
❹ Epirus and the west	❾ The Dodecanese	⓬ The Ionian Islands

Although you may have some difficulty understanding people in isolated villages or on remote islands, the effect of the centralized Greek education system, and of films and TV, has been to decrease the number of dialect characteristics. If you use the pronunciation system given in this book, you won't have any difficulties making yourself understood.

		Standard Greek	
omission of final vowel	χέρι	kheri	
unstressed e becomes i	φεγγάρι	fengari	
unstressed o becomes oo	κορίτσι	korítsi	
l before i is like l-y	πολιτικά	politika	
n before i is like the 'ni' in onion	πυκνή	pikni	
k becomes ts	κεφάλι	kefali	
g becomes dz	γιατί	yati	
k becomes ch before i and e	και	ke	
	κιλό	kilo	
g becomes j (as in joke) before i and e	ανάγκη	anangi	
	εγκαίρως	engeros	
kh becomes sh before i and e	μαχαίρι	makheri	
	όχι	okhi	

The table below contains examples of the key deviations from standard Greek that can be found in regional accents throughout the country:

Northern Greece	Peloponnese	Crete
kher	kheri	kheri
figar	fengari	fengari
kooritsi	koritsi	koritsi
politika	pol-yitika	politika
pikni	pik-nyi	pikni
kefali	tsefali	kefali
yati	yati	dzati
ke	ke	che
kilo	kilo	chilo
anangi	anangi	ananji
engeros	engeros	enjeros
makheri	makheri	masheri
okhi	okhi	oshi

SCENARIOS

Download these scenarios as MP3s from
www.roughguides.com/phrasebooks

1. Accommodation

▶ Is there an inexpensive hotel you can recommend?
Υπάρχει κάποιο φτηνό ξενοδοχείο που μπορείτε να μου συστήσετε;
iparkhi kapio ftino xenothokhio poo boriteh na moo sistiseteh?

▶▶ I'm sorry, they all seem to be fully booked.
Λυπάμαι, φαίνεται ότι είναι όλα κλεισμένα.
lipameh, feneteh oti ineh ola klismena.

▶ Can you give me the name of a good middle-range hotel?
Μπορείτε να μου πείτε το όνομα ενός ξενοδοχείου μεσαίας κατηγορίας;
boriteh na moo piteh to onoma enos xenothokhioo meseas katigorias?

▶▶ Let me have a look; do you want to be in the centre?
Δώστε μου να δω: θέλετε να είστε στο κέντρο της πόλης;
thosteh moo na tho; THeleteh na isteh sto kendro tis polis?

▶ If possible.
Αν είναι δυνατό.
an ineh thinato

▶▶ Do you mind being a little way out of town?
Θα σας πείραζε να είστε λίγο έξω από την πόλη;
THa sas pirazeh na isteh ligo exo apo tin poli?

▶ Not too far out.
Όχι πολύ μακριά.
okhi poli makria

▶ Where is it on the map?
Πού είναι στον χάρτη;
poo ineh ston kharti?

▶ Can you write the name and address down?
Μπορείτε να μου γράψετε το όνομα και τη διεύθυνση;
boriteh na moo grapseteh to onoma keh ti di-efтHinsi?

▶ I'm looking for a room in a private house.
Ψάχνω για ένα δωμάτιο σε πανσιόν.
psakhno ya ena thomatio seh pansion

2. Banks

bank account	ο τραπεζικός	o trapezikos
	λογαριασμός	logariasmos
to change money	αλλάζω χρήματα	alazo khrimata
cheque	μιά επιταγή	mia epitayi
to deposit	κάνω κατάθεση	kano kataтнesi
euro	ένα ευρώ	ena evro
pin number	ο κωδικός	o kothikos
pound	η λίρα Αγγλίας	i lira anglias
to withdraw	κάνω ανάληψη	kano analipsi

▶ Can you change this into euros?
Μπορείτε να αλλάξετε αυτά σε ευρώ;
boriteh na alaxeteh afta seh evro?

▶▶ How would you like the money?
Πώς θέλετε τα χρήματα;
pos тнeleteh ta khrimata?

▶ Small notes.
Χαρτονομίσματα μικρής αξίας.
khartonomismata mikris axias

▶ Big notes.
Χαρτονομίσματα μεγάλης αξίας.
khartonomismata megalis axias

▶ Do you have information in English about opening an account?
Έχετε πληροφορίες στα Αγγλικά για να ανοίξω έναν λογαριασμό;
ekheteh plirofories sta Anglika ya na anixo enan logariasmo?

▶▶ Yes, what sort of account do you want?
Ναι, τί είδος λογαριασμού θέλετε;
neh, ti ithos logariasmoo тнeleteh?

▶ I'd like a current account.
Θα ήθελα έναν τρέχοντα λογαριασμό.
тнa iтнela enan trekhonda logariasmo

▶▶ Your passport, please.
Το διαβατήριό σας, παρακαλώ.
to thiavatirio sas, parakalo

▶ Can I use this card to draw some cash?
Μπορώ να κάνω ανάληψη μετρητών με αυτή την κάρτα;
boro na kano analipsi metriton me afti tin karta?

▶▶ You have to go to the cashier's desk.
Πρέπει να πάτε στο ταμείο.
prepi na pateh sto tamio

▶ I want to transfer this to my account at National Bank.
Θέλω να μεταφέρω αυτά στον λογαριασμό μου στην Εθνική Τράπεζα.
THelo na metafero afta ston logariasmo moo stin ETHniki Trapeza

▶▶ OK, but we'll have to charge you for the phonecall.
Εντάξει, αλλά θα πρέπει να σας χρεώσουμε για το τηλεφώνημα.
endaxi, ala THa prepi na sas khreosoomeh ya to tilefonima

3. Booking a room

payphone in the lobby	το καρτοτηλέφωνο στη ρεσεψιόν	to kartotilefono sti resepsion
shower	το ντους	to doos
telephone in the room	το τηλέφωνο στο δωμάτιο	to tilefono sto thomatio

▶ Do you have any rooms?
Έχετε δωμάτια;
ekheteh thomatia?

▶▶ For how many people?
Για πόσα άτομα;
ya posa atoma?

▶ For one/for two.
Για ένα/για δύο.
ya ena/ya thio

▶▶ Yes, we have rooms free.
Ναι, έχουμε ελεύθερα δωμάτια.
neh, ekhoomeh elefTHera thomatia

▶▶ For how many nights?
Για πόσα βράδυα;
ya posa vrathia?

▶ Just for one night.
Μόνο για ένα βράδυ;
mono ya ena vrathi

▶ How much is it?
Πόσο κάνει;
poso kani?

▶▶ 90 euros with bathroom and 70 euros without bathroom.
Ενενήντα ευρώ με λουτρό και εβδομήντα ευρώ χωρίς λουτρό.
eneninda evro meh lootro keh evthominda evro khoris lootro

▶ Does that include breakfast?
Αυτό περιλαμβάνει και πρωινό;
afto perilamvani keh pro-ino?

▶ Can I see a room with bathroom?
Μπορώ να δω ένα δωμάτιο με λουτρό;
boro na tho ena thomatio meh lootro?

▶ OK, I'll take it.
Εντάξει, θα το κλείσω.
endaxi, THa to kliso

▶ When do I have to check out?
Πότε πρέπει να κάνω check-out;
poteh prepi na kano check-out?

▶ Is there anywhere I can leave luggage?
Μπορώ να αφήσω τις αποσκευές μου κάπου;
boro na afiso tis aposkeves moo kapoo?

4. Car hire

automatic	το αυτόματο	to aftomato
full tank	το γεμάτο τεπόζιτο	to yemato tepozito
manual	το σειριακό	to siriako
rented car	το νοικιασμένο αυτοκίνητο	to nikiasmeno aftokinito

▶ I'd like to rent a car.
Θα ήθελα να νοικιάσω ένα αυτοκίνητο.
THA iTHela na nikiaso ena aftokinito

▶▶ For how long?
Για πόσο καιρό;
ya poso kero?

▶ Two days.
Για δύο ημέρες.
ya thio imeres

▶ I'll take the…
Θα πάρω το…
THA paro to…

▶ Is that with unlimited mileage?
Έχει απεριόριστο αριθμό χιλιομέτρων;
ekhi aperioristo arithmo khiliometron?

▶▶ It is.
Ναι.
neh

▶▶ Can I see your driving licence, please?
Παρακαλώ, μπορώ να δω την άδεια οδήγησης;
parakalo, boro na tho tin athia othiyisis?

▶▶ And your passport.
Και το διαβατήριό σας.
keh to thiavatirio sas

▶ Is insurance included?
Περιλαμβάνεται η ασφάλεια;
perilamvaneteh i asfalia?

▶▶ Yes, but you have to pay the first 100 euros.
Ναι, αλλά πρέπει να πληρώσετε τα πρώτα εκατό ευρώ.
neh, ala prepi na pliroseteh ta prota ekato evro

▶▶ Can you leave a deposit of 100 euros?
Μπορείτε να δώσετε εγγύηση εκατό ευρώ.
boriteh na thoseteh engi-isi ekato evro?

▶ And if this office is closed, where do I leave the keys?
Και αν αυτό το γραφείο είναι κλειστό, πού μπορώ να αφήσω τα κλειδιά;
keh an afto to grafio ineh klisto, poo boro na afiso ta klithia?

▶▶ You drop them in that box.
Τα ρίχνετε σε αυτό το κουτί.
ta rikhneteh se afto to kooti

5. Car problems

brakes	τα φρένα	ta frena
to break down	παθαίνω βλάβη	paтнeno vlavi
clutch	ο συμπλέκτης	o siblektis
diesel	η diesel	i dizel
flat battery	η πεσμένη μπαταρία	i pesmeni bataria
flat tyre	το σκασμένο λάστιχο	to skasmeno lastikho
petrol	η βενζίνη	i venzini

▶ Excuse me, where is the nearest petrol station?
Με συγχωρείτε, πού είναι το πλησιέστερο βενζινάδικο;
meh sinkhoriteh, poo ineh to plisi-estero venzinathiko?

▶▶ In the next town, about 5km away.
Στην επόμενη πόλη, περίπου πέντε χιλιόμετρα μακριά.
stin epomeni poli, peripoo pendeh khiliometra makria

▶ The car has broken down.
Το αυτοκίνητο έπαθε βλάβη.
to aftokinito epaтнeh vlavi

▶▶ Can you tell me what happened?
Μπορείτε να μου πείτε τι συνέβη;
boriteh na moo piteh ti sinevi?

▶ I've got a flat tyre.
Έχω σκασμένο λάστιχο.
ekho skasmeno lastikho

▶ I think the battery is flat.
Νομίζω ότι η μπαταρία είναι πεσμένη.
nomizo oti i bataria ineh pesmeni

▶▶ Can you tell me exactly where you are?
Μπορείτε να μου πείτε πού ακριβώς βρίσκεστε;
boriteh na moo piteh poo akrivos vriskesteh?

▶ I'm about 2km outside of Lamia on the Ethniki motorway.
Είμαι περίπου δύο χιλιόμετρα έξω από τη Λαμία, στην Εθνική οδό.
imeh peripoo thio khiliometra exo apo ti lamia, stin eтнiki otho

▶▶ What type of car? What colour?
Τι αυτοκίνητο έχετε; Τι χρώμα;
ti aftokinito ekheteh? ti khroma?

▶ Can you send a tow truck?
Μπορείτε να στείλετε γερανό;
boriteh na stileteh yerano?

6. Children

baby	το μωρό	to moro
boy	το αγόρι	to agori
child	το παιδί	to pethi
children	τα παιδιά	ta pethia
cot	η κούνια	i koonia
formula	το παρασκεύασμα	to paraskevasma
girl	το κορίτσι	to koritsi
highchair	το καρεκλάκι μωρού	to kareklaki moroo
nappies (diapers)	οι πάνες	i panes

▶ We need a babysitter for tomorrow evening.
Χρειάζομαστε μία baby-sitter για αύριο το βράδυ.
khriazomasteh mia babysitter ya avrio to vrathi

▶▶ For what time?
Για πόσες ώρες;
ya poses ores?

▶ From 7.30 to 11.00.
Από τις επτάμιση μέχρι τις εντεκάμιση.
apo tis eptamisi mekhri tis endekamisi

▶▶ How many children? How old are they?
Πόσα παιδιά έχετε; Πόσο χρονών;
posa pethia ekheteh? poso khronon?

▶ Two children, aged four and eighteen months.
Δύο παιδιά, το ένα τεσσάρων χρονών και το άλλο δεκαοχτώ μηνών.
thIo pethia, to ena tesaron khronon keh to alo theka-okhto minon

---

▶ Where can I change the baby?
Πού μπορώ να αλλάξω το μωρό;
poo boro na alaxo to moro?

▶ Could you please warm this bottle for me?
Θα μπορούσες σε παρακαλώ να ζεστάνεις το γάλα στο μπιμπερό;
THa borooses seh parakalo na zestanis to gala sto bibero?

▶ Can you give us a child's portion?
Μπορείτε να μας δώσετε παιδική μερίδα;
boriteh na mas thoseteh pethiki meritha?

▶ We need two child seats.
Χρειάζομαστε δύο παιδικά καρεκλάκια αυτοκινήτου.
khriazomasteh thIo pethika kareklakia aftokinitoo

▶ Is there a discount for children?
Υπάρχει έκπτωση για παιδιά;
iparkhi ekptosi ya pethia?

7. Communications: Internet

@, at sign	το παπάκι	to papaki
computer	ο υπολογιστής	o ipolo-yistis
email	το email	to email
Internet	το Internet	to Internet
keyboard	το πληκτρολόγιο	to pliktrolo-yio
mouse	το ποντίκι	to pondiki

▶ Is there somewhere I can check my emails?
Υπάρχει κάποιο μέρος που μπορώ να δω τα emails μου;
iparkhi kapio meros poo boro na tho ta emails moo?

▶ Do you have Wi-Fi?
Έχετε wifi;
ekheteh wi-fi?

▶ Is there an Internet café around here?
Υπάρχει Internet café εδώ γύρω;
iparkhi Internet café etho yiro?

▶▶ Yes, there's one in the shopping centre.
Ναι, υπάρχει στο εμπορικό κέντρο.
neh, iparkhi sto emboriko kendro

▶▶ Do you want fifteen minutes, thirty minutes or one hour?
Θέλετε δεκαπέντε λεπτά, τριάντα λεπτά ή μισή ώρα;
THeleteh thekapendeh lepta, trianda lepta i misi ora?

▶ Thirty minutes please. Can you help me log on?
Τριάντα λεπτά παρακαλώ. Μπορείτε να με βοηθήσετε να κάνω είσοδο;
trianda lepta parakalo, boriteh na meh vo-iTHiseteh na kano isotho?

▶▶ OK, here's your password.
Εντάξει, εδώ είναι ο κωδικός σας.
endaxi, etho ineh o kothikos sas

▶ Can you change this to an English keyboard?
Μπορείτε να αλλάξετε αυτό σε βρετανικό πληκτρολόγιο;
boriteh na alaxeteh afto seh vretaniko pliktrolo-yio?

▶ I'll take another quarter of an hour.
Θα ήθελα να το χρησιμοποιήσω ακόμη ένα τέταρτο.
THa iTHela na to khrisimopi-iso akomi ena tetarto

▶ Is there a printer I can use?
Υπάρχει εκτυπωτής που μπορώ να χρησιμοποιήσω;
iparkhi ektipotis poo boro na khrisimopi-iso?

8. Communications: phones

mobile phone (cell)	το κινητό	to kinito
payphone	το τηλέφωνο με κέρματα	to tilefono meh kermata
phone call	η τηλεφωνική κλήση	i tilefoniki klisi
phone card	η τηλεκάρτα	i tilekarta
phone charger	ο φορτιστής τηλεφώνου	o fortistis tilefonoo
SIM card	η κάρτα SIM	i karta SIM

▶ Can I call abroad from here?
Μπορώ να καλέσω στο εξωτερικό από εδώ;
boro na kaleso sto exoteriko apo etho?

▶ How do I get an outside line?
Πώς μπορώ να πιάσω γραμμή;
pos boro na piaso grami?

▶ What's the code to call the UK/US from here?

Ποιός είναι ο κωδικός αριθμός για να καλέσω Ηνωμένο Βασίλειο/ΗΠΑ από εδώ;
pios ineh o kothikos ariTHmos ya na kaleso inomeno vasili-o/ipa apo etho?

zero	μηδέν	mithen
one	ένα	ena
two	δύο	thio
three	τρία	tria
four	τέσσερα	tesera
five	πέντε	pendeh
six	έξι	exi
seven	επτά	epta
eight	οχτώ	okhto
nine	εννιά	enia

▶ Hello, can I speak to Costas?

Γεια σας, μπορώ να μιλήσω στον Κώστα;
Ya sas, boro na miliso ston Kosta?

▶▶ Yes, that's me speaking.
Ναι, ο ίδιος.
neh, o ithios

▶ Do you have a charger for this?

Έχετε φορτιστή για αυτό;
ekheteh fortisti ya afto?

▶ Can I buy a SIM card for this phone?

Μπορώ να αγοράσω μία κάρτα SIM για αυτό το τηλέφωνο;
boro na agoraso mia karta SIM ya afto to tilefono?

9. Directions

just after	αμέσως μετά	amesos meta
opposite	απέναντι από	apenandi apo
on the left	στα αριστερά	sta aristera
over there	εκεί	eki
next	επόμενος	epomenos
straight ahead	ευθεία	efTHia
near	κοντά	konda
past the...	μετά το...	meta to...
in front of	μπροστά	brosta
street	η οδός	i othos
further	παραπέρα	parapera
back	πίσω	piso
turn off	στρίβω	strivo
on the right	στα δεξιά	sta thexia

▶ Hi, I'm looking for Panepistimiou Street.

Γειά σας, ψάχνω την οδό Πανεπιστημίου.
ya sas, psakhno ya tin otho Panepistimioo

▶ Hi, Panepistimiou Street, do you know where it is?

Γειά σας, η οδός Πανεπιστημίου ξέρετε πού είναι;

ya sas, i othos Panepistimioo xereteh poo ineh?

▶▶ Sorry, never heard of it.

Λυπάμαι, δεν την έχω ακουστά.

lipameh, then tin ekho akoosta

▶ Hi, can you tell me where Panepistimiou Street is?

Γειά σας, μπορείτε να μου πείτε πού είναι η οδός Πανεπιστημίου;

ya sas, boriteh na moo piteh poo ineh i othos Panepistimioo?

▶▶ I'm a stranger here too.

Είμαι και εγώ ξένος εδώ.

imeh keh ego xenos etho

▶ Where?

Πού.

poo?

▶ Which direction?

Προς ποιά κατεύθυνση.

pros pia katefтнinsi?

▶▶ Around the corner.

Στη γωνία.

sti gonia

▶▶ Left at the second traffic lights.

Αριστερά στα δεύτερα φανάρια.

aristera sta theftera fanaria

▶▶ Then it's the first street on the right.

Κατόπιν, είναι ο πρώτος δρόμος στα δεξιά.

katopin, ineh o protos thromos sta thexia

10. Emergencies

accident	το ατύχημα	to atikhima
ambulance	το πρώτων βοηθειών	to proton vo-iTHion
consul	ο πρόξενος	o proxenos
embassy	η πρεσβεία	i presvia
fire brigade	η πυροσβεστική	i pirosvestiki
police	η αστυνομία	i astinomia

▶ Help!
Βοήθεια!
vo-íTHia

▶ Can you help me?
Μπορείτε να με βοηθήσετε;
boriteh na meh vo-íTHiseteh?

▶ Please come with me! It's really very urgent.
Ελάτε, παρακαλώ, μαζί μου! Είναι πραγματικά πολύ επείγον.
elateh, parakalo, mazi moo! ineh pragmatika poli epigon

▶ I've lost my keys.
Έχασα τα κλειδιά μου.
ekhasa ta klithia moo

▶ My car is not working.
Το αυτοκίνητό μου δεν λειτουργεί.
to aftokinito moo then litooryi

▶ My purse has been stolen.
Έκλεψαν το πορτοφόλι μου.
eklepsan to portofoli moo

▶ I've been mugged.
Με λήστεψαν.
meh listepsan

▶▶ What's your name?
Πώς σας λένε;
pos sas leneh?

▶▶ I need to see your passport.
Χρειάζεται να δω το διαβατήριό σας.
khriazeteh na tho to thiavatirio sas

▶ I'm sorry, all my papers have been stolen.
Λυπάμαι, μου έκλεψαν όλα τα στοιχεία ταυτότητας.
lipameh, moo eklepsan ola ta stikhia taftotitas

11. Friends

▶ Hi, how're you doing?
Γειά σου, τί κάνεις;
ya soo, ti kanis?

▶▶ OK, and you?
Καλά, και εσύ;
kala, keh esi?

▶ Yeah, fine.
Ναι, ωραία.
neh, orea

▶ Not bad.
Όχι άσχημα.
okhi askhima

▶ Do you know Mark?
Ξέρεις τον Μάρκ;
xeris ton Mark?

▶ And this is Hannah.
Και αυτή είναι η Χάννα.
keh afti ineh i khana

▶▶ Yeah, we know each other.
Ναι, γνωριζόμαστε.
neh, gnorizomasteh

▶ Where do you know each other from?
Από που γνωρίζεστε;
apo poo gnorizesteh?

▶▶ We met at Yanis' place.
Συναντηθήκαμε στο σπίτι του Γιάννη.
sinandiTHikameh sto spiti too Yani

▶ That was some party, eh?
Πολύ ωραίο πάρτυ, ε;
poli oreo parti, eh?

▶▶ The best.
Το καλύτερο.
to kalitero

▶ Are you guys coming for a beer?
Έρχεστε για μιά μπύρα;
erkhesteh ya mia bira?

▶▶ Cool, let's go.
Cool, πάμε.
cool, pameh

▶▶ No, I'm meeting Maria.
Όχι, θα συναντήσω τη Μαρία.
okhi, THa sinandiso ti Maria

▶ See you at Yanis' place tonight.
Τα λέμε στο σπίτι του Γιάννη απόψε.
ta lemeh sto spiti too Yani apopseh

▶▶ See you.
Τα λέμε.
ta lemeh

12. Health

antibiotics	το αντιβιοτικό	to andiviotiko
antiseptic ointment	η αντισηπτική αλοιφή	i andisiptiki alifi
cystitis	η κυστίτιδα	i kistititha
dentist	ο/η οδοντίατρος	o/i othondiatros
diarrhoea	η διάρροια	i thiari-a
doctor	ο γιατρός	o yatros
hospital	το νοσοκομείο	to nosokomio
ill	άρρωστος	arostos
medicine	το φάρμακο	to farmako
painkillers	τα παυσίπονα	ta pafsipona
pharmacy	το φαρμακείο	to farmakio
to prescribe	γράφω συνταγή	grafo sinda-yi
thrush	η στοματίτιδα	i stomatitida

▶ I'm not feeling very well.
Δεν αισθάνομαι πολύ καλά.
then esTHanomeh poli kala

▶ Can you get a doctor?
Μπορείτε να φέρετε έναν γιατρό;
boriteh na fereteh enan yatro?

▶▶ Where does it hurt?
Πού πονάει;
poo pona-i?

▶ It hurts here.
Πονάει εδώ.
pona-i etho

▶▶ Is the pain constant?
Πονάει συνεχώς;
pona-i sinekhos?

▶ It's not a constant pain.
Δεν πονάει συνεχώς.
then pona-i sinekhos

- -

▶ Can I make an appointment?
Μπορώ να κλείσω ένα ραντεβού;
boro na kliso ena randevoo?

▶ Can you give me something for…?
Μπορείτε να μου δώσετε κάτι για…;
boriteh na moo thoseteh kati ya…?

▶ Yes, I have insurance.
Ναι, έχω ασφάλεια.
neh, ekho asfalia

13. Hotels

maid	η καμαριέρα	i kamari-era
manager	ο διευθυντής	o thi-efтнindis
room service	η υπηρεσία δωματίου	i ipiresia thomatioo

▶ Hello, we've booked a double room in the name of Cameron.
Γεια σας, έχουμε κλείσει ένα διπλό δωμάτιο στο όνομα Κάμερον.
ya sas, ekhoomeh klisi ena thiplo thomatio sto onoma kameron

▶▶ That was for four nights, wasn't it?
Μάλιστα, για τέσσερα βράδια, σωστά;
malista, ya tesera vrathia, sosta?

▶ Yes, we're leaving on Saturday.
Ναι, φεύγουμε το Σάββατο.
neh, fevgoomeh to savato

▶▶ Can I see your passport please?
Μπορώ να δω το διαβατήριο σας, παρακαλώ;
boro na tho to thiavatirio sas, parakalo?

▶▶ There you are, room 321 on the third floor.
Ορίστε, δωμάτιο τριακόσια είκοσι ένα στον τρίτο όροφο.
oristeh, thomatio triakosia ikosi ena ston trito orofo

▶ I can't get this keycard to work.
Δεν μπορώ να ανοίξω με την κάρτα-κλειδί.
then boro na aníxo me tin karta-klithí

>> Sorry, I need to reactivate it.
Συγνώμη, πρέπει να την ενεργοποιήσω εκ νέου.
signomi, prepi na tin energopi-iso ek neoo

▶ What time is breakfast?
Τι ώρα σερβίρεται το πρωινό;
ti ora servireteh to pro-ino?

▶ There aren't any towels in my room.
Δεν υπάρχουν πετσέτες στο δωμάτιο μου.
then iparkhoon petsetes sto thomatio moo

▶ My flight isn't until this evening, can I keep the room a bit longer?
Επειδή η πτήση μου είναι σήμερα το βράδυ, θα μπορούσα να κρατήσω το δωμάτιο λίγο περισσότερο;
epithi i ptisi moo ineh simera to vrathi, тна boroosa na kratiso to thomatio ligo perisotero?

▶ Can I settle up? Is this card ok?
Μπορώ να σας πληρώσω; Είναι εντάξει αυτή η κάρτα;
boro na sas pliroso? ineh endaxi afti i karta?

14. Language difficulties

a few words	λίγες λέξεις	liyes lexis
interpreter	ο/η διερμηνέας	o/i thi-ermineas
to translate	μεταφράζω	metafrazo

>> Your credit card has been refused.
Η πιστωτική σας κάρτα δεν έγινε δεκτή.
i pistotiki sas karta then eyineh thekti

▶ What, I don't understand; do you speak English?
Τί; δεν καταλαβαίνω, μιλάτε Αγγλικά;
ti? then katalaveno; milateh Anglika?

>> This isn't valid.
Αυτή δεν ισχύει.
afti then iskhi-i

► Could you say that again?   ► Slowly.
Μπορείτε να το ξαναπείτε αυτό;   Αργά.
boriteh na to xanapiteh afto?   arga

► I understand very little Greek.
Καταλαβαίνω πολύ λίγα Ελληνικά.
katalaveno poli liga Elinika

► I speak Greek very badly.
Δεν μιλάω καθόλου καλά Ελληνικά.
then milao kaTHoloo kala Elinika

>> You can't use this card to pay.
Δεν μπορείτε να πληρώσετε με αυτή την κάρτα.
then boriteh na pliroseteh meh afti tin karta

>> Do you understand?
Καταλαβαίνετε;
katalaveneteh?

► Sorry, no.
Όχι, λυπάμαι.
okhi, lipameh

► Is there someone who speaks English?
Μιλάει κανείς εδώ Αγγλικά;
mila-i kanis etho Anglika?

► Oh, now I understand.
Α, τώρα καταλαβαίνω.
ah, tora katalaveno

► Is that OK now?
Είναι εντάξει τώρα;
ineh endaxi tora?

15. Meeting people

► Hello.
Γειά σας.
ya sas

>> Hello, my name's Katerina.
Γειά σας, με λένε Κατερίνα.
ya sas, meh leneh Katerina

► Graham, from England, Thirsk.
Με λένε Graham και είμαι από το Thirsk στην Αγγλία.
meh leneh Graham keh imeh apo to Thirsk stin Anglia

> ► ► Don't know that, where is it?
>
> Δεν το ξέρω, πού βρίσκεται;
> then to xero, poo vrisketeh?

► Not far from York, in the North; and you?

Όχι μακριά από το York στον Βορρά, και εσύ;
okhi makria apo to York ston vora; keh esi?

> > ► ► I'm from Thessaloniki; here by yourself?
> >
> > Εγώ είμαι από τη Θεσσαλονίκη: είσαι εδώ μόνος σου;
> > ego imeh apo ti THesaloniki; iseh etho monos soo?

► No, I'm with my wife and two kids.

Όχι, είμαι με τη γυναίκα μου και τα δύο μου παιδιά.
okhi, imeh meh ti yineka moo keh ta thio moo pethia

► What do you do?

Τί δουλειά κάνεις;
ti thoolia kanis?

> > ► ► I'm in computers.
> >
> > Είμαι στους υπολογιστές.
> > imeh stoos ipolo-yistes

► Me too.

Κι εγώ επίσης.
ki ego episis

► Here's my wife now.

Να και η γυναίκα μου.
na keh i yineka moo

> > ► ► Nice to meet you.
> >
> > Χαίρω πολύ.
> > khero poli

16. Nightlife

electro	η ελέκτρο	i electro
folk	η φολκ	i folk
heavy metal	η χέβι-μέταλ	i heavy metal
hip-hop	η χιπ-χοπ	i hip-hop
jazz	η τζαζ	i jazz
rock	η ροκ	i rock

▶ What's a good club for...?
Πού υπάρχει ένα καλό κλαμπ για...;
poo iparkhi ena kalo club ya...?

▶▶ There's going to be a great gig at Malakasa tomorrow night.
Πρόκειται να πραγματοποιηθεί μια εξαιρετική συναυλία στη Μαλακάσα αύριο το βράδυ.
prokiteh na pragmatopi-iTHi mia exeretiki sinavlia sti malakasa avrio to vrathi

▶ Where can I hear some local music?
Πού μπορώ να ακούσω λίγη ντόπια μουσική;
poo boro na akooso liyi dopia moosiki?

▶ What's a good place for dancing?
Πού υπάρχει ένα καλό μέρος για χορό;
poo iparkhi ena kalo meros ya khoro?

▶ Can you write down the names of the best bars around here?
Μπορείτε να γράψετε τα ονόματα των καλύτερων μπαρ εδώ γύρω;
boriteh na grapseteh ta onomata ton kaliteron bar etho yiro?

▶▶ That depends what you're looking for.
Εξαρτάται από το τι ψάχνετε.
exartateh apo to ti psakhneteh

▶ The place where the locals go.

Τα μέρη όπου συχνάζουν οι ντόπιοι.

ta meri opoo sikhnazoon i dopi-i

▶ A place for a quiet drink.

Ένα ήσυχο μέρος για ποτό.

ena isikho meros ya poto

▶▶ The casino across the bay is very good.

Το καζίνο που βρίσκεται κατά μήκος του κόλπου είναι πολύ καλό.

to kasino poo vrisketeh kata mikos too kolpoo ineh poli kalo

▶ I suppose they have a dress code.

Υποθέτω ότι έχουν κώδικα ενδυμασίας.

ipoTHeto oti ekhoon koTHika enthimasias

▶▶ You can wear what you like.

Μπορείτε να φορέσετε ό,τι θέλετε.

boriteh na foreseteh oti THeleteh

▶ What time does it close?

Τι ώρα κλείνει;

ti ora klini?

17. Post offices

airmail	αεροπορικώς	a-eroporikos
post card	η κάρτα	i karta
post office	το ταχυδρομείο	to takhithromio
stamp	το γραμματόσημο	to gramatosimo

▶ What time does the post office close?

Τί ώρα κλείνει το ταχυδρομείο;

ti ora klini to takhithromio?

▶▶ Five o'clock weekdays.

Τις καθημερινές στις 5.

tis kaTHimerines stis pendeh

▶ Is the post office open on Saturdays?

Είναι ανοιχτά το ταχυδρομείο το Σάββατο;

ineh anikhta to takhithromio to Savato?

▶▶ Until midday.
Μέχρι το μεσημέρι.
mekhri to mesimeri

▶ I'd like to send this registered to England.
Θα ήθελα να στείλω αυτό συστημένο στην Αγγλία.
THa iTHela na stilo afto sistimeno stin Anglia

▶▶ Certainly, that will cost 10 euros.
Βεβαίως, κάνει 10 ευρώ.
veveos, kani theka evro

▶ And also two stamps for
England, please.
Και δύο γραμματόσημα για την
Αγγλία, παρακαλώ.
keh thio gramatosima ya tin Anglia,
parakalo

ΓΡΑΜΜΑΤΑ	letters
ΔΕΜΑΤΑ	parcels
ΕΞΩΤΕΡΙΚΟΥ	international
ΕΣΩΤΕΡΙΚΟΥ	domestic
ΠΟΣΤ-ΡΕΣΤΑΝΤ	poste restante

▶ Do you have some airmail stickers?
Έχετε αυτοκόλλητα Αεροπορικώς;
ekheteh aftokolita a-eroporikos?

▶ Do you have any mail for me?
Έχετε γράμματα για μένα;
ekheteh gramata ya mena?

18. Restaurants

bill	ο λογαριασμός	o logariasmos
menu	ο κατάλογος	o katalogos
table	το τραπέζι	to trapezi

▶ Can we have a non-smoking table?
Μπορούμε να έχουμε ένα τραπέζι για μη-καπνιστές;
boroomeh na ekhoomeh ena trapezi ya mi-kapnistes?

▶ There are two of us.
Είμαστε δύο άτομα.
imasteh thio atoma

▶ There are four of us.
Είμαστε τέσσερα άτομα.
imasteh tesera atoma

▶ What's this?
Τί είναι αυτό;
ti ineh afto?

▶▶ It's a type of fish.
Είναι ένα είδος ψαριού.
ineh ena ithos psarioo

▶▶ It's a local speciality.
Είναι μιά τοπική σπεσιαλιτέ.
ineh mia topiki spesialiteh

▶▶ Come inside and I'll show you.
Ελάτε μέσα και θα σας δείξω.
elateh mesa keh THa sas thixo

▶ We would like two of these, one of these, and one of those.
Θα θέλαμε δύο από αυτά, ένα από αυτά και ένα από εκείνα.
THa THelameh thio apo afta, ena apo afta keh ena apo ekina

▶▶ And to drink?
Και τί θα πιείτε;
keh ti THa pi-iteh?

▶ Red wine.   ▶ White wine.
κόκκινο κρασί.   Λευκό κρασί.
kokino krasi   lefko krasi

▶ A beer and two orange juices.
Μιά μπύρα και δύο πορτοκαλάδες.
mia bira keh thio portokalathes

▶ Some more bread please.
Ακόμη λίγο ψωμί, παρακαλώ.
akomi ligo psomi, parakalo

▶▶ How was your meal?
Σας άρεσε το γεύμα;
sas areseh to yevma?

▶ Excellent, very nice!
Έξοχο!, πολύ νόστιμο!
exokho!, poli nostimo!

▶▶ Anything else?
Τίποτα άλλο;
tipota alo?

▶ Just the bill, thanks.
Μόνο τον λογαριασμό, ευχαριστώ.
mono ton logariasmo, efkharisto

19. Self-catering accommodation

air-conditioning	ο κλιματισμός	ο klimatismos
apartment	το διαμέρισμα	to thiamerisma
cooker	η ηλεκτρική κουζίνα	i ilektriki koozina
fridge	το ψυγείο	to psiyio
heating	η θέρμανση	i THermansi
hot water	ζεστό νερό	zesto nero
lightbulb	η λάμπα	i lamba
toilet	η τουαλέτα	i tooaleta

▶ The toilet's broken, can you get someone to fix it?
Η τουαλέτα έχει χαλάσει, μπορείτε να φέρετε κάποιον να την φτιάξει;
i tooaleta ekhi khalasi, boriteh na fereteh kapion na tin ftiaxi?

▶ There's no hot water.
Δεν έχει ζεστό νερό.
den ekhi zesto nero

▶ Can you show me how the air-conditioning works?
Μπορείτε να μου δείξετε πως λειτουργεί ο κλιματισμός;
boriteh na moo thixeteh pos litooryi o klimatismos?

▶▶ OK, what apartment are you in?
Εντάξει, σε ποιό διαμέρισμα είστε;
endaxi, seh pio thiamerisma isteh?

▶ We're in number five.
Είμαστε στον αριθμό πέντε.
imasteh ston ariTHmo pendeh

▶ Can you move us to a quieter apartment?
Μπορείτε να μας μεταφέρετε σε ένα πιο ήσυχο διαμέρισμα;
boriteh na mas metafereteh seh ena pio isikho thiamerisma?

▶ Is there a supermarket nearby?
Υπάρχει σουπερμάρκετ εδώ κοντά;
iparkhi supermarket etho konda?

▶▶ Have you enjoyed your stay?
Απολαύσατε τη διαμονή σας;
apolafsateh ti thiamoni sas?

▶ Brilliant holiday, thanks!
Καταπληκτικές διακοπές, ευχαριστώ!
katapliktikes thiakopes, efkharisto!

20. Shopping

▶▶ Can I help you?
Μπορώ να σας βοηθήσω;
boro na sas vo-iTHiso?

▶ Can I just have a look around?
Μπορώ να κοιτάξω μόνο γύρω;
boro na kitaxo mono yiro?

▶ Yes, I'm looking for…
Ναι, ψάχνω για…
neh, psakhno ya…

▶ How much is this?
Πόσο κάνει αυτό;
poso kani afto?

▶▶ Thirty-two euros.
Τριάντα δύο ευρώ.
trianda thio evro

▶ OK, I think I'll have to leave it; it's a little too expensive for me.
Εντάξει, νομίζω ότι δεν θα το πάρω, είναι λίγο ακριβό για μένα.
endaxi, nomizo oti then THa to paro; ineh ligo akrivo ya mena

▶▶ How about this?
Αυτό πώς σας φαίνεται;
afto pos sas feneteh?

▶ Can I pay by credit card?
Μπορώ να πληρώσω με πιστωτική κάρτα;
boro na pliroso meh pistotiki karta?

▶ It's too big.
Είναι πολύ μεγάλο.
ineh poli megalo

▶ It's too small.
Είναι πολύ μικρό.
ineh poli mikro

▶ It's for my son – he's about this high.
Είναι για τον γιό μου – είναι περίπου τόσο ψηλός.
ineh ya ton yo moo – ineh peripoo toso psilos

▶▶ Will there be anything else?
Θέλετε τίποτα άλλο;
THeleteh tipota alo?

▶ That's all, thanks.
Μόνο αυτό, ευχαριστώ.
mono afto, efkharisto

▶ Make it twenty euros and I'll take it.
Θα το πάρω αν μου το δώσετε
για 20 ευρώ.
THa to paro an moo to thoseteh ya
ikosi evro

ΑΛΛΑΓΕΣ	to exchange
ΑΝΟΙΧΤΑ	open
ΕΚΠΤΩΣΕΙΣ	sale
ΚΛΕΙΣΤΑ	closed
ΤΑΜΕΙΟ	cash desk

▶ Fine, I'll take it.
Ωραία, θα το πάρω.
orea, THa to paro

21. Shopping for clothes

to alter	μεταποιώ	metapio
bigger	μεγαλύτερος	megaliteros
just right	αυτό ακριβώς	afto akrivos
smaller	μικρότερος	mikroteros
to try on	δοκιμάζω	thokimazo

▶▶ Can I help you?
Μπορώ να σας βοηθήσω;
boro na sas vo-iTHiso?

▶ No thanks, I'm just looking.
Όχι ευχαριστώ, απλά ρίχνω μια ματιά.
okhi efkharisto, apla rikhno mia matia

▶▶ Do you want to try that on?
Θέλετε να το δοκιμάσετε;
THeleteh na to thokimaseteh?

▶ Yes, and I'll try this one too.
Ναι, και θα δοκιμάσω και αυτό επίσης.
neh, keh THa thokimaso keh afto episis

▶ Do you have it in a bigger size?
Το έχετε σε μεγαλύτερο μέγεθος;
to ekheteh seh megalitero meyeTHos?

▶ Do you have it in a different colour?
Το έχετε σε άλλο χρώμα;
to ekheteh seh alo khroma?

▶▶ That looks good on you.
Αυτό σας πηγαίνει.
afto sas piyeni

▶ Can you shorten this?
Μπορείτε να το κοντύνετε;
boriteh na to kondineteh?

▶▶ Sure, it'll be ready on Friday, after 12.00.
Βεβαίως, θα είναι έτοιμο την Παρασκευή, στις δώδεκα.
veveos, THa ineh etimo tin paraskevi, stis thotheka

22. Sightseeing

art gallery	η πινακοθήκη	i pinakoTHiki
bus tour	η ξενάγηση με λεωφορείο	i xenayisi meh leoforio
city centre	το κέντρο της πόλης	to kendro tis polis
closed	κλειστά	klista
guide	ο/η ξεναγός	o/i xenagos
museum	το μουσείο	to moosio
open	ανοιχτός	anikhtos

▶ I'm interested in seeing the old town.
Θα με ενδιέφερε να δω την παλιά πόλη.
THa meh enthiefereh na tho tin palia poli

▶ Are there guided tours?
Υπάρχουν ξεναγήσεις;
iparkhoon xenayisis?

▶▶ I'm sorry, it's fully booked.
Λυπάμαι, είναι όλα κλεισμένα.
lipameh, ineh ola klismena

▶ How much would you charge to drive us around for four hours?
Πόσα θα χρεώσετε για να μας πάτε βόλτα για τέσσερις ώρες;
posa THa khreoseteh ya na mas pateh volta ya teseris ores?

▶ Can we book tickets for the concert here?
Μπορούμε να κλείσουμε εδώ εισιτήρια για το κονσέρτο;
boroomeh na klisoomeh etho isitiria ya to konserto?

▶▶ Yes, in what name?
Ναί, σε τί όνομα;
neh, seh ti onoma?

▶▶ Which credit card?
Ποιά πιστωτική κάρτα;
pia pistotiki karta?

▶ Where do we get the tickets?
Πού θα πάρουμε τα εισιτήρια;
poo tha paroomeh ta isitiria?

▶▶ Just pick them up at the entrance.
Θα τα πάρετε στην είσοδο.
THa ta pareteh stin isotho

▶ Is it open on Sundays?
Είναι ανοικτά την Κυριακή;
ineh anikta tin Kiriaki?

▶ How much is it to get in?
Πόσο κάνει η είσοδος;
poso kani i isothos?

▶ Are there reductions for groups of six?
Υπάρχει έκπτωση για ομάδα έξι ατόμων;
iparkhi ekptosi ya omatha exi atomon?

▶ That was really impressive!
Αυτό ήταν πραγματικά εντυπωσιακό!
afto itan pragmatika endiposiako!

23. Taxis

▶ Can you get us a taxi?
Μπορείτε να μας καλέσετε ένα ταξί;
boriteh na mas kaleseteh ena taxi?

▶▶ For now? Where are you going?
Για τώρα; Πού πηγαίνετε;
ya tora? poo piyeneteh?

▶ To the town centre.
Στο κέντρο της πόλης.
sto kendro tis polis

▶ I'd like to book a taxi to the airport for tomorrow.
Θα ήθελα να κλείσω ένα ταξί για το αεροδρόμιο για αύριο.
THa iTHela na kliso ena taxi ya to aerothromio ya avrio

▶▶ Sure, at what time? How many people?
Φυσικά, τι ώρα; Πόσα άτομα;
fisika, ti ora? posa atoma?

▶ How much is it to Eleftherios Venizelos?
Πόσο κάνει μέχρι το Ελευθέριος Βενιζέλος;
poso kani mekhri to elefTHerios venizelos?

▶ Right here is fine, thanks.
Ακριβώς εδώ είναι εντάξει, ευχαριστώ.
akrivos etho ineh endaxi, efkharisto

▶ Can you wait here and take us back?
Μπορείτε να περιμένετε εδώ και να μας γυρίσετε πίσω;
boriteh na perimeneteh etho keh na mas yiriseteh piso?

▶▶ How long are you going to be?
Πόση ώρα θα κάνετε;
posi ora THa kaneteh?

24. Trains

to change trains	αλλάζω τρένο	alazo treno
platform	η πλατφόρμα	i platforma
return	ένα εισιτήριο	ena isitirio
	με επιστροφή	meh epistrofi
single	ένα εισιτήριο απλό	ena isitirio aplo
station	ο σταθμός	o staTHmos
stop	η στάση	i stasi
ticket	ένα εισιτήριο	ena isitirio

▶ How much is...?
Πόσο κάνει...;
poso kani...?

▶ A single, second class to...
Ένα εισιτήριο απλό, δεύτερη θέση για...
ena isitirio aplo, thefteri THesi ya...

▶ Two returns, second class to...
Δύο εισιτήρια με επιστροφή, δεύτερη θέση για...
thio isitiria meh epistrofi, thefteri THesi ya...

▶ For today.
Για σήμερα.
ya simera

▶ For tomorrow.
Για αύριο.
ya avrio

▶ For next Tuesday.
Για την άλλη Τρίτη.
ya tin ali Triti

▶▶ Do you want to make a seat reservation?
Θέλετε να κρατήσετε θέση;
THeleteh na kratiseteh THesi?

Προς Κηφισιά
To Kifissia

▶▶ You have to change at Lamia.
Πρέπει να αλλάξετε στη Λαμία.
prepi na alaxeteh sti Lamia

▶ What time is the last train to Corinth?
Τι ώρα είναι το τελευταίο τρένο για την Κόρινθο;
ti ora ineh to telefteo treno ya tin KorinTHO?

▶ Is this seat free?
Είναι ελεύθερη αυτή η θέση;
ineh elefTHeri afti i THesi?

▶ Excuse me, which station are we at?
Με συγχωρείτε, σε ποιό σταθμό είμαστε;
meh sinkhoriteh, seh pio staTHmo imasteh?

▶ Is this where I change for Thessaloniki?
Εδώ πρέπει να αλλάξω τρένο για τη Θεσσαλονίκη;
etho prepi na alaxo treno ya ti THesaloniki?

ENGLISH
→ GREEK

A

a, an enas, mia, ena
about: about 20 peripoo íkosi
   it's about 5 o'clock íneh yíro
   stis péndeh
   a film about Greece
   ena ergo ya tin Elatha
above pano apo
abroad sto exoteriko
absolutely! (I agree) apolitos!
accelerator to gazi
accept thekhomeh
accident to thistikhima
   there's been an accident
   eyineh ena thistikhima
accommodation i thiamoni
accurate akrivis
ache o ponos
   my back aches
   pona-i i plati moo
across: across the road
   apenandi sto thromo
adapter to polaplo
   (for voltage change) i briza taf
address i thi-efTHinsi
   what's your address?
   pia ineh i thi-efTHinsi soo?
address book i adzenda ton
   thi-efTHinseon
admission charge timi isothoo
adult (male/female) o enilikos/
   i eniliki
advance: in advance
   prokatavolika
aeroplane to a-eroplano

after meta
   after you meta apo sas
   after lunch meta apo to
   yevma
afternoon apo-yevma
   in the afternoon
   kata to apo-yevma
   this afternoon
   afto to apo-yevma
aftershave i kolonia meta to
   xirisma
aftersun cream to galaktoma
   ya ton ilio
afterwards meta
again xana
against enandion
age i ilikia
ago: a week ago
   prin apo mia evthomatha
   an hour ago prin apo mia ora
agree: I agree simfono
AIDS to AIDS
air o a-eras
   by air a-eroporikos
air-conditioning o klimatismos
airmail: by airmail a-eroporikos
airmail envelope o a-eroporikos
   fakelos
airport to a-erothromio
   to the airport, please
   sto a-erothromio, parakalo
airport bus to leoforio
   a-erothromi-oo
aisle seat THesi thipla sto
   thiathromo
alarm clock to xipnitiri
Albania i Alvania

Albanian (*adj*) Alvanik**o**s

alcohol to alko-**o**l

alcoholic inopnevmat**o**this

all: all the boys **o**la ta ag**o**ria

 all the girls **o**la ta kor**i**tsia

 all the men **o**li i **a**ndres

 all the women **o**les i yin**e**kes

 all of it ol**o**kliro

 all of them **o**la aft**a**

 that's all, thanks aft**a** **i**neh **o**la, efkharist**o**

allergic: I'm allergic to… **i**meh aleryik**o**s meh…

allowed: is it allowed? epitr**e**peteh?

all right end**a**xi

 I'm all right **i**meh end**a**xi

 are you all right? (*adj*) **i**seh end**a**xi?

 (*plural or polite*) es**i**s end**a**xi?

almond to amigthalo

almost skheth**o**n

alone m**o**nos

alphabet to alf**a**vito
 see page 9

already **i**thi

also ep**i**sis

although an keh

altogether sinolik**a**

always p**a**nda

am: I am **i**meh

am: at 7am stis eft**a** pro mesimvr**i**as

amazing (*surprising*) ekpliktik**o**s

 (*very good*) thavmas**i**os

ambulance to asthenof**o**ro

 call an ambulance! kal**e**steh **e**na asthenof**o**ro!

America i Amerik**i**

American (*adj*) Amerik**a**nikos

 I'm American (*male/female*) **i**meh Amerik**a**nos/Amerik**a**na

among an**a**mesa

amount to pos**o**

 (*money*) ta khr**i**mata

amp: a 13-amp fuse m**i**a asf**a**lia thekatr**i**a amp**e**r

amphitheatre to amf**i**theatro

Ancient Greece i arkh**e**a El**a**tha

Ancient Greek ta arkh**e**a Elinik**a**

and keh

angry thimom**e**nos

animal to zo-**o**

ankle o astr**a**galos

anniversary (*wedding*) i ep**e**tios too g**a**moo

annoy: this man's annoying me aft**o**s o **a**ndras meh enokhl**i**

annoying enokhlitik**o**s

another **a**los, **a**li, **a**lo

 can we have another room? bor**oo**meh na ekh**oo**meh **e**na **a**lo thom**a**tio?

 another beer, please **a**li m**i**a b**i**ra, parakal**o**

antibiotics to andiviotik**o**

antihistamine to andi-istaminik**o** f**a**rmako

antique: is it an antique? **i**neh ant**i**ka?

antique shop to paleopolio

antiseptic to andisiptiko

**any: have you got any bread/
tomatoes?** ekheteh psomi/
domates?

DIALOGUE

do you have any change?
ekhis katholoo psila?

sorry, I don't have any
lipameh, then ekho
katholoo

anybody kanis

**does anybody speak
English?** mila-i kanis Anglika?

there wasn't anybody there
then itan kanis eki

anything otithipoteh

DIALOGUE

anything else? tipoteh alo?

nothing else, thanks
tipoteh, efkharisto

**would you like anything
to drink?** THa THelateh na
pi-iteh kati?

**I don't want anything,
thanks** then THelo tipoteh,
efkharisto

apart from ektos apo

apartment to thiamerisma

appendicitis i skoliko-ithitis

appetizer to proto piato

  appetizers ta orektika

aperitif to aperitif

apology i signomi

apple to milo

appointment to randevoo

DIALOGUE

**good afternoon, sir, how
can I help you?** kalispera
sas, kiri-eh, pos boro na sas
vo-ithiso?

**I'd like to make an
appointment** THa iThela
na kliso ena randevoo

what time would you like?
ti ora THeleteh?

three o'clock tris i ora

**I'm afraid that's not
possible; is four o'clock
all right?** fovameh oti afto
then yineteh; boriteh stis
teseris?

yes, that will be fine
neh, poli kala

the name was…?
to onoma sas?

apricot to verikoko

April o Aprilios

archaeology i arkheoloyia

are: we are imasteh

  you are isteh

  they are ineh

area i periokhi

area code o kothikos arithmos

arm to kheri

**arrange: will you arrange it
for us?** THa to kanonisis ya
mas?

arrival i afixi

arrive ftano

  when do we arrive?
poteh ftanoomeh?

  has my fax arrived yet?

eftaseh to fax moo?

we arrived today
ftasameh simera

art i tekhni

art gallery i pinakoTHiki

artist (*male/female*) o kalitekhnis/i
kalitekhnitha

as: as big as... megalo san...

as soon as possible
oso pio grigora yineteh

ashtray to tasaki,
to stokhto-thokhio

ask roto

I didn't ask for this
then zitisa afto

could you ask him to...?
boris na too pis na...?

asleep: she's asleep kimateh

aspirin i aspirini

asthma to asthma

astonishing ekpliktikos

at: at the hotel sto xenothokhio

at the station sto staTHmo

at six o'clock stis exi i ora

at Yanni's stoo Yanni

Athens i ATHina

athletics o aTHlitismos

@, at sign to papaki

attractive elkistikos

aubergine i melidzana

August o Avgoostos

aunt i THia

Australia i Afstralia

Australian (*adj*) Afstralezikos

I'm Australian (*male/female*)
imeh Afstralos/Afstraleza

automatic (*adj*) aftomatos
(car) to aftomato aftokinito

automatic teller i mikhani ya
metrita

autumn to ftHinoporo

in the autumn sto ftHinoporo

avenue i leoforos

average (not good) metrio

on average kata meson oro

awake: is he awake?
ineh xipnios?

away: go away! fiyeh

is it far away?
ineh poli makria?

awful apesios

axle o axonas

B

baby to moro

baby food i pethiki trofi

baby's bottle to bibero

baby-sitter i baby-sitter

back (of body) i plati
(back part) piso

at the back sto piso meros

**can I have my money
back?** boro na ekho ta lefta
moo piso?

to come/go back
epistrefo, yirizo piso

backache ponos stin plati

bacon to bacon

bad kakos

a bad headache enas
askhimos ponokefalos

badly askhima
bag i tsanda
  (suitcase) i valitsa
baggage i aposkeves
baggage check o khoros filaxis
  aposkevon
baggage claim anazitisi
  aposkevon
bakery o foornaris
balcony to balkoni
  a room with a balcony
  ena thomatio meh balkoni
bald falakros
ball (large) i bala
  (small) to balaki
ballet to baleto
banana i banana
band (musical) to singrotima
bandage o epithesmos
Bandaid to lefkoplast
bank i trapeza
bank account o trapezikos

logariasmos
bar to bar
  a bar of chocolate
  mia sokolata
barber's to koorio
basket to kalaтнi
basketball to basketball,
  i kalaтнosferisi
bath to banio
  can I have a bath? boro na
  kano ena banio?
bathroom to lootro, to banio
  with a private bathroom
  meh ithiotiko lootro
bath towel i petseta too banioo
battery i bataria
bay o kolpos
be imeh
beach i paralia
beach mat i psaтнa
beach umbrella i ombrela
beans ta fasolia

green beans ta fasolakia

runner beans ta fasolakia freska

broad beans ta kookia

beard ta yenia

beautiful oreos

because epithi

because of... exetias...

bed to krevati

I'm going to bed now pao ya ipno tora

bed and breakfast thomatio meh pro-ino

bedroom to ipnothomatio

beef to moskhari

beer i bira

two beers, please thio bires, parakalo

before prin

begin arkhizo

when does it begin? poteh arkhizi?

beginner (*male/female*) o arkharios/i arkharia

beginning: at the beginning kat arkhas

behind piso

behind me apo piso moo

beige bez

believe pistevo

belly-dancing to tsifteteli

below apo kato

belt i zoni

bend (in road) i strofi

berth (on ship) i klini

beside: beside the... thipla sto...

best aristos

better kaliteros

better than... kaliteros apo...

are you feeling better? esthaneseh kalitera?

between metaxi

beyond pera apo

bicycle to pothilato

big megalos

too big poli megalo

it's not big enough then ineh arketa megalo

bike to pothilato

(motorbike) to mikhanaki

bikini to bikini

bill o logariasmos

(US) to khartonomisma

could I have the bill, please? boro na ekho ton logariasmo, parakalo?

> **Travel tip** With falling visitor numbers at many popular destinations, bill-padding has become common in restaurants, as a few extra euros per party adds up over time. If the itemized bill is in Greek script, ensure that the number and cost of items tally with what you've ordered, and be wary of waiters bringing things you haven't asked for.

bin o skoopithotenekes

bin liners i sakoola skoopithion

bird to pooli

biro to stilo

birthday ta yeneTHlia

   happy birthday! khronia pola!

biscuit to biskoto

bit: a little bit ligo

   a big bit ena megalo komati

   a bit of… ligo apo…

   a bit expensive ligo akrivo, akrivootsiko

bite (by insect) to tsibima

   (by dog) i thagonia

bitter (taste etc) pikros

black mavros

blanket i kooverta

bleach (for toilet) to Harpik

bless you! ya soo!

blind tiflos

blinds ta pantzooria

blister i fooskala

blocked (road, pipe) frakarismenos

   (sink) voolomenos

block of flats i polikatikia

blond xanTHos

blood to ema

   high blood pressure ipsili pi-esi ematos

blouse i blooza

blow-dry to khtenisma

   I'd like a cut and blow-dry THa iTHela kopsimo keh khtenisma

blue bleh

   blue eyes galana matia

blusher i poothra

boarding house i pansion

boarding pass i karta epivivaseos

boat (small) to ka-iki

   (for passengers) to plio

body to soma

boil (*verb*) vrazo

boiled egg to vrasto avgo

boiler o vrastiras

bone to kokalo

bonnet (of car) to kapo

book to vivlio

   (*verb*) klino

   can I book a seat? boro na kliso mia THesi?

I'd like to book a table for two THa iThela na kliso ena trapezi ya thio atoma

what time would you like it booked for? ti ora to THeleteh?

half past seven stis efta keh misi

that's fine endaxi

and your name? to onoma sas, parakalo?

bookshop to vivliopolio

boot (footwear) i bota

   (of car) to port-bagaz

border (of country) ta sinora

bored: I'm bored vari-emeh

boring varetos

born: I was born in Manchester yeniTHika sto Manchester

   I was born in 1960 yeniTHika to 1960 (khilia eniakosia exinda)

borrow thanizomeh

  may I borrow…?
  boro na thanisto…?

both keh i thio

bother: sorry to bother you
signomi poo sas enokhlo

bottle to bookali

  a bottle of house red ena
  bookali kokino spitiko krasi

bottle-opener to anikhtiri

bottom (of person) o kolos

  at the bottom of the hill
  sto vaтнos too lofoo

  at the bottom of the road
  sto telos too thromoo

box to kooti

box office to tamio

boy to agori

boyfriend o filos

bra to sooti-en

bracelet to vrakhioli

brake to freno

  (*verb*) frenaro

brandy to koniak

bread to psomi

  white bread to aspro psomi

  brown bread to mavro psomi

  wholemeal bread
  to starenio psomi

break (*verb*) spao

  I've broken the… espasa to…

  I think I've broken my wrist
  nomizo oti espasa ton karpo
  moo

break down (car) paтнeno vlavi

  I've broken down khalaseh
  to aftokinito moo

breakdown (car) i vlavi

breakdown service
  i vlaves aftokiniton

breakfast to pro-ino

break-in: I've had a break-in
  meh listepsan

breast to stiтнos

breathe anapneo

breeze to aeraki

bridge (over river) i yefira

brief sindomos

briefcase o khartofilakas

bright (light etc) fotinos

  bright red khtipitos kokinos

brilliant (idea, person)
  katapliktikos

bring ferno

  I'll bring it back later
  тнa to fero piso argotera

Britain i Vretania

British Vretanikos

brochure to prospektoos

broken spasmenos

  it's broken ineh spasmeno

bronchitis i vronkhititha

brooch i karfitsa

broom i skoopa

brother o athelfos

brother-in-law o gambros

brown kafeh

  brown hair kastana malia

  brown eyes kastana matia

bruise i melania

brush i voortsa

  (for hair) i voortsa ya ta malia

  (artist's) to pinelo

bucket o koovas

buffet car to boofeh

buggy (for child) to pethiko amaxaki

building to ktirio

bulb (light bulb) i lamba

Bulgaria i Voolgaria

Bulgarian (*adj*) Voolgarikos

bumper o profilaktiras

bunk i kooketa

bureau de change Sinalagma

burglary i thiarixi

burn (*noun*) to kapsimo (*verb*) keo

burnt: this is burnt afto ineh kameno

burst: a burst pipe mia spasmeni solina

bus to leoforio

  what number bus is it to...? ti arithmo ekhi to leoforio ya...?

  when is the next bus to...? poteh ineh to epomeno leoforio ya...?

  what time is the last bus? ti ora ineh to telefteo leoforio?

  could you let me know when we get there? boriteh na moo to piteh, otan ftasoomeh eki?

  does this bus go to...? piyeni afto to leoforio sto...?

  no, you need a number... okhi, prepi na pareteh to leoforio arithmos...

business i thooli-es

bus station to praktorio leoforion, o stathmos leoforion

bus stop i stasi leoforioo

bust (sculpture) i protomi (measurement) to stithos

busy (restaurant etc) polisikhnastos

  I'm busy tomorrow imeh apaskholimenos avrio

but ala

butcher's o khasapis

butter to vootiro

button to koobi

buy agorazo

  where can I buy...? poo boro na agoraso...?

by: by bus/car meh to leoforio/ aftokinito

  written by... grameno apo...

  by the window thipla sto parathiro

  by the sea konda sti thalasa

  by Thursday prin apo tin Pempti

bye yasoo

C

cabbage to lakhano

cabin (on ship) i kabina

cable car to teleferik

café i kafeteria, to kafenio

cagoule to athiavrokho

cake to cake

cake shop to zakharoplastio

call fonazo

(to phone) tilefono

what's it called? pos to leneh?

he/she is called…
ton/tin leneh…

please call a doctor
seh parakalo, tilefoniseh seh
ena yatro

**please give me a call at
7.30am tomorrow**
seh parakalo, tilefoniseh moo
avrio to pro-i stis efta keh misi

please ask him to call me
seh parakalo, pes too na moo
tilefonisi

call back: I'll call back later THA xanartho argotera

(phone back) THA seh paro piso

**call round: I'll call round
tomorrow** THA peraso avrio

camcorder i mikhani lipseos

camera i fotografiki mikhani

camera shop to katastima
fotografikon ithon

camp (*verb*) kataskinono

can we camp here?
boroomeh na kataskinosoomeh
etho?

camping gas to igra-erio

campsite to kambing

can to kooti, i konserva

a can of beer
mia bira seh kooti

can: can you…? boriteh na…?

can I have…? boro na ekho…?

I can't… then boro…

Canada o Kanathas

Canadian Kanathezikos

I'm Canadian (*male/female*)
imeh Kanathos/Kanatheza

canal to kanali

cancel akirono

candies i karameles

candle to keri

canoe to kano

canoeing kano kano

can-opener to anikhtiri

cap (hat) to kapelo

(of bottle) to kapaki

car to aftokinito

by car meh to aftokinito

carafe i karafa

**a carafe of house white,
please** mia karafa aspro
spitiko krasi, parakalo

caravan to trokhospito

caravan site topothesia ya
trokhospita

carburettor to karbirater

card (birthday etc) i karta

here's my (business) card
oristeh, i karta moo

cardigan i zaketa

cardphone i tilekarta

careful prosektikos

be careful! prosekheh!

caretaker o/i epistatis

car ferry to feri-bot

car hire enikiasis aftokiniton

car park to parking

carpet to khali

(fitted) i moketa

carriage (of train) to vagoni

carrier bag i sakoola

carrot to karoto

carry metafero

carry-cot to port-beh-beh

carton i koota

carwash to plindirio aftokiniton

case (suitcase) i valitsa

cash ta metrita

  will you cash this for me?
тна moo to exaryiroseteh?

cash desk to tamio

cash dispenser
i mikhani ya metrita

cashier o/i tamias

cassette i kaseta

cassette recorder to kasetofono

castle to kastro

casualty department
Protes Vo-iтнi-es

cat i gata

catch piano

  **where do we catch the bus
to…?** apo poo тна paroomeh
to leoforio?

cathedral o katнethrikos naos

Catholic (adj) katнolikos

cauliflower to koonoopithi

cave i spilia

ceiling to tavani

celery to selino

cellar (for wine) to kelari

cell phone to kinito

cemetery to nekrotafio

Centigrade Kelsioo

centimetre ena ekatosto

central kendrikos

central heating
i kendriki тнermansi

centre to kendro

  **how do we get to the city
centre?** pos тна pameh sto
kendro?

cereal ta cornflakes

certainly sigoora

  certainly not fisika okhi

chair i karekla

champagne i sampania

change (money) ta resta

  (verb: money, trains) alazo

  can I change this for…?
boro na alaxo afto ya…?

  I don't have any change
then ekho psila

  **can you give me change
for a 50 euro note?**
boriteh na moo khalaseteh
peninda evro?

**do we have to change
(trains)?** prepi na
alaxoomeh treno?

**yes, change at Corinth/
no, it's a direct train**
neh, alaxteh stin Korintнo/
okhi, piyeni katefrнian

changed: to get changed
alazo rookha

chapel to eklisaki

charge i timi, i thapani

  (verb) khreono

charge card i pistotiki karta

cheap ftinos

  **do you have anything
cheaper?** ekheteh tipoteh
ftinotero?

check (*verb*) epaliтнevo

   (cheque) i epitayi

   (bill) o logariasmos

   could you check the…, please? boriteh na elenxeteh to…, parakalo?

checkbook to karneh epitagon

check-in to check-in

check in kano check-in

   where do we have to check in? poo prepi na kanoomeh check-in?

cheek (on face) to magoolo

cheerio! yasoo!

cheers! (toast) stin iya sas!, is iyian!

cheese to tiri

chemist's to farmakio

cheque i epitayi

   do you take cheques? perneteh epitayes?

cheque book to karneh epitagon

cheque card i karta epitagon

cherry to kerasi

chess to skaki

chest to stiтнos

chewing gum i tsikhla

chicken to kotopoolo

chickenpox i anemovloyia

child to pethi

   children ta pethia

child minder i dada

children's pool i pisina ton pethion

children's portion i pethiki meritha

> Travel tip Children are worshipped and indulged in Greece. They are always welcome at family tavernas, where they are expected to eat the same as adults, and are quickly socialized into the Greek routine of late hours. However, outside of certain all-inclusive resorts with children's programmes, there are few amusements specifically for them.

chin to pigooni

china i porselani

Chinese (*adj*) Kinezikos

chips i tiganites patates

chocolate i sokolata

   milk chocolate i sokolata galaktos

   plain chocolate sokolata sketi

   a hot chocolate i zesti sokolata, mia sokolata rofima

choose thialego

Christian name to mikro onoma

Christmas ta khristooyena

   Christmas Eve i paramoni ton khristooyenon

   merry Christmas! kala khristooyena!

church i eklisia

cicada o tzitzikas

cider cider

cigar to pooro

cigarette to tsigaro

cigarette lighter o anaptiras

cinema o kinimatografos, to sinema

circle o kiklos
(in theatre) o exostis

city i poli

city centre to kendro tis polis

clean (adj) kaтнaros

can you clean these for me? moo pleneteh afta?

cleaning solution (for contact lenses) to kaтнaristiko thialima

cleansing lotion to galaktoma kaтнarismoo

clear kaтнaros
(obvious) profanis

clever exipnos

cliff o apotomos vrakhos

climbing i orivasia

cling film to na-ilon

clinic i kliniki

cloakroom i gardaroba

clock to rolo-i

close klino

what time do you close? ti ora klineteh?

we close at 8pm on weekdays and 6pm on Saturdays klinoomeh stis okto to vrathi tis kaтнimerines keh stis exi to apoyevma ta Savata

do you close for lunch? klineteh ya mesimeriano fayito?

yes, between 1 and 3.30pm neh, apo ti mia mekhri tis tris keh misi

closed klistos

cloth (fabric) to ifasma
(for cleaning etc) to pani

clothes ta rookha

clothes line i aplostra

clothes peg to mandalaki

cloud to sinefo

cloudy sinefiasmenos

clutch to debrayaz, o siblektis

coach (bus) to poolman
(on train) to vagoni

coach station o staтнmos iperastikon leoforion

coach trip to taxithi meh poolman

coast i akti

on the coast stin akti

coat (long coat) to palto
(jacket) to sakaki

coathanger i kremastra

cockroach i katsaritha

cocoa to kakao

coconut i karitha

code (for phoning) o kothikos

what's the (dialling) code for Athens? pios ineh o kothikos ya tin Aтнina?

coffee o kafes

two Greek coffees, please thio Elinikoos kafethes, parakalo

coin to kerma

Coke i koka-kola

cold krios

I'm cold kriono

I have a cold imeh kriomenos

The Rough Guide Greek Phrasebook > ENGLISH→GREEK

collapse: he's collapsed
katarefseh

collar o yakas

collect paralamvano

I've come to collect...
ilтнa ya na paro...

collect call tilefono collect

college to koleyio

colour to khroma

do you have this in other colours? to ekheteh seh ala khromata?

colour film to enkhromo film

comb i khtena

come erkhomeh

where do you come from?
apo poo iseh?

I come from Edinburgh
imeh apo to Ethimvoorgo

come back epistrefo

I'll come back tomorrow
тнa epistrepso avrio

come in beno mesa

comfortable (chair) anapaftikos
(clothes) anetos
(room, hotel) volikos

compact disc to compact disc

company (business) i eteria

compartment (on train) to koopeh

compass i pixitha

complain paraponoomeh

complaint to parapono

I have a complaint
ekho ena parapono

completely telios

computer o ipolo-yistis

concert i sinavlia

concussion i thiasisi engefaloo

conditioner (for hair) to kondisioner

condom to profilaktik**o**
conference to sin**e**thrio
confirm epiveve**o**no
congratulations! sinkharit**i**ria!
connecting flight s**i**nthesi pt**i**sis
connection (travel) i s**i**nthesi
conscious sinesтнan**o**menos
constipation i thiskili**o**tis
consulate to prox**e**nio
contact erkhomeh seh epaf**i**
contact lenses i fak**i** epaf**i**s
contraceptive (pill) to andisiliptik**o**
(condom) to profilaktik**o**
convenient volik**o**s
that's not convenient
then meh vol**e**vi
convent to monast**i**ri
cook (*verb*) ma-yir**e**vo
not cooked misopsim**e**no
cooker i kooz**i**na
cookie to bisk**o**to
cooking utensils ta ma-yirik**a**
skev**i**
cool throser**o**s
Corfu i K**e**rkira
cork o fel**o**s
corkscrew to anikht**i**ri
corner: on the corner sti gon**i**a
in the corner sti gon**i**a
cornflakes ta cornflakes
correct (right) sost**o**s
corridor o thi**a**thromos
cosmetics ta kalindik**a**
cost (*verb*) stikh**i**zo
how much does it cost?
p**o**so k**a**ni?

cot i ko**o**nia
cotton to vamvak**i**
cotton wool to vamvak**i**
couch o kanap**e**s
couchette i kook**e**ta
cough o v**i**khas
cough medicine to farmako ya
ton v**i**kha
could: could you…?
bor**i**teh na…?
could I have…?
bor**o** na **e**kho…?
I couldn't… then bor**oo**sa na…
country (nation) i kh**o**ra
(countryside) i exokh**i**
countryside i exokh**i**
couple (man and woman) to zevg**a**ri
a couple of… th**i**o ap**o**…
courgette to kolokiтн**a**ki
courier o/i sin**o**thos
course (main course etc) to pi**a**to
of course v**e**veh-a
of course not fisik**a** **o**khi
cousin (*male/female*) o xath**e**lfos/
i xath**e**lfi
cow i a-yel**a**tha
crab to kav**oo**ri
cracker to kraker**a**ki
craft shop to ergast**i**ri
crash i s**i**groosi
I've had a crash trak**a**ra
crazy trel**o**s
cream (on milk, in cake) i kr**e**ma
(lotion) i kr**e**ma therm**a**tos
(colour) krem
creche o pethik**o**s staтнm**o**s

credit card i pistotiki karta

can I pay by credit card? boro na pliroso meh pistotiki karta?

which card do you want to use? ti karta THeleteh na khrisimopi-iseteh?

yes, sir endaxi, kiri-eh

what's the number? ti ariTHmo ekhi?

and the expiry date? keh poteh ineh i imerominia lixeos?

credit crunch i khrimatopistotiki krisi

Crete i Kriti

crisps ta tsips

crockery ta piatika

crossing (by sea) to THalasio taxithi

crossroads to stavrothromi

crowd o kosmos

crowded yematos kosmo

crown (on tooth) i korona

cruise i krooazi-era

crutches i pateritses

cry (weep) kleo

(shout) fonazo

cucumber to agoori

cup to flidzani

a cup of..., please ena flidzani..., parakalo

cupboard to doolapi

cure i THerapia

curly sgooros, katsaros

current to revma

curtains i koortines

cushion to maxilaraki

custom to eTHimo

Customs to Telonio

cut to kopsimo

(verb) kovo

I've cut myself kopika

cutlery ta makheropiroona

cycling i pothilasia

cyclist o/i pothilatis

Cyprus i Kipros

D

dad o babas

daily kaTHimerina

damage (verb) katastrefo

damaged katastrafikeh

I'm sorry, I've damaged this lipameh, to khalasa

damn! na pari i oryi!

damp (adj) igros

dance o khoros

(verb) khorevo

would you like to dance? THelis na khorepsoomeh?

dangerous epikinthinos

Danish thanos

dark (adj: colour) skotinos

(hair) mavros

it's getting dark skotiniazi

date: what's the date today? poso ekhi o minas simera?

let's make a date for next Monday as sinandiTHoomeh

tin epomeni theftera

dates (fruit) i khoormathes

daughter i kori

daughter-in-law i nifi

dawn i avyi

  at dawn tin avyi

day i mera

  the day after
  tin epomeni mera

  the day after tomorrow
  meтнavrio

  the day before
  tin pro-igoomeni mera

  the day before yesterday
  prokhtes

  every day kaтнeh mera

  all day oli tin imera

  in two days' time meta apo
  thio meres

day trip to taxithi afтнimeron

dead peтнamenos, nekros

deaf koofos

deal (business) i simfonia

  it's a deal simfonisameh,
  endaxi

death o тнanatos

decaffeinated coffee o kafes
  khoris kafe-ini

December o Thekemvrios

decide apofasizo

  we haven't decided yet then
  ekhoomeh apofasisi akoma

decision i apofasi

deck (on ship) to katastroma

deckchair i poliтнrona, i sez long

deduct afero

deep vaтнis

definitely oposthipoteh

  definitely not seh kamia
  periptosi

degree (qualification) to ptikhio

delay i kaтнisterisi

deliberately epitithes

delicatessen ta delicatessen

delicious nostimotatos

deliver thianemo

delivery (of mail) i thianomi,
  i parathosi

demotic i dimotiki

Denmark i thania

dental floss to othondiko nima

dentist o/i othondiatros

dentures i masela

deodorant to aposmitiko

department to tmima

department store
  to megalo katastima

departure i anakhorisi

departure lounge
  i eтноosa anakhoriseos

depend: it depends exartateh

  it depends on…
  exartateh apo…

deposit (as security) i kataтнesi
  (as part payment) i prokatavoli

description i perigrafi

dessert to glikisma

destination o pro-orismos

develop anaptiso

diabetic (*male/female*) o thiavitikos/i thiavitiki

   diabetic foods i thiavitiki trofi

dial (*verb*) kalo, perno ariTHmo

dialling code o kothikos ariTHmos

diamond to thiamandi

diaper i pana

diarrhoea i thiaria

diary to imerolo-yio

dictionary to lexiko

didn't *see* not

die peTHeno

diesel i dizel

diet i thi-eta

   I'm on a diet kano thi-eta

   I have to follow a special diet prepi na kano ithiki thi-eta

difference i thiafora

   what's the difference? pia ineh i thiafora?

different thiaforetikos

   this one is different afto etho ineh thiaforetiko

   a different table ena alo trapezi

difficult thiskolos

difficulty i thiskolia

dinghy to zodiak

dining room i trapezaria

dinner (evening meal) to thipno

   to have dinner tro-o vrathino

direct (*adj*) kat-efrHian

is there a direct train? iparkhi kat-efrHian treno ya…?

direction i katefrHinsi

   which direction is it? pros ta poo ineh?

   is it in this direction? ineh pros afti tin katefrHinsi?

directory enquiries i plirofori-es

dirt i vroma

dirty vromikos

disabled anapiros

   is there access for the disabled? iparkhi prosvasi ya toos anapiroos?

disappear exafanizomeh

   it's disappeared exafanistikeh

disappointed apogo-itevmenos

disappointing apogo-iteftiko

disaster i katastrofi

disco i diskotek

discount i ekptosi

   is there a discount? kaneteh ekptosi?

disease i arostia

disgusting a-ithiastikos

dish (meal) to piato

   (bowl) to bol

dishcloth i patsavoora

disinfectant to apolimandiko

disk (for computer) i thisketa

disposable nappies (diapers) i khartines panes

distance i apostasi

   in the distance eki kato

distilled water apestagmeno nero

district i sinikia

disturb enokhlo

diversion (detour) i parakampsi

diving board i sanitha vootias

divorced: I'm divorced
(*male/female*) khorismenos/
khorismeni

dizzy: I feel dizzy zalizomeh

do kano

what shall we do?
ti THa kanoomeh?

how do you do it?
pos to kaneteh?

will you do it for me?
boriteh na moo to kaneteh?

DIALOGUE

how do you do?
ti kaneteh?

nice to meet you
kharika ya ti gnorimia

what do you do?
ti thoolia kaneteh?

I'm a teacher, and you?
imeh thaskalos, ki esis?

I'm a student imeh fititis

**what are you doing this
evening?** ti THa kaneteh
apopseh?

**we're going out for a
drink; do you want to
join us?** THa pameh ya
ena poto – THeleteh na
elTHeteh mazi mas?

do you want cream?
THeleteh krema?

I do, but she doesn't
ego neh, ekini, omos, okhi

doctor o/i yatros

we need a doctor
khriazomasteh enan yatro

please call a doctor seh
parakalo, kaleseh enan yatro

DIALOGUE

where does it hurt?
poo ponateh?

right here akrivos etho

does that hurt more?
sas pona-i afto pio poli?

yes neh

take this to a chemist
thosteh afto seh ena
farmaki-o

document to engrafo

dog o skilos

doll i kookla

domestic flight ptisi esoterikoo

donkey o ga-itharos

don't! mi!

don't do that! min to kanis
afto!
(stop) stamata!
see **not**

door i porta

doorman o THiroros

double thiplo

double bed to thiplo krevati

double room to thiplo
thomatio

doughnut to donat

down kato

down here etho kato

put it down over there
valeh to eki kato

it's down there on the right
vrisketeh eki kato sta thexia

it's further down the road

ineh ligo parakato

download (*verb*) katevazo

downmarket (restaurant etc)
ftinos

downstairs kato

dozen mia doozina

half a dozen misi doozina

drain o okhetos

draught beer varelisia bira

draughty: it's draughty
kani revma

drawer to sirtari

drawing to skhethio

dreadful friktos

dream to oniro

dress to forema

dressed: to get dressed
dinomeh

dressing (for cut) i gaza
(for salad) to lathoxitho

dressing gown i roba

drink to poto
(*verb*) pino

a cold drink to anapsiktiko

can I get you a drink? boro
na seh keraso kanena poto?

what would you like (to
drink)? ti THa THelateh na
pi-iteh?

no thanks, I don't drink
okhi, efkharisto, then pino

I'll just have a drink of
water THa paro monon ena
potiri nero

drinking water to posimo nero

is this drinking water?
ineh posimo afto to nero?

drive othiga-o

we drove here
othiyisameh etho

I'll drive you home
THa seh pao spiti

driver o/i othigos

driving licence i athia
othiyiseos, to thiploma
othiyiseos

drop: just a drop, please
(of drink) poli ligo, parakalo

drug to farmako

drugs (narcotics) ta narkotika

drunk (adj) meтHismenos

drunken driving methismeno
othiyima

> **Travel tip** Drunkenness
> has always been held in
> contempt in Greece,
> where the inability to hold
> one's liquor is considered
> unmanly and shameful.
> Inebriation will be viewed
> as an aggravating factor if
> you're arrested for some-
> thing else, not an excuse.

dry (adj) stegnos
(wine) xiros

dry-cleaner to stegno-
kaтHaristirio

duck i papia

**due: he was due to arrive
yesterday** eprokito na ftasi
khtes

when is the train due?
poteh ftani to treno?

dull (pain) exasтHenimenos
(weather) moondos
(boring) varetos

dummy (baby's) i pipila

during kata ti thiarkia

dust i skoni

dusty skonismeno

dustbin o skoopithodenekes

duty-free (goods)
ta aforolo-yita

duty-free shop to katastima
aforolo-yiton

duvet to paploma

DVD to DVD

E

each kaтHeh

how much are they each?
poso ekhi to kaтHena?

ear to afti

earache: I have earache
ekho pono sto afti

early noris

early in the morning
noris to pro-i

I called by earlier
perasa pro-igoomenos

earrings ta skoolarikia

east i anatoli

in the east stin anatoli

Easter to Paskha

Easter Sunday i Kiriaki too
Paskha

easy efkolos

eat tro-o

**we've already eaten,
thanks** fagameh ithi,
efkharisto

eau de toilette i kolonia

EC i eok

economy class tooristiki тHesi

egg to avgo

hard-boiled egg avgo sfikhto

fried egg tiganito avgo

eggplant i melidzana

either: either... or... i... i...

either of them opio naneh

elastic to lastikho

elastic band to lastikhaki

elbow o angonas

electric ilektrikos

electrical appliances
ilektrikes siskeves

electric fire i ilektriki somba

electrician o ilektrologos

electricity to ilektriko revma

elevator to asanser

else: something else
kati alo

somewhere else kapoo aloo

DIALOGUE

would you like anything else? THa THelateh tipoteh alo?

no, nothing else, thanks okhi, tipoteh alo, efkharisto

e-mail to e-mail

(*verb*: file) stelno meh
e-mail

(person) stelno e-mail seh

embassy i presvia

emergency i ektakti anangi

this is an emergency!
ineh epigon!

emergency exit i exothos
kinthinoo

empty (*adj*) athios

end to telos

(*verb*) teliono

at the end of the street
sto telos too thromoo

when does it end?
poteh telioni?

engaged (toilet, telephone)
katilimenos

(to be married: *male/female*)
aravoniasmenos/
aravoniasmeni

engine (car) i mikhani too
aftokinitoo

England i Anglia

English ta Anglika

I'm English (*male/female*)
imeh Anglos/Anglitha

do you speak English?
milateh anglika?

enjoy: to enjoy oneself
thiaskethazo

DIALOGUE

how did you like the film?
pos soo fanikeh to ergo?

I enjoyed it very much; did you enjoy it? moo areseh
para poli; esena soo areseh?

enjoyable efkharistos

enlargement (of photo)
i me-yenTHisi

enormous terastios

enough arketa

there's not enough
then iparkhi arketo

it's not big enough
then ineh arketa megalo

that's enough ftani, arki

entrance i isothos

envelope o fakelos

epileptic (*male/female*)
o epiliptikos/i epiliptiki

equipment o exoplismos

error to lathos

especially ithika

essential vasikos, aparetitos

   it is essential that…
   ineh aparetito na…

EU Evropa-iki Enosi

euro to evro

Eurocheque to Eurocheque

Eurocheque card
   i karta Eurocheque

Europe i Evropi

European (*adj*) Evropa-ikos

European Union
   Evropa-iki Enosi

even: even the Greeks
   akoma keh i Elines

   even if… akoma ki an…

evening to vrathi

   this evening simera to vrathi

   in the evening to vrathi

evening meal to thipno

eventually telika

ever poteh

**have you ever been to
   Crete?** ekheteh pa-i poteh
   stin Kriti?

**yes, I was there two years
   ago** neh, imoon eki prin
   apo thio khronia

every kaTHeh

   every day kaTHeh mera

everyone oli

everything kaTHeh ti

everywhere pandoo

exactly! akrivos!

exam to thiagonisma

example to parathigma

   for example
   parathigmatos kharin

excellent exokhos

   excellent! exokha!

except ektos

excess baggage to ipervaro

exchange rate
   sinalagmatiki isotimia

exciting sinarpastikos

excuse me (to get past)
   signomi
   (to get attention) parakalo
   (to say sorry) meh sinkhoriteh

exhaust (pipe) i exatmisi

exhausted (tired) exandlimenos

exhibition i ekTHesi

exit i exothos

   where's the nearest exit?
   poo ineh i plisi-esteri
   exothos?

expect perimeno

expensive akrivos

experienced embiros

explain exigo

   can you explain that?
   boris na moo to exiyisis?

express mail to katepigon

express train to treno
   express

extension (telephone)
   i sinthesi tilefonoo

could you get me extension 221, please? meh sintheh-eteh meh to 221 (thiak**o**sia **i**kosi **e**na), parakal**o**?

extension lead i pro-**e**ktasi

extra: can we have an extra chair? bor**oo**meh na **e**kh**oo**meh m**i**a kar**e**kla ak**o**ma?

do you charge extra for that? khre**o**neteh epipl**e**on ya afto?

extraordinary asini**rn**istos

extremely ipervolik**a**

eye to m**a**ti

will you keep an eye on my suitcase for me? **rn**a moo to pros**e**kheteh?

eyebrow pencil to mol**i**vi ya ta fr**i**thia

eye drops i stag**o**nes ya ta m**a**tia

eyeglasses ta yiali**a**

eyeliner to eyeliner

eye make-up remover to gal**a**ktoma ka**rn**arism**oo**

eye shadow i ski**a** mati**o**n

F

face to pr**o**sopo

factory to ergost**a**sio

Fahrenheit va**rn**m**i** Farena-it

faint (*verb*) lipo**rn**im**a**o

she's fainted lipo**rn**im**i**seh

I feel faint es**rn**anomeh lipo**rn**im**i**a

fair (funfair) to paniy**i**ri

(trade) i **e**k**rn**esi

(*adj*) th**i**keos

fairly arket**a**

fake i apom**i**misi

fall (autumn) to fr**rn**in**o**poro

in the fall sto fr**rn**in**o**poro

fall (*verb*) p**e**fto

she's had a fall **e**peseh

false ps**e**ftikos

family i iko-y**e**nia

famous thi**a**simos

fan (electrical) o anemist**i**ras

(hand held) i vent**a**lia

(sports) o/i opath**o**s

fan belt to vendilat**e**r

fantastic fandastik**o**s

far makri**a**

DIALOGUE

is it far from here? **i**neh makri**a** ap**o** eth**o**?

no, not very far **o**khi, **o**khi keh pol**i** makri**a**

well how far? p**o**so makri**a**, thilath**i**?

it's about 20 kilometres **i**neh per**i**poo **i**kosi khili**o**metra

fare i tim**i** too isitir**i**oo

farm to agr**o**ktima

fashionable tis m**o**thas

fast gr**i**goros

fat (person) pakh**i**s

(on meat) to l**i**pos

father o pat**e**ras

father-in-law o pe**rn**er**o**s

faucet i vr**i**si

fault to el**a**toma

sorry, it was my fault
signomi, itan sfalma moo

it's not my fault
then fteo ego

faulty elatomatikos

favourite agapimenos

fax to fax

(*verb:* person) stelno fax seh…

(document) stelno seh fax

February o Fevrooarios

feel estHanomeh

I feel hot zestenomeh

I feel unwell then
estHanomeh kala

I feel like going for a walk
ekho orexi na pao mia volta

how are you feeling?
pos estHaneseh?

I'm feeling better
estHanomeh kalitera

felt-tip pen o markathoros

fence o fraktis

fender o profilaktiras

ferry to feri bot

festival to festival

Travel tip With some kind
of saint listed literally every
day in the Greek Orthodox
calendar, there are scores
of religious ceremonies and
festivals. You're unlikely to
travel around the islands for
long without stumbling on a
celebration of the patron of
the parish church or some
other observance, celebrated
with gusto and always with
respect to local tradition.

fetch pa-o na fero

I'll fetch him THa pa-o na ton
fero

**will you come and fetch me
later?** THa elthis na meh paris
argotera?

feverish empiretos

few: a few liyi, liyes, liga

a few days liyes meres

fiancé o aravoniastikos

fiancée i aravoniastikia

field to khorafi

fight o agonas

figs ta sika

file (computer) to arkhio

fill yemizo

fill in yemizo

do I have to fill this in?
prepi na to yemiso?

fill up yemizo telios

fill it up, please yemisteh tin,
parakalo

filling (in cake, sandwich) i yemisi

(in tooth) to sfra-yisma

film to film

filter coffee o kafes filtroo

filter papers ta filtra ya kafeh

filthy vromeros

find vrisko

I can't find it then to vrisko

I've found it to vrika

find out anakalipto

could you find out for me?
boris na mathis?

fine (weather) oreos

(punishment) to prostimo

finger to thakhtilo
finish teliono
  I haven't finished yet then ekho teliosi akomi
  when does it finish? poteh telioni?
fire: fire! pirkaya!
  can we light a fire here? boroomeh na anapsoomeh fotia etho?
  it's on fire pireh fotia
fire alarm o sinayermos pirkayas
fire brigade i pirosvestiki ipiresia
fire escape i exothos pirkayas
fire extinguisher o pirosvestiras
first protos
  I was first imoon protos
  at first stin arkhi
  the first time i proti fora
  first on the left protos sta aristera
first aid i protes vo-iTHi-es
first aid kit to kooti proton vo-iTHi-on
first class (travel etc) proti THesi
first floor to proto patoma
  (US) to iso-yio

first name to onoma
fish to psari
fisherman o psaras
fishing village to psarokhori
fishmonger's to psarathiko
fit (attack) i prosvoli
  it doesn't fit me then moo khora-i
fitting room to thokimastirio
fix ftiakhno
  (arrange) kanonizo
  can you fix this? boris na to ftiaxis?
fizzy meh anTHrakiko
flag i simea
flannel to sfoogari
flash (for camera) to flas
flat (apartment) to thiamerisma
  (adj) epipethos

I've got a flat tyre
me epiaseh lastikho

flavour i gefsi

flea o psilos

flight i ptisi

flight number ariτHmos ptisis

flippers ta vatrakhopethila

flood i plimira

floor (of room) to patoma

(of building) o orofos

on the floor sto patoma

florist o anτHopolis

flour to alevri

flower to looloothi

flu i gripi

**fluent: he speaks fluent
Greek** mila-i aptesta elinika

fly i miga

(verb) peto

can we fly there? boroomeh
na pameh eki a-eroporikos?

fly in peta-o pros

fly out peta-o apo

fog i omikhli

foggy: it's foggy
ekhi omikhli

folk dancing
i thimotiki khori

folk music i thimotiki moosiki

follow akolooτHo

follow me akolootha meh

food to fa-yito

food poisoning trofiki
thilitiriasi

food shop/store to bakaliko

foot to pothi

on foot meh ta pothia

football (game) to pothosfero

(ball) i bala

football match
o pothosferikos agonas

for ya

**do you have something
for...?** (headache/diarrhoea etc)
ekheteh kati ya...?

DIALOGUE

who's the moussaka for?
ya pion ineh o moosakas?

that's for me ya mena

and this one? ki afto etho?

that's for her afto ineh ya
ekini

**where do I get the bus
for Akropolis?** apo poo
τHa paro to leoforio ya tin
Akropoli?

**the bus for Acropolis
leaves from Stathiou
Street** to leoforio ya tin
Akropoli fevyi apo tin Otho
Stathioo

**how long have you been
here for?** poso kero iseh
etho pera?

**I've been here for two
days, how about you?**
vriskomeh etho pera etho
keh thio meres, esi?

I've been here for a week
vriskomeh etho pera etho
keh mia vthomatha

forehead to metopo
foreign xenos
foreigner (*male/female*)
o xenos/i xeni
forest to thasos
forget xekhno
I forget xekhno
I've forgotten xekhasa
fork (for eating) to pirooni
(in road) i thiaklathosi
form (document) i etisi
formal (dress) episimos
fortnight to theka-penтнimero
fortunately eftikhos
**forward: could you forward
my mail?** boriteh na moo
stileteh ta gramata moo?
forwarding address
i thi-efтнinsi apostolis
foundation cream krema
prosopoo ya makiyaz
fountain i piyi
foyer to foyer
fracture to katagma
free elefтнeros
(no charge) thorean
is it free of charge?
ineh thorean?
freeway i eтнniki othos
freezer i katapsixi
French (*adj*) galikos
(language) ta galika
French fries i tiganites patates
frequent sikhnos
**how frequent is the bus to
Corinth?** kaтнeh poteh ekhi
leoforio ya tin KorinтнO?

fresh (weather, breeze) throseros
(fruit etc) freskos
fresh orange o freskos khimos
portokali
Friday i Paraskevi
fridge to psiyio
fried tiganismenos
fried egg to tiganito avgo
friend (*male/female*) o filos/i fili
friendly filikos
from apo
**when does the next train
from Patras arrive?**
poteh ftani to epomeno treno
apo tin Patra?
from Monday to Friday
apo theftera os Paraskevi
from next Thursday
apo tin ali Pempti

front to mbrostino meros
in front mbrosta
in front of the hotel
mbrosta apo to xenothokhio
at the front
sto mbrostino meros
frost i pagonia, o pa-yetos
frozen pagomenos
frozen food i katepsiymeni trofi
fruit ta froota
fruit juice o khimos frooton
fry tiganizo

frying pan to tigani

full yematos

   it's full of… ineh yemato
meh…

   I'm full khortasa

full board fool pansion

fun: it was fun kala itan,
kanameh kefi

funeral i kithia

funny (strange) paraxenos

   (amusing) astios

furniture ta epipla

further parapera

   it's further down the road
ineh akoma parakato

DIALOGUE

   **how much further is it to
Piraeus?** poso ineh akomi
mekhri ton Pirea?

   about 5 kilometres yiro sta
pendeh khiliometra

fuse i asfalia

   the lights have fused
ka-ikaneh ta fota

fuse box to kooti meh tis
asfali-es

fuse wire to sirma asfalias

future to melon

   in future sto melon

G

gallon ena galoni

game (cards etc) to pekhnithi

   (match) o agonas

   (meat) to kiniyi

garage (for fuel)
to venzinathiko

   (for repairs) to sineryio

   (for parking) to garaz

garden o kipos

garlic to skortho

gas to gazi

gas cylinder (camping gas)
i fiali gazi

gasoline i venzini

gas permeable lenses
i imiskliri faki epafis

gas station to venzinathiko

gate i avloporta

   (at airport) i exothos

gay (adj) omofilofilos

gay bar to gay bar

gears i takhitita

gearbox to kivotio
takhititon

gear lever o levi-es takhititon

general yenikos

gents (toilet) i too-aleta ton
anthron

genuine (antique etc)
afrнendikos

German (adj) Yermanikos

   (language) ta Yermanika

German measles
i eritнra

Germany i Yermania

get (fetch) perno

   **will you get me another
one, please?** тнa moo paris
alo ena, parakalo?

   how do I get to…?
pos boro na pao sto…?

do you know where I can get them? mipos χereteh poo boro na vro tetia?

can I get you a drink? na seh keraso kanena poto?

no, I'll get this one, what would you like? okhi, ego kernao afti ti fora; ti тнa iтнeles?

a glass of red wine ena potiri kokino krasi

get back (return) epistrefo
get in (arrive) ftano
get off kateveno

  where do I get off? poo тнa katevo?

get on (to train etc) aneveno
get out (of car etc) vyeno
get up (in the morning) sikonomeh
gift to thoro
gift shop katastima thoron, ithi thoron
gin to tzin

  a gin and tonic, please ena tzin meh tonik, parakalo

girl to koritsi
girlfriend i filenatha
give thino

  can you give me some change? boriteh na moo thoseteh psila?

  I gave it to him to ethosa seh afton

  will you give this to…? to thinis afto ston…?

how much do you want for this? posa тнelis ya afto?

100 euros ekato evro
I'll give you 70 euros soo thino evthominda evro

give back epistrefo, thino piso
glad efkharistimenos
glass (material) to yali

  (tumbler, wine glass) to potiri

  a glass of wine ena potiri krasi

glasses ta yalia
gloves ta gandia
glue i kola
go pao

  we'd like to go to the… theloomeh na pamch sto…

  where are you going? poo pateh?

  where does this bus go? poo pa-i afto to leoforio?

  let's go! pameh!

  she's gone (left) efiyeh

  where has he gone? poo piyeh aftos?

  I went there last week piga eki tin perasmeni evthomatha

  hamburger to go khamboorger ya to spiti

go away fevgo

  go away! fiyeh!

go back (return) epistrefo
go down (the stairs etc) kateveno

go in beno

go out (in the evening) v-yeno

  do you want to go out tonight? theleteh na pateh exo apopseh?

go through thiaskhizo, pao thia mesoo

go up (the stairs etc) aneveno

goat i katsika

goat's cheese to katsikisio tiri

God o THEos

goggles i maska

gold o khrisos

golf to golf

golf course to yipetho golf

good kalos

  good! kala!

  it's no good (product etc) afto then ineh kalo

  (not worth trying) then ofeli

goodbye ya khara, adio

good evening kalispera

Good Friday i Megali Paraskevi

good morning kalimera

good night kalinikhta

goose i khina

got: we've got to... prepi na...

  have you got any...? ekheteh katholoo...?

government i kivernisi

gradually siga-siga

grammar i gramatiki

gram(me) ena gramario

granddaughter i egoni

grandfather o papoos

grandmother i ya-ya

grandson o egonos

grapefruit to grapefruit

grapefruit juice o khimos grapefruit

grapes ta stafilia

grass to khortari, to grasithi

grateful evgnomon

gravy o zomos too kreatos

great (excellent) poli kalo

  that's great! iperokha!

  it's a great success ineh megali epitikhia

Great Britain i Megali Vretania

Greece i Elatha

greedy akhortagos

Greek (adj) Elinikos

  (language) ta Elinika

  (man) o Elinas

  (woman) i Elinitha

  the Greeks i Elines

Greek coffee Elinikos kafes

Greek-Cypriot (adj) Elinokiprios

Greek Orthodox Elinikos OrTHothoxos

green prasinos

green card (car insurance) i asfalia ya othiyisi sto exoteriko

greengrocer's o manavis

grey grizos

grill i psistaria

grilled psitos sti skhara

grocer's to bakaliko

ground to ethafos

  on the ground sto ethafos

ground floor to iso-yio

group to groop

guarantee i engi-isi

  is it guaranteed?
  ineh engi-imeno?

guest (*male/female*)
o filoxen**oo**menos/
i filoxen**oo**meni

guesthouse i pansi**o**n

guide o/i xenag**o**s

guidebook o tooristik**o**s othig**o**s

guided tour i xen**a**yisi

guitar i kiтн**a**ra

gum (in mouth) to **oo**lo

gun (pistol) to pist**o**li

  (rifle) to **o**plo

gym to yimnast**i**rio

H

hair ta mali**a**

hairbrush i v**oo**rtsa ya mali**a**,
i kht**e**na

haircut (man's) to k**oo**rema

  (woman's) to k**o**psimo

hairdresser's to komot**i**rio

  (men's) to k**oo**rio

hairdryer to pistol**a**ki

hair gel o afr**o**s mali**o**n

hairgrips ta piastr**a**kia
mali**o**n

hair spray to spray ya
ta mali**a**

half mis**o**s

  half an hour misi **o**ra

  half a litre mis**o** l**i**tro

  about half that per**i**poo to
mis**o** ap**o** aft**o**

half board demi-pansi**o**n

half-bottle mis**o** bookali

half fare mis**o** isit**i**rio

half price misotim**i**s

ham to zamb**o**n

hamburger to khamb**oo**rger

hammer to sfir**i**

hand to kh**e**ri

handbag i ts**a**nda

handbrake to khir**o**freno

handkerchief to mand**i**li

  (paper) to khartom**a**ndilo

handle to kher**oo**li

hand luggage to sakvooa-y**a**z

hang-gliding i anemopor**i**a

hangover o ponok**e**falos

  I've got a hangover ekho
ponok**e**falo

happen s**i**mv**e**ni

  what's happening?
ti simv**e**ni?

  what has happened?
ti sin**e**vi?

happy eftikhism**e**nos

  I'm not happy about this
then **i**meh efkharistim**e**nos
meh aft**o**

harbour to lim**a**ni

hard sklir**o**s

  (difficult) th**i**skolos

hard-boiled egg to sfikht**o** avg**o**

hard lenses i sklir**i** fak**i**

hardly met**a** v**i**as

  hardly ever s-kheth**o**n pot**e**h

hardware shop
ta **i**thi kingaler**i**as

hat to kapelo
hate miso
have ekho
  can I have a…? boro na ekho ena…?
  do you have…? ekheteh…?
  what'll you have? ti THa pilteh?
  I have to leave now prepi na piyeno tora
  do I have to…? prepi na…?
  can we have some…? boroomeh na ekhoomeh merika…?
hayfever aler-yia sti yiri
hazelnuts to foondooki
he aftos
  is he here? ineh etho?
head to kefali
headache o ponokefalos
headlights i provolis
headphones ta akoostika
health food shop katastima iyi-inon trofon
healthy iyi-is
hear akoo-o

DIALOGUE
  can you hear me? meh akoos?
  I can't hear you, could you repeat that? then seh akoo-o, boris na to epanalavis?

hearing aid ta akoostika
heart i karthia
heart attack i karthiaki prosvoli

heat i zesti
heater i THermansi
  (radiator) to kalorifer
heating i THermansi
heavy varis
heel (of foot) i fterna
  (of shoe) to takooni
  could you heel these? boriteh na moo valeteh kenooryia takoonia safta?
heelbar o tsagaris
height to ipsos
helicopter to elikoptero
hello ya sas
  (*familiar*) ya soo
  (answer on phone) embros
helmet (for motorcycle) to kranos
help i vo-iTHia
  (*verb*) vo-iTHo
  help! vo-iTHia!
  can you help me? boriteh na meh vo-iTHiseteh?
  thank you very much for your help efkharisto ya ti vo-iTHia sas
helpful exipiretikos
hepatitis i ipatititha
her: I haven't seen her then tin ekho thi
  to her saftin
  with her mazi tis
  for her yaftin
  that's her afti ineh
  that's her towel afti ineh i petseta tis
herbal tea tsa-i too voonoo

herbs ta vo**t**ana

here eth**o**

  here is/are… na…

  here you are (offering) or**i**steh

hers thik**o** tis

  that's hers aft**o** ineh thik**o** tis

hey! eh!

hi! (hello) ya soo

hide (something) kr**i**vo

  (oneself) kr**i**vomeh

high psil**o**s

highchair to karekl**a**ki
  mor**oo**

highway i e**TH**nik**i** oth**o**s

hill o l**o**fos

him: I haven't seen him
  then ton **e**kho thi

  to him saft**o**n

  with him maz**i** too

  for him yaft**o**n

  that's him aft**o**s ineh

hip o gof**o**s

hire nik**i**-a**z**o

  for hire eniki-a**z**onteh

  where can I hire a bike?
  poo bor**o** na nik**i**-a**s**o **e**na
  poth**i**lato?

his: it's his car ineh to aftok**i**nito
  too

  that's his ineh thik**o** too

hit khtip**a**o

hitch-hike k**a**no otost**o**p

hobby to kh**o**bi

hold krat**a**o

hole i tr**i**pa

holiday i thiakop**e**s

  on holiday seh thiakop**e**s

Holy Week i Megali Evthom**a**tha

home to sp**i**ti

  at home (in my house etc)
  sto sp**i**ti

  (in my country) stin patr**i**tha moo

we go home tomorrow
piyeno stin patritha moo avrio
honest timios
honey to meli
honeymoon o minas too melitos
hood (US: of car) to kapo
hope elpizo
I hope so etsi elpizo
I hope not elpizo pos okhi
hopefully meh kali tikhi
horn (of car) to klaxon
horrible friktos
horse to alogo
horse riding i ipasia
hospital to nosokomio
hospitality i filoxenia
thank you for your hospitality sas efkharisto ya ti filoxenia sas
hot zestos
(spicy) kafteros, kaftos
I'm hot zestenomeh
it's hot today kani poli zesti simera
hotel to xenothokhio
hotel room: in my hotel room sto thomatio too xenothokhioo
hour i ora
house to spiti
house wine to krasi too magazioo
hovercraft to hovercraft, o a-erolisTHitiras
how pos
how many? posi?
how do you do? khero poli

DIALOGUE

how are you? pos iseh?
fine, thanks, and you?
poli kala, efkharisto; ki esi?

how much is it?
poso kani afto?
50 euros peninda evro
I'll take it THa to paro

humid igros
humour to khioomor
hungry pinasmenos
are you hungry? pinas?
hurry (verb) viazomeh
I'm in a hurry viazomeh
there's no hurry
then iparkhi via
hurry up! viasoo!
hurt travmatizomeh
it really hurts pona-i poli
husband o sizigos
hydrofoil to iptameno thelfini

I

I ego
ice o pagos
with ice meh pago
no ice, thanks khoris pago, efkharisto
ice cream to pagoto
ice-cream cone to pagoto khonaki
iced coffee to frapeh
ice lolly to pagoto xilaki

idea i ithea

idiot o vlakas

if an

ignition i miza

ill arostos

I feel ill imeh arostos

illness i arostia

imitation (leather etc) i apomimisi

immediately amesos

important spootheos

it's very important
ineh poli simandiko

it's not important
then ineh spootheo

impossible athinaton

impressive endiposiakos

improve veltiono

I want to improve my Greek
THelo na kaliterepso ta Elinika
moo

in: it's in the centre
ineh sto kendro

in my car mesa sto aftokinito
moo

in Athens stin ATHina

in two days from now
seh thio meres apo tora

in May sto Ma-io

in English sta Anglika

in Greek sta Elinika

is he in? ineh eki?

in five minutes
seh pendeh lepta

inch i intsa

include perilamvano

does that include meals?
afto perilamvani keh fayito?

is that included in the price?
perilamvaneth stin timi?

inconvenient akatalilos, avolos

incredible apiTHanos

Indian (adj) Inthikos

indicator to flas, o thiktis

indigestion i thispepsia

indoor pool i esoteriki pisina

indoors mesa

inexpensive ftinos
see **cheap**

inner tube (for tyre) i sabrela

infection i molinsi

infectious kolitikos

inflammation i anaflexi

informal anepisimos

information i plirofori-es

**do you have any
information about…?**
ekheteh tipoteh plirofori-es
skhetika meh…?

information desk i plirofori-es

injection i enesi

injured travmatismenos

she's been injured khtipiseh

in-laws ta peTHerika

innocent atHo-os

insect to endomo

insect bite to tsibima endomoo

**do you have anything for
insect bites?** ekheteh tipoteh
ya tsibimata apo endoma?

insect repellent to AUTAN

inside mesa

inside the hotel mesa sto
xenothokhio

let's sit inside
as katsoomeh mesa

insist epimeno

I insist epimeno

insomnia i a-ipnia

instant coffee to neskafeh

instead andi

give me that one instead
thosteh moo afto sti THesi too aloo

instead of... sti THesi too...

insulin i insoolini

insurance i asfalia

intelligent exipnos

interested: I'm interested in...
enthiaferomeh poli ya...

interesting enthiaferon

that's very interesting
ineh poli enthiaferon

international thi-ethnis

internet to Internet

interpret thi-erminevo

interpreter o/i thi-ermineas

intersection to stavrothromi

interval (at theatre) to thi-alima

into mesa

I'm not into...
then moo aresi...

introduce sistino

may I introduce...?
boro na sas sistiso ton...?

invitation i prosklisi

invite proskalo

Ionian Sea to I-onio pelagos

Ireland i Irlanthia

Irish Irlanthos

I'm Irish (*male/female*)
imeh Irlanthos/Irlantheza

iron (for ironing) to ilektriko sithero

can you iron these for me?
boriteh na moo ta sitheroseteh?

is ineh

island to nisi

it afto

it is... ineh...

is it...? ineh...?

where is it? poo ineh?

it's him ineh aftos

it was... itan...

Italian (*adj*) Italos
(language) ta Italika

Italy i Italia

itch: it itches meh tro-i

J

jack (for car) o grilos

jacket to sakaki

jar to vazaki

jam i marmelatha

jammed: it's jammed
ineh frakarismeno

January o I-anooarios

jaw to sagoni

jazz i tzaz

jealous ziliaris

jeans ta tzins

jellyfish i tsookhtra

jersey to fanelaki

jetty o molos

Jewish Evra-ikos

jeweller's to khrisokho-io

jewellery ta kosmimata

job i thoolia

jogging to jogging

to go jogging
pao ya jogging

joke to astio

journey to taxithi

have a good journey!
kalo taxithi!

jug i kanata

a jug of water
mia kanata nero

juice o khimos

July o I-oolios

jump pithao

jumper to poolover

jump leads ta kalothia batarias

junction i thiastavrosi

June o I-oonios

just (only) monon

just two mono thio

just for me mono ya mena

just here akrivos etho

not just now okhi tora

we've just arrived
molis ftasameh

K

keep krato

keep the change
krata ta resta

can I keep it?
boro na to kratiso?

please keep it
kratisteh to, sas parakalo

ketchup to ketsap

kettle i booyota,
o vrastiras

key to klithi

**the key for room 201,
please** to klithi ya to 201
(thiakosia ena), parakalo

key ring to brelok

kidneys ta nefra

kill skotono

kilo ena kilo

kilometre ena khiliometro

**how many kilometres is it
to…?** posa khiliometra ineh
mekhri to…?

kind (generous) evyenikos

that's very kind
ineh poli evyeniko

---

king o vasilias

kiosk to periptero

kiss to fili
(verb) filao

kitchen i koozina

kitchenette i koozinoola

Kleenex ta khartomandila

knee to gonato

knickers i kilota

knife to makheri

knitwear plekta rookha

knock khtipo

knock down khtipo

he's been knocked down
khtipiTHikeh

knock over (object)
anapotho-yirizo

(pedestrian) khtipo

know (somebody) gnorizo

(something, a place) xero

I don't know then xero

I didn't know that then to ixera

**do you know where I can
find…?** mipos xereteh poo
boro na vro…?

L

label i etiketa

ladies' (toilets) i too-aleta ton
yinekon

ladies' wear yinekia ithi

lady i kiria

lager i bira

lake i limni

lamb (meat) to arni

lamp i lamba

lane (on motorway) i loritha

(small road) i parothos

language i glosa

language course
maTHimata xenis glosas

laptop o foritos ipolo-yistis

large megalos

last telefteos

last week i perasmeni
evthomatha

last Friday tin perasmeni
Paraskevi

last night kh-THes vrathi

**what time is the last
train to Salonika?** ti ora
ineh to telefteo treno ya tin
THesaloniki?

late arga

sorry I'm late meh
sinkhoriteh poo arisa

the train was late to treno
ikheh kaTHisterisi

we must go – we'll be late
prepi na piyenoomeh – THa
aryisoomeh

it's getting late nikhtoni

later argotera

I'll come back later
THa yiriso argotera

see you later adio, THa ta
xanapoomeh

later on argotera

latest o pi-o prosfatos

by Wednesday at the latest
tin Tetarti to argotero

laugh yelo

launderette to plindirio rookhon

laundromat to plindirio rookhon

laundry (clothes) i boogatha,
ta aplita

(place) to kaTHaristirio

lavatory i too-aleta

law o nomos

lawn to grasithi

lawyer o/i thikigoros

laxative to kaTHartiko

lazy tebelis

lead (electrical) o agogos

(verb) othigo

where does this lead to?
poo othiyi afto?

leaf to filo

leaflet to thiafimistiko

leak i thiaro-i

(*verb*) stazo

the roof leaks i steyi stazi

learn maтнeno

least: not in the least katholoo

at least toolakhiston

leather to therma

leave (bag etc) afino

(go away) fevgo

(forget) xekhnao

I am leaving tomorrow
fevgo avrio

he left yesterday
efiyeh kh-тнes

may I leave this here?
boro nafiso afto etho?

I left my coat in the bar
afisa tin tsanda moo sto bar

**when does the bus for
Athens leave?** poteh fevyi to
leoforio ya tin Aтнina?

leeks ta prasa

left aristera

on the left pros ta aristera

to the left pros ta aristera

turn left stripseh aristera

there's none left then
emineh tipoteh

left-handed aristerokhiras

left luggage (office) o khoros
filaxis aposkevon

leg to pothi

lemon to lemoni

lemonade i lemonatha

lemon tea tsai meh lemoni

lend thanizo

will you lend me your... ?
тнa moo thanisis to thiko
soo...?

lens (of camera) o fakos

lesbian i lesvia

less ligotero

less than ligotero apo

less expensive ligotero akrivo

lesson to maтнima

let (allow) epitrepo

will you let me know?
тнa moo to pis?

I'll let you know тнa soo po

**let's go for something to
eat** pameh na fameh kati

let off katevazo

will you let me off at...?
тнa meh katevaseteh sto...?

letter to grama

**do you have any letters for
me?** ekho kanena grama?

letterbox to gramatokivotio

lettuce to marooli

lever o levi-es

library i vivlioтнiki

licence i athi-a

lid to kapaki

lie (tell untruth) leo psemata

lie down xaplono

life i zo-i

lifebelt i zoni asfalias

lifeguard o navagosostis

life jacket to sosivio**

lift (in building) to asanser

  could you give me a lift?
boriteh na meh pateh?

  would you like a lift?
THeleteh na sas pao?

light to fos

  (not heavy) elafros

  do you have a light?
(for cigarette) ekhis fotia?

  light green anikhto prasino

light bulb i lamba, o glombos

  I need a new light bulb
khriazomeh mia kenoorya
lamba

lighter (cigarette) o anaptiras

lightning i astrapi

like (*verb*) moo aresi

  I like it moo aresi afto

  I like going for walks
moo aresi na piyeno peripato

I like you moo aresis

I don't like it
then moo aresi afto

do you like it? soo aresi afto?

I'd like to go swimming
THa iTHela na pao ya kolimbi

I'd like a beer
THa iTHela mia bira

would you like a drink?
THa iTHeles ena poto?

**would you like to go for a
walk?** THa iTHeles na pameh
mia volta?

what's it like? meh ti miazi?

I want one like this
THelo ena san ki afto

lime to moskholemono

lime cordial to lime

line (on paper) i grami

  (phone) i tilefoniki grami

could you give me an outside line? тна moo тноseteh grami?

lips ta khilia

lip salve to vootiro kakao

lipstick to krayon

liqueur to liker

listen akoo-o

litre ena litro

  a litre of white wine ena litro aspro krasi

little mikros

  just a little, thanks ligo mono, efkharisto

  a little milk ligo gala

  a little bit more ligo akomi

live zo

  we live together sizoomeh

  where do you live? poo menis?

  I live in London meno sto Lonthino

lively thrastirios

liver to sikoti

loaf i fradzola

lobby (in hotel) to saloni

lobster o astakos

local dopios

  can you recommend a local wine/restaurant? boriteh na mas sistiseteh ena dopio krasi/ estiatorio?

lock i klitharia

  (*verb*) klithono

  it's locked ineh klithomeno

lock in klithono mesa

lock out klithono apo exo

  I've locked myself out klithoтHika apexo

locker (for luggage etc) i тнiritha

lollipop to glifidzoori

London to Lonтнino

long makris

  how long will it take to fix it? poso kero тнa pari ya na to ftiaxeteh?

  how long does it take? posi ora kani?

  a long time polis keros, poli ora

  one day/two days longer mia mera/thio meres parapano

long-distance call to iperastiko tilefonima

look: I'm just looking, thanks efkharisto, vlepo mono

  you don't look well then feneseh kala

  look out! prosexe!

  can I have a look? boro na tho?

look after prosekho, frondizo

look at kitazo

look for psakhno

  I'm looking for… psakhno ya…

look forward to perimeno meh khara

  I'm looking forward to it to perimeno pos keh pos

loose (handle etc) khalaros

lorry to fortigo

lose khano

    I've lost my way ekho khaтнi

    I'm lost, I want to get to…
    ekho khaтнi, тнelo na pao
    sto…

> **Travel tip** If you're lost, the
> pavement kiosk is the first
> place to go for directions.
> Positioned on squares and
> strategic thoroughfares all
> over Greece, they keep long
> hours and contribute con-
> siderably to the air of public
> street-safety after dark. Their
> stock in trade is predictable:
> newspapers, magazines,
> sweets, tissues, bus tickets,
> cigarettes, mobile top-up
> cards and cold drinks.

    I've lost my (hand)bag
    ekhasa tin tsanda moo

lost property (office)
    to grafio apolesтнendon

lot: a lot, lots pola

    not a lot okhi pola

    a lot of people poli anтнropi

    a lot bigger poli megalitero

    I like it a lot moo aresi poli

lotion i losion

loud thinatos

lounge to saloni

love i agapi

    (*verb*) agapo

    I love Greece latrevo tin
    Elatha

lovely oreos

low khamilos

luck i tikhi

    good luck! kali tikhi!

luggage i aposkeves

luggage trolley to karotsaki ya
    tis aposkeves

lump (on body) to priximo

lunch to yevma

lungs o pnevmonas

luxurious (hotel, furnishings)
    politelis

luxury politelias

M

Macedonia i Makethonia

machine i mikhani

mad (insane) trelos
    (angry) trelos apo тнimo

magazine to periothiko

maid (in hotel) i kamari-era

maiden name to patronimo

mail ta gramata, to takhithromio
    (*verb*) takhithromo

    is there any mail for me?
    ekho kanena grama?

mailbox to gramatokivotio

main kirios

main course to kirio piato

Mainland Greece
    i Ipirotiki Elatha

main post office
    kendriko takhithromio

main road (in town)
    o kendrikos thromos
    (in country) o aftokinito-thromos

main switch
    o kendrikos thiakoptis

make (brand name) i marka
  (verb) kano

  I make it 60 euros
  ipolo-yizo oti kani exinda evro

  what is it made of?
  apo ti ineh ftiagmeno?

make-up to make-up

man o andras

manager o thi-efтнindis,
  o manager

  can I see the manager?
  boro na tho ton thi-efтнindi?

manageress i thi-efтнindria

manual to aftokinito meh
  kanonikes takhitites

many pola

  not many liga, okhi pola

map o khartis

March o Martios

margarine i margarini

market i agora

marmalade i marmelatha

married: I'm married (said
  by a man/woman) imeh
  pandremenos/pandremeni

  are you married? (said
  to a man/woman) isteh
  pandremenos/pandremeni?

mascara i maskara

match (football etc) to mats,
  o agonas

matches ta spirta

material (fabric) to ifasma

matter: it doesn't matter
  then pirazi

  what's the matter?
  ti simveni?

mattress to stroma

May o Ma-ios

**may: may I have another
  one?** тнa iтнela ki alo ena?

  may I come in? boro na bo?

  may I see it? boro na to tho?

  may I sit here? boro na
  kaтнiso etho?

maybe isos

mayonnaise i ma-yoneza

me emena

  that's for me afto ineh ya
  mena

  send it to me stilteh to seh
  mena

  me too ki ego episis

meal to fa-yito

did you enjoy your meal?
sas areseh to fayito?

**it was excellent, thank
you** itan poli nostimo,
efkharisto

DIALOGUE

mean: what do you mean?
  ti eno-iteh?

**what does this word
mean?** ti simeni afti i lexi?

it means… in English
simeni… sta Anglika

DIALOGUE

measles i ilara

meat to kreas

mechanic o mikhanikos

medicine to farmako

Mediterranean i Meso-yios

medium (adj: size) metrios

medium-dry imixiro krasi

medium-rare misopsimeno

medium-sized
metrio meyeтнos

meet sinandao

  nice to meet you
  kharika poo sas gnorisa

  where shall I meet you?
  poo тнa sas sinandiso?

meeting i sinandisi

meeting place
to meros sinandisis

melon to peponi

memory stick to stik mnimis

men i anthres

mend thiorтнono

  **could you mend this for
  me?** boriteh na moo to
  ftiaxeteh?

menswear ta anthrika ithi

mention anafero

  don't mention it parakalo

menu to menoo

  **may I see the menu,
  please?** boro na tho to
  menoo, parakalo?

  see Menu Reader

message to minima

  **are there any messages for
  me?** iparkhi kanena minima
  ya mena?

  **I want to leave a message
  for...** thelo nafiso ena minima
  ya...

metal to metalo

metre to metro

microwave (oven) o foornos

  mikrokimaton, to microwave

midday to mesimeri

  at midday to mesimeri

middle: in the middle sti mesi

  in the middle of the night
  arga ti nikhta

  the middle one to meseo

midnight ta mesanikhta

  at midnight ta mesanikhta

might: I might тнa boroosa

  I might not then тнa boroosa

  **I might want to stay
  another day** bori na тнelo na
  mino akomi mia mera

migraine i imikrania

mild (weather) eтнrios

  (taste) elafros

mile ena mili

milk to gala

milkshake to milkshake

millimetre ena khiliosto

minced meat o kimas

mind: never mind then pirazi

  I've changed my mind
  alaxa gnomi

DIALOGUE

**do you mind if I open the
window?** seh pirazi an
anixo to paraтнiro?

no, I don't mind okhi, then
meh pirazi

---

mine: it's mine ineh thiko moo

mineral water
to emfialomeno nero

mint (sweet) i menda

minute to lepto

in a minute seh ena lepto

just a minute ena lepto

mirror o kaтнreftis

Miss thespinis

miss khano

I missed the bus
ekhasa to leoforio

missing lipi

one of my… is missing
lipi ena…

there's a suitcase missing
lipi mia valitsa

mist i katakhnia

mistake to laтнos

I think there's a mistake
nomizo oti iparkhi ena laтнos
etho

sorry, I've made a mistake
meh sinkhoriteh, ekana
laтнos

misunderstanding i parexiyisi

**mix-up: sorry, there's been
a mix-up** meh sinkhoriteh,
iparkhi ena berthema

mobile phone to kinito

modern modernos

modern art gallery i galeri
modernas tekhnis

Modern Greek ta Nea Elinika

moisturizer i ithatiki krema

**moment: I won't be a
moment** mia stigmi parakalo

monastery to monastiri

Monday i theftera

money ta lefta

month o minas

monument to mnimio

moon to fengari

moped to mikhanaki

more perisoteros

**can I have some more
water, please?**
akomi ligo nero, parakalo

more expensive/interesting
pio akrivo/enthiaferon

more than 50
perisotero apo peninda

more than that
pio poli ap afto

a lot more poli perisotero

**would you like some
more?** тна тнelateh ligo
akomi?

**no, no more for me,
thanks** okhi, okhi alo ya
mena, efkharisto

how about you? ki esis?

**I don't want any more,
thanks** then тнelo alo,
efkharisto

morning to pro-i

this morning simera to pro-i

in the morning to pro-i

mosquito to koonoopi

mosquito repellent to fithaki ya
ta koonoopia

**most: I like this one most
of all** afto moo aresi pio poli
apo ola

most of the time siniтнos

most tourists i perisoteri
tooristes

mostly kirios

mother i mitera

motorbike i motosikleta

motorboat i varka meh mikhani

motorway i ethniki othos

mountain to voono

  in the mountains pano sta voona

mountaineering i orivasia

mouse to pondiki

moustache to moostaki

mouth to stoma

mouth ulcer pliyi sto stoma

move metakino

  he's moved to another room piyeh seh alo thomatio

  could you move your car? boriteh na metakiniseteh to aftokinito sas?

  could you move up a little? boriteh na metakinithiteh ligo?

  where has it moved to? poo metaferthikeh?

movie to film

movie theater o kinimato- grafos, to sinema

MP3 format i morfi MP3

Mr kiri-eh

Mrs kiria

Ms thespinis

much poli

  much better/worse poli kalitera/khirotera

  much hotter poli pio zesta

  not much okhi poli

  not very much okhi para poli

  I don't want very much then thelo para poli

mud i laspi

mug (for drinking) i koopa

  I've been mugged meh listepsan

mum i mama

mumps i parotititha

museum to moosio

mushrooms ta manitaria

music i moosiki

musician o/i moosikos

Muslim (adj) Moosoolmanikos

mussels ta mithia

must: I must... prepi na...

  I mustn't drink alcohol then prepi na pio alko-ol

mustard i moostartha

my o/i/to... moo

myself: I'll do it myself tha to kano o ithios

  by myself apo monos moo

N

nail (finger) to nikhi
  (metal) to karfi

nailbrush i voortsa ya ta nikhia

nail varnish to mano

name to onoma

  my name's John meh leneh John

  what's your name? pos seh leneh?

  what is the name of this

street? pos leneh afto to thromo?

napkin i petseta

nappy i pana

narrow (street) stenos

nasty (person) apesios (weather, accident) askhimos

national еTHnikos

nationality i еTHnikotita

natural fisikos

nausea i naftia

navy (blue) ble maren

near konda

   is it near the city centre? ineh konda sto kendro tis polis?

   do you go near the Acropolis? pernateh apo tin Akropoli?

   where is the nearest…? poo ineh to plisi-estero…?

nearby etho konda

nearly skhethon

necessary aparetitos, anangeos

neck o lemos

necklace to koli-e

necktie i gravata

need: I need… khriazomeh…

   do I need to pay? khriazeteh na pliroso?

needle i velona

negative (film) to arnitiko

neither: neither (one) of them kanenas apo aftoos

   neither… nor… ooteh… ooteh…

nephew o anipsios

net (in sport) to thikhti

network map o khartis othikoo thiktioo

never poteh

have you ever been to Athens? ekheteh pa-i poteh stin ATHina?

no, never, I've never been there okhi, poteh, then ekho pa-i poteh eki

new neos, kenooryos

news (radio, TV etc) ta nea

newsagent's to praktorio efimerithon

newspaper i efimeritha

newspaper kiosk to periptero meh efimerithes

New Year to neo etos

Happy New Year! eftikhismenos o kenooryos khronos!

New Year's Eve i protokhronia

New Zealand i Nea Zilanthia

New Zealander: I'm a New Zealander (*male/female*) imeh Neozilanthos/Neozilantheza

next epomenos

the next turning on the left i epomeni strofi sta aristera

the next street on the left o epomenos thromos sta aristera

at the next stop stin epomeni stasi

next week tin ali evthomatha

next to thipla apo

nice (food) nostimos

(looks, view etc) oreos

(person) kalos

---

niece i anipsia

night i nikhta

at night to vrathi

good night kalinikhta

do you have a single room for one night? ekheteh ena mono thomatio ya mia nikhta?

yes, madam malista, kiria moo

how much is it per night? poso kani ti mia nikhta?

it's 60 euros for one night ineh exinda evro ya mia nikhta

thank you, I'll take it efkharisto, THa to kliso

---

nightclub to nait-klab

nightdress to nikhtiko

night porter o nikhterinos THiroros

no okhi

I've no change then ekho psila

there's no... left then emineh katHoloo...

no way! apokli-eteh!

oh no! (upset) okh!, o okhi!

nobody kanenas

there's nobody there then ineh kanis eki

noise i fasaria

noisy: it's too noisy ekhi poli fasaria

non-alcoholic khoris alko-ol

none kanis

non-smoking compartment
o khoros ya mi kapnizondes

noon to mesimeri

no-one kanenas

nor: nor do I ooteh kego

normal fisiolo-yikos

north o voras

  in the north sta vori-a

  north of Athens
  vori-a tis ATHinas

northeast o vorio-anatolikos

northwest o vorio-thitikos

northern vorios

Northern Ireland i Vorios
Irlanthia

Norway i Norviyia

Norwegian (*adj*) Norviyikos

nose i miti

nosebleed i emorayia sti miti

not then

  no, I'm not hungry
  okhi, then pina-o

  I don't want any, thank you
  efkharisto, then THelo

  it's not necessary
  then ineh aparetito

  I didn't know that
  then to ixera

  not that one – this one
  okhi afto – to alo

note (banknote) to khartonomisma

notebook to blokaki,
to simiomatario

notepaper (for letters)
to kharti alilografias

nothing tipoteh

  nothing for me, thanks
  tipoteh ya mena, efkharisto

  nothing else tipoteh alo

novel to miTHistorima

November o No-emvrios

now tora

number o ariTHmos

  I've got the wrong
  number pira laTHos
  noomero

  what is your phone
  number? pio ineh to tilefono
  soo?

number plate i pinakitha

nurse (*male/female*)
o nosokomos/i nosokoma

nursery slope i pista
ekmaTHisis

nut (for bolt) to paximathi

nuts to karithi

O

o'clock i ora

occupied (toilet) katilimenos

October o Oktovrios

odd (strange) paraxenos

of too

off (lights) klisto

  it's just off Omonia Square
  ligo pio eki apo tin Omoni-a

  we're off tomorrow
  fevgoomeh avrio

offensive (language, behaviour)
prosvlitikos

office (place of work) to grafio

officer (said to policeman)
astinomeh

often sikhna

not often okhi sikhna

how often are the buses?
katheh poteh ekhi leoforia?

oil (for car) ta lathia

(for salad) to lathi

ointment i alifi

OK endaxi

are you OK? iseh kala?

is that OK with you?
iseh efkharistimenos etsi?

is it OK to…? pirazi na…?

that's OK thanks (it doesn't
matter) ineh endaxi, efkharisto

I'm OK (nothing for me)
tipoteh ya mena

(I feel OK) imeh mia khara

is this train OK for…?
afto ineh to treno ya…?

I said I'm sorry, OK?
soo ipa signomi, endaxi?

old (person) yeros

(thing) palios

how old are you?
poso khronon iseh?

I'm twenty-five imeh ikosi-
pendeh khronon

and you? ki esi?

old-fashioned demodeh

old town (old part of town)
i palia poli

in the old town stin palia poli

olive oil to eleolatho

olives i eli-es

omelette i omeleta

on pano

(lights) anikhto

on the street/beach
sto thromo/stin paralia

is it on this road? ineh safto
to thromo?

on the plane mesa sto
a-eroplano

on Saturday to Savato

on television stin tileorasi

I haven't got it on me
then to ekho mazi moo

this one's on me (drink)
ego kernao afti ti fora

the light wasn't on
to fos then itan anikhto

what's on tonight?
ti pezi simera?

once (one time) mia fora

at once (immediately) amesos

one enas, mia, ena

the white one to aspro

**one-way ticket: a one-way
ticket to…** ena aplo ya…

onion to kremithi

online (book, check) online

only mono

only one mono ena

it's only 6 o'clock
ineh mono exi i ora

I've only just got here
molis eftasa

on/off switch o thiakoptis

open (adj) aniktos

(verb: door, shop) anigo

when do you open?
poteh aniyeteh?

I can't get it open
then boro na to anixo

in the open air stin ipethro

opening times ores litooryias

open ticket isitirio meh anikhti
epistrofi

opera i opera

operation (medical) i enkhirisi

operator (telephone: *male/female*)
o tilefonitis/i tilefonitria

**opposite: the opposite
direction** stin anditheti
katefrhinsi

the bar opposite
to bar apenandi

opposite my hotel apenandi
apo to xenothokhio moo

optician o optikos

or i

orange (fruit) to portokali
(colour) portokali

orange juice i portokalatha

orchestra i orkhistra

order: can we order now?
(in restaurant) boroomeh na
paragiloomeh tora?

**I've already ordered,
thanks** ekho ithi paragili,
efkharisto

I didn't order this
then paragila afto

out of order then litooryi

ordinary kanonikos

other alos, ali, alo

the other one to alo

the other day tis pro-ales

I'm waiting for the others
perimeno toos aloos

do you have any others?
ekheteh tipoteh ala?

otherwise thiaforetika

our o/i/to… mas

ours thikos mas

out: he's out then ineh etho

**three kilometres out of
town** tria khiliometra exo apo
tin poli

outdoors exo

outside… exo…

can we sit outside?
borroomeh na kathisoomeh
exo?

oven o foornos

over: over here etho

over there eki, eki pera

over 500 pano apo pendakosia

it's over teliosa

**overcharge: you've
overcharged me** meh
khreosateh parapano

overcoat to palto

**overlook: I'd like a room
overlooking the courtyard**
тна irHela ena thomatio meh
тнеa stin avli

overnight (travel) oloniktio

overtake prosperno

**owe: how much do I owe
you?** poso sas khrostao?

own: my own… thiko moo…

are you on your own?
iseh monos soo?

I'm on my own imeh monos moo

owner (*male/female*) o ithioktitis/ i ithioktitria

P

pack (*verb*) ftiakhno tis valitses

   a pack of... ena paketo...

package (parcel) to paketo

package holiday i organomeni ekthromi

packed lunch to etimo mesimeriano

packet: a packet of cigarettes ena paketo tsigara

padlock to looketo, i klitharia

page (of book) i selitha

   could you page Mr...? boriteh na fonaxeteh ton kirio...?

pain o ponos

   I have a pain here esthanomeh ena pono etho

painful othiniros

painkillers to pafsipono

paint i boya

painting o pinakas zografikis

pair: a pair of... ena zevgari...

Pakistani (*adj*) Pakistanikos

palace to palati

pale khlomos

   pale blue galazios

pan to tapsi

panties to slip, i kilotes

pants (underwear: men's) to sovrako

(women's) to slip, i kilotes

(trousers) to pandaloni

pantyhose to kalson

paper to kharti

   (newspaper) i efimeriTHa

   a piece of paper ena komati kharti

paper handkerchiefs ta khartomandila

parcel to thema

pardon (me)? (didn't understand/ hear) signomi?

parents: my parents i gonis moo

parents-in-law ta peTHerika

park to parko

   (*verb*) parkaro

   can I park here? boro na parkaro etho?

parking lot to parking

part to meros

partner (boyfriend, girlfriend) o filos, i fili

party (group) i omatha

   (celebration) to parti

pass (in mountains) to perasma

passenger o/i epivatis

passport to thiavatirio

password o kothikos prosvasis

past: in the past sto parelTHon

   just past the information office amesos meta to grafio pliroforion

path to monopati

pattern to s-khethio

pavement to pezothromio

   on the pavement sto pezothromio

pavement café
kafenio sto thromo

pay plirono

can I pay, please?
boro na pliroso, parakalo?

it's already paid for
ineh ithi pliromeno

who's paying? pios тна
plirosi?

I'll pay ego тна pliroso

**no, you paid last time, I'll
pay** okhi, esi pliroses tin
teleftea fora, ego тна pliroso

payphone to tilefono meh
kermata

peaceful irinikos

peach to rothakino

peanuts fistikia arapika

pear to akhlathi

peas ta bizelia

peculiar (taste, custom)
paraxenos

pedestrian crossing
i thiavasi pezon

pedestrian precinct
o pezo-thromos

peg (for washing) to mandalaki
(for tent) to palooki

pen to stilo

pencil to molivi

penfriend (male/female) o filos
thi' alilografias/i fili thi'
alilografias

penicillin i penikilini

penknife o soo-yias

pensioner o/i sindaxiookhos

people i anтнropi

**the other people in the
hotel** i ali anтнropi sto xenothokhio

too many people ipervolika
poli anтнropi

pepper (spice) to piperi
(vegetable) i piperia

peppermint (sweet) i menda

per: per night tin vrathia

how much per day?
poso tin imera?

percent tis ekato

perfect telios

perfume to aroma

perhaps isos

perhaps not isos okhi

period (time, menstruation)
i periothos

perm i permanand

permit i athia

person to atomo

petrol i venzini

petrol can ena thokhio
venzinis

petrol station to venzinathiko

pharmacy to farmakio

phone to tilefono
(verb) perno tilefono, tilefono

phone book o tilefonikos
katalogos

phonecard i tilekarta

phone charger
o fortistis tilefonoo

phone number
o ariтнmos tilefonoo

photo i fotografia

excuse me, could you take a photo of us? meh sinkhoriteh, тна boroosateh na mas pareteh mia fotografia?

phrase book to vivlio thialogon

piano to piano

pickpocket o portofolas

pick up: will you be there to pick me up? тна iseh eki na meh paris?

picnic to piknik

picture i ikona

pie i pita

(meat) i kreatopita

(fruit) i frootopita

piece to komati

a piece of... ena komati...

pill to khapi

I'm on the pill perno antisiliptika khapia

pillow to maxilari

pillow case i maxilaroтнiki

pin i karfitsa

pineapple o ananas

pineapple juice o khimos anana

pink roz

pipe (for smoking) i pipa, to tsibooki

(for water) o solinas

pipe cleaners катнaristis pipas

Piraeus o Pireas

pistachio nuts fistiki-a Eyinis

pity: it's a pity ineh krima

pizza i pitsa

place to meros

is this place taken? ineh piasmeni afti i тнesi?

at your place sti тнesi soo

at his place sti тнesi too

plain (not patterned) monokhromo

plane to a-eroplano

by plane meh to a-eroplano

plant to fito

plaster cast o yipsos

plasters to lefkoplast

plastic plastikos

(credit cards) i pistotiki karta

plastic bag i plastiki sakoola

plate to piato

plate-smashing spasimo pi-aton

platform i platforma

which platform is for Patras, please? pia platforma ya tin Patra, parakalo?

play (in theatre) to тнeatriko ergo

(verb) pezo

playground to yipetho

pleasant efkharistos

please parakalo

yes please neh, parakalo

could you please...? тна boroosateh, parakalo, na...?

please don't stamata, seh parakalo

pleased to meet you kharika poli

pleasure: i efkharistisi

my pleasure efkharistisi moo

plenty: plenty of... poli/pola...

there's plenty of time iparkhi arketi ora

that's plenty, thanks efkharisto, arki

pliers i pensa
plug (electrical) i briza
  (for car) to boozi
  (in sink) i tapa
plumber o ithravlikos
pm meta mesimvrias
poached egg to avgo poseh
pocket i tsepi
point: two point five thio koma pendeh
  there's no point then iparkhi logos
points (in car) i platines
poisonous thilitiriothis
police i astinomia
  call the police! kalesteh tin astinomia!
policeman o astifilakas
police station to astinomiko tmima
policewoman i astinomikos

polish to verniki
polite evgenikos
polluted molismenos
pony to poni
pool (for swimming) i pisina
poor (not rich) ftokhos
  (quality) kakos
pop music i moosiki pop
pop singer o tragoothistis pop, i tragoothistria pop
population o plithismos
pork to khirino
port (for boats) to limani
  (drink) i mavrothafni
porter (in hotel) o akh-тноforos
portrait to portreto
posh (restaurant) akrivos
  (people) kiriles
possible thinatos
  is it possible to...? ineh thinaton na...?

as... as possible oso to
thinaton...

post (mail) ta gramata
(*verb*) takhithromo

**could you post this for
me?** boriteh na moo to
takhithromiseteh?

postbox to gramatokivotio

postcard i kartpostal

postcode o takhithromikos
kothikos

poster (for room) to poster
(in street) i afisa

post office to takhithromio

poste restante post restand

pots and pans (cooking
implements) katsaroles keh
tigania

potato i patata

potato chips ta tsips

pottery ta keramika

pound (money) i lira
(weight) i libra

power cut i thiakopi revmatos

power point o revmatothotis

**practise: I want to practise
my Greek** THElo na exaskiso
ta Elinika moo

prawns i garithes
(larger) i karavitha

prefer: I prefer... protimo...

pregnant engios

prescription (for chemist)
i sindayi

present (gift) to thoro

president (of country) o pro-ethros

pretty (beautiful) omorfos, oreos

(quite) arketa

it's pretty expensive
ineh arketa akrivo

price i timi

priest o papas

prime minister
o proTHi-poorgos

printed matter ta endipa

priority (in driving) i protereotita

prison i filaki

private ithiotikos

private bathroom
to ithiotiko banio

probably piTHanon

problem to provlima

no problem! kanena provlima!

program(me) to programa

promise: I promise
iposkhomeh

**pronounce: how is this
pronounced?**
pos to proferis afto?

properly (repaired, locked etc)
opos prepi

protection factor (of suntan
lotion) o vaTHmos prostasias

Protestant o thiamartiromenos

public convenience
i kinokhristi tooaleta

public holiday i thimosia aryia

pudding (dessert) to glikisma

pull travao

pullover to poolover

puncture to foo-it

purple mov

purse (for money) to portofoli
(US: handbag) i tsanda

push sprokhno

pushchair to karotsaki

put vazo

   where can I put…?
   poo boro na valo…?

   **could you put us up for
   the night?** boriteh na mas
   filoxeniseteh ya ena vrathi?

pyjamas i pitzames

Q

quality i piotita

quarantine i karantina

quarter to tetarto

quayside: on the quayside
   stin provlita

question i erotisi

queue i oora

quick grigora

   that was quick
   afto itan grigoro

   **what's the quickest way
   there?** pios ineh o pio grigoros
   thromos?

   fancy a quick drink?
   ekhis orexi ya ena poto sta
   grigora?

quickly grigora

quiet (place, hotel) isikhos

   quiet! siopi!

quince to kithoni

quite (fairly) arketa
   (very) telios

   that's quite right
   poli sosta

   quite a lot arketa

R

rabbit o lagos

race (for runners, cars) i koorsa

racket i raketa

radiator (in room) to kalorifer
   (of car) to psiyio aftokinitoo

radio to rathiofono

   on the radio sto rathiofono

rail: by rail sithirothromikos

railway o sithirothromos

rain i vrokhi

   in the rain mes tin vrokhi

   it's raining vrekhi

raincoat i kabardina,
   to athiavrokho

rape o viasmos

rare (steak) okhi poli psimeno

rash (on skin) to exanтнima

raspberry to vatomooro

rat o arooreos

rate (for changing money)
   i timi sinalagmatos

rather: it's rather good
   ineh malon kalo

   I'd rather… тна protimoosa
   na…

razor (dry) to xirafaki
   (electric) i xiristiki mikhani

razor blades to xirafaki

read thiavazo

ready etimos

   are you ready? (to man/
   woman) iseh etimos/etimi?

   I'm not ready yet then imeh
   etimos akomi

when will it be ready?
poteh tha ineh etimo?

it should be ready in a couple of days tha prepi na ineh etimo seh mia-thio meres

real pragmatikos

really pragmatika

(very) poli

really! (surprise, doubt) psemata!

really? (interest) alithia?

rearview mirror o kathreftis aftokinitoo

reasonable (prices etc) loyikos

receipt i apothixi

recently prosfata

reception (in hotel) i resepsion

(for guests) i thexiosi

at reception stin paralavi

reception desk to grafio ipothokhis

receptionist i/o resepsionist

recognize anagnorizo

recommend: could you recommend…? boriteh na moo sistiseteh…?

record (music) o thiskos

red kokinos

red wine to kokino krasi

refund i epistrofi khrimaton

can I have a refund? moo epistrefondeh khrimata?

region i periokhi

registered: by registered mail sistimeno

registration number o arithmos kikloforias

relative o/i singenis

religion i thriskia

remember: I don't remember then thimameh

I remember thimameh

do you remember? thimaseh?

rent (for apartment etc) to enikio

(verb) niki-azo

to/for rent eniki-azonteh

rented car to enikiasmeno aftokinito

repair i episkevi

can you repair it? boriteh na to episkevaseteh?

repeat epanalamvano

could you repeat that? boriteh na to epanalaveteh?

reservation (train, bus) to klisimo thesis

I have a reservation ekho kani mia kratisi

yes sir, what name please? malista, kiri-eh; seh ti onoma, parakalo?

reserve krato

can I reserve a table for tonight? boro na kliso ena trapezi ya apopseh?

yes madam, for how many people? malista, kiria moo; ya posa atoma?

for two ya thio
and for what time? keh ya
ti ora?
for eight o'clock ya tis
okhto
**and could I have your
name please?** to onoma
sas, parakalo?
see alphabet on p.9 for spelling

rest: I need a rest khriazomeh
xekoorasi
  the rest of the group
  to ipolipo groop
restaurant to estiatorio
rest room i too-aleta
retired: I'm retired imeh seh
sindaxi
return: a return to… ena isitirio
met epistrofis ya to…
reverse charge call
to tilefonima kolekt
reverse gear i opisthen
revolting apesios
Rhodes i Rothos
rib to plevro
rice to rizi
rich (person) ploosios
  (food) varis
ridiculous yelios
right (correct) sostos
  (not left) thexia
  you were right ikhes thikio
  that's right sosta
  this can't be right afto then
  bori na ineh sosto

right! endaxi!
is this the right road for…?
ineh aftos o sostos thromos
ya…?
  on the right sta thexia
  turn right stripseh thexia
right-hand drive meh thexio
timoni
ring (on finger) to thaktilithi
  I'll ring you тна soo tilefoniso
ring back тна seh paro piso
ripe (fruit) orimos
rip-off: it's a rip-off ineh listia
rip-off prices astronomikes
times
risky ripsokinthinos
river to potami
road (country) o thromos
  (in town) i othos
  is this the road for…?
  ineh aftos o thromos ya…?
  down the road parakato
road accident to aftokinitistiko
thistikhima
road map o othikos khartis
roadsign i pinakitha
rob: I've been robbed
meh listepsan
rock o vrakhos
  (music) i rok moosiki
  on the rocks (with ice)
  meh pagakia
roll (bread) to psomaki
roof i orofi, i steyi
  (flat) i taratsa
roof rack i s-khara aftokinitoo
room to thomatio

(space) to meros

in my room sto thomatio moo

room service to servis thomatioo

rope to skhini

rosé (wine) to rozeh

roughly (approximately) pano-kato

round: it's my round
ineh i sira moo

roundabout (for traffic)
o kikloforiakos komvos, i platia

**round trip ticket: a round trip
ticket to...** ena isitirio met
epistrofis ya to…

route i poria

what's the best route for...?
pios ineh o kaliteros thromos
ya…?

rubber (material) lastikho
(eraser) i svistra, i goma

rubber band to lastikhaki

rubbish (waste) ta skoopithia

(poor quality goods) kaki piotita

rubbish! (nonsense) trikhes!

rucksack to sakithio

rude a-yenis

ruins ta eripia, i arkheotites

rum to roomi

rum and Coke ena roomi
meh koka kola

run (person) trekho

**how often do the buses
run?** poso sikh-na pernoon
ta leoforia?

I've run out of money
moo teliosan ta khrimata

rush hour ora ekhmis

S

sad lipimenos

saddle i sela

safe (not in danger) asfalis

(not dangerous) akinthinos, avlavis

safety pin i paramana

sail to pani

sailboard to windsurf

sailboarding to windsurf

salad i salata

salad dressing to lathoxitho

sale: for sale politeh

salmon o solomos

Salonika i THesaloniki

salt to alati

same: the same o ithios

  the same as this
to ithio opos afto

  the same again, please
to ithio xana, parakalo

  it's all the same to me
to ithio moo kani

sand i amos

sandals ta santhalia

sandwich to sandwich

sanitary towels/napkins
i servi-etes

sardines i sartheles

Saturday to Savato

sauce i saltsa

saucepan i katsarola

saucer to piataki

sauna i sa-oona

sausage to lookaniko

say: how do you say...
  in Greek? pos to leneh...
sta Elinika?

  what did he say? ti ipeh?

  I said... ipa...

  he said... ipeh...

could you say that again?
boriteh na to xanapiteh?,
boriteh na to epanalaveteh?

scarf (for neck) to kaskol
  (for head) to mandili

scenery to topio

schedule to programa

scheduled flight
i programatismeni ptisi

school to skholio

scissors: a pair of scissors
to psalithi

scooter to skooter

Travel tip Small motor
scooters are good transport
for all but the hilliest terrain,
and are available for rent on
many islands and in popular
mainland resorts. Accidents
are common if riding two to
an underpowered scooter,
so don't be tempted by this
apparent economy; you're
likely to face an exorbitant
repair bill if you wipe out.
Helmet-wearing is also
required by law.

---

scotch to skots whisky

Scotch tape to sellotape

Scotland i Skotia

Scottish Skotsezikos

  I'm Scottish (male/female)
imeh Skotsezos/Skotseza

scrambled eggs ta khtipita
avga

scratch i gratzoonia

screw i vitha

screwdriver to katsavithi

scuba diving i anapnefstiki siskevi katathiti

sea i THalasa

  by the sea konda sti THalasa

seafood ta THalasina

seafood restaurant i psaro-taverna

seafront i paralia

  on the seafront stin paralia

seagull o glaros

search psakh-no

seashell i akhivaTHa

seasick: I feel seasick esthanomeh naftia

  I get seasick meh piani i THalasa

seaside: by the seaside konda stin paralia

seat i THesi

  is this anyone's seat? ineh kanenos afti i THesi?

seat belt i zoni asfalias

sea urchin o akhinos

seaweed ta fikia

secluded apomeros

second (of time) to theftero-lepto

  (adj) thefteros

  just a second! mia stigmi!

second class (travel) thefteri THesi

second floor o thefteros orofos

  (US) o tritos orofos

second-hand apo theftero kheri

see vlepo, kitazo

  can I see? boro na tho?

have you seen...? ekhis thi...?

see you! ta xanalemeh!

I see (I understand) katalava

I saw him this morning ton itha simera to pro-i

self-catering apartment to anexartito thiamerisma

self-service self-servis

sell poolo

  do you sell...? poolateh...?

Sellotape to sellotape

send stelno

  I want to send this to England thelo na stilo afto stin Anglia

senior citizen o/i sindaxi-ookhos

separate (adj) khoristos

separated: I'm separated (male/female) imeh khorismenos/khorismeni

separately (pay, travel) xekhorista

September o Septemvrios

septic siptikos

serious sovaros

service charge (in restaurant) to filothorima

service station to venzinathiko

serviette i hartopetseta, i petseta

set menu to tabl-dot

several arketi

sew ravo

  could you sew this back on? boriteh na to rapseteh pali sti THesi too?

sex to sex

shade: in the shade
sti skia

shake: let's shake hands
as thosoomeh ta kheria

shallow (water) rikha nera

shame: what a shame!
ti krima!

shampoo to samboo-an

a shampoo and set
ena loosimo meh mizampli

share (*verb*: room, table etc)
mirazomeh

sharp (knife etc) kofteros

(taste, pain) thinatos

shattered (very tired)
exandlimenos

shaver i xiristiki mikhani

shaving foam
o afros xirismatos

shaving point
i priza xiristikis mikhanis

she afti

is she here? ineh etho?

sheet (for bed) to sendoni

shelf to rafi

shellfish ta ostraka

sherry to seri

ship to plio

by ship meh plio

shirt to pookamiso

shit! skata!

shock to sok

**I got an electric shock from
the...** ilektristika meh...

shock-absorber to amortiser

shocking (behaviour, prices)
exofrenikos

shoe to papootsi

a pair of shoes ena zevgari
papootsia

shoelaces ta korthonia
papootsion

shoe polish to verniki
papootsion

shoe repairer o tsangaris

shop to magazi

shopping: I'm going shopping
pao ya psonia

shopping centre
to emboriko kendro

shop window i vitrina

shore i akti

short (person) kondos

(time) ligos

(journey) sindomos

shortcut o sindomos
thromos

shorts to sorts

should: what should I do?
ti prepi na kano?

he shouldn't be long
then prepi na aryisi

you should have told me
eprepeh na moo to ikhes pi

shoulder o omos

shout (*verb*) fonazo

show (in theatre) to ergo

could you show me?
boriteh na moo thixeteh?

shower (in bathroom) to doos

(rain) i bora

with shower meh doos

shower gel to afrolootro

shut (*verb*) klino

when do you shut?
poteh klineteh?

when do they shut?
poteh klinoon?

they're shut ineh klista

I've shut myself out
klistika apexo

shut up! skaseh!

shutter (on camera)
to thiafragma

(on window) to exofilo,
to pandzoori

shy dropalos

sick (ill) arostos

see **ill**

I'm going to be sick (vomit)
ekho tasi pros emeto

side i plevra

the other side of town
i ali akri tis polis

side lights ta khamila fota

side salad i salata ya garnitoora

side street to thromaki

sidewalk to pezothromio

sight: the sights of…
ta axioтнeata too…

**sightseeing: we're going
sightseeing** pameh na
thoomeh ta axioтнeata

sightseeing tour i xenayisi sta
axioтнeata

sign (roadsign etc) to sima

signal: he didn't give a signal
then ekaneh sima

signature i ipografi

signpost i pinakitha, i tabela

silence i siopi

silk to metaxi

silly ano-itos

silver to asimi

silver foil to aloominokharto

similar omios

simple (easy) aplos

since: since yesterday
apo kh-тнes

since I got here apo toteh
poo irтнa etho

sing tragootho

singer (*male/female*) o tragoo-
thistis/i tragoothistria

single (*male/female*) monos

a single to… ena aplo ya…

I'm single imeh elefтнeros/
elefтнeri

single bed to mono krevati

single room to mono thomatio

sink (in kitchen) o nerokhitis

sister i athelfi

sister-in-law (brother's wife)
i nifi

(wife's sister) i kooniatha

sit: can I sit here? boro na
kaтнiso etho?

is anyone sitting here?
kaтнeteh kanis etho?

sit down kaтнomeh

sit down! katseh kato!

site to axioтнeato

(archaeological) arkheoloyikos
khoros

size to meh-yeтнos

skin to therma

skindiving i katathisis

skinny kokaliaris

skirt i f**oo**sta

sky o ooran**o**s

sleep (*verb*) kim**a**meh

did you sleep well?
kimi-тнikes kal**a**?

I need a good sleep
khri**a**zomeh **e**na kal**o** **i**pno

sleeper (on train) i kook**e**ta

sleeping bag to sleeping bag

sleeping car i klin**a**maxa,
i kook**e**ta

sleeping pill to ipnotik**o** khapi

sleepy: I'm feeling sleepy
nist**a**zo

sleeve to man**i**ki

slide (photographic) to slide

slip (under dress) to misof**o**ri

slippery glister**o**s

slow arg**o**s

slow down! pi**o** arg**a**

slowly siga-siga

could you say it slowly?
bor**i**teh na to p**i**teh arg**a**-arg**a**?

very slowly pol**i** arg**a**

small mikr**o**s

smell: it smells (smells bad)
vrom**a**-i

smile (*verb*) khamo-yel**o**

smoke o kapn**o**s

do you mind if I smoke?
sas pir**a**zi an kapn**i**so?

I don't smoke then kapn**i**zo

do you smoke? kapn**i**zeteh?

snack: I'd just like a snack
тнa **i**тнela na f**a**o k**a**ti
pr**o**khiyo

snake to f**i**thi

sneeze to ftarn**i**sma

snorkel o anapnefst**i**ras

Travel tip When snorkelling
in deeper water, you may
spot a brightly coloured
moray eel sliding back and
forth out of its rocky lair.
Keep a respectful distance
– their slightly comical air
and clown-colours belie
an irritable temper and the
ability to inflict nasty bites
or even sever fingers.

---

snow to khi**o**ni

so: it's so good **i**neh pol**i** kal**o**

not so fast **o**khi t**o**so gr**i**gora

so am I keh eg**o** to **i**thio

so do I keh eg**o** ep**i**sis

so-so **e**tsi ki **e**tsi

soaking solution (for contact
lenses) igr**o** sind**i**risis fak**o**n
epaf**i**s

soap to sap**oo**ni

soap powder to aporipandik**o**

sober xemeтн**i**stos

socks i k**a**ltses

socket (electrical) i pr**i**za

soda (water) i s**o**tha

sofa o kanap**e**s

soft (material etc) apal**o**s

soft-boiled egg to mel**a**to avg**o**

soft drink to anapsiktik**o**

soft lenses i malak**i** fak**i**

sole i s**o**la

**could you put new soles on
these?** bor**i**teh na moo val**e**teh
ken**oo**ryi-es s**o**les saft**a**?

some: can I have some water/rolls? moo thineteh ligo nero?/liga psomakia?

can I have some? boro na paro ligo?

somebody, someone kapios

something kati

something to drink kati na pi-iteh

sometimes merikes fores

somewhere kapoo

son o yos

song to tragoothi

son-in-law o gambros

soon sindoma

I'll be back soon THA yiriso sindoma

as soon as possible oso to thinaton grigorotera

sore: it's sore ineh ereTHismeno

sore throat pona-i o lemos moo

sorry: (I'm) sorry signomi

sorry? (didn't understand/hear) pardon?, signomi?

sort: what sort of...? ti ithos...?

soup i soopa

sour (taste) xinos

south notos

south of noti-a

in the south sto noto

to the south noti-a

South Africa i Noti-os Afriki

South African (adj) Notio-afrikanos

I'm South African (male/

female) imeh Notio-afrikanos/ Notio-afrikana

southeast notio-anatolikos

southwest notio-thitikos

souvenir to enTHimio

Spain i Ispania

Spanish (adj) ispanikos

(language) ta ispanika

spanner to klithi

spare part ta andalaktika

spare tyre i rezerva

spark plug to boozi

speak: do you speak English? milateh Anglika?

I don't speak... then milao...

DIALOGUE

can I speak to Costas? boro na miliso ston Kosta, parakalo?

who's calling? pios ton zita-i?

it's Patricia i Patricia

I'm sorry, he's not in, can I take a message? lipameh, then ineh etho, boro na too thoso kapio minima?

no thanks, I'll call back later okhi, efkharisto, THA xanaparo argotera

please tell him I called parakalo, piteh too pos tilefonisa

speciality i spesialiteh

spectacles ta yali-a

speed i takhitita

speed limit to orio takhititas

speedometer to konder

spell: how do you spell it?
pos to grafeteh?
see alphabet on p.9
spend xothevo
spider i arakhni
spin-dryer to stegnotirio
splinter i agitha
spoke (in wheel) i aktina
spoon to kootali
sport to spor
sprain: I've sprained my...
straboolixa to...
spring (season) i anixi
(in seat etc) to elatirio
square (in town) i platia
stairs ta skalopatia, i skales
stale (bread, taste) bayatikos
stall: the engine keeps stalling i mikhani sinekhos stamata
stamp to gramatosimo

DIALOGUE

a stamp for England, please ena gramatosimo ya Anglia, parakalo
what are you sending? ti тнa stileteh?
this postcard afti tin karta

star to asteri
(in film) o/i star
start i arkhi, to xekinima
(*verb*) arkhizo
when does it start? poteh arkhizi?
the car won't start to aftokinito then xekina

starter (of car) i miza
(food) to proto piato
starters ta orektika
starving: I'm starving peтнeno tis pinas
state (in country) i politia
the States (USA) i Inomenes Politi-es
station o staтнmos
statue to agalma
stay: where are you staying? poo meneteh?
I'm staying at... meno sto...
I'd like to stay another two nights тнa irтнela na mino ales thio nikhtes
steak i brizola
steal klevo
my bag has been stolen klepsaneh tin tsanda moo
steep (hill) apotomos
steering to timoni
step: on the steps sta skalopati-a
stereo to stereofoniko singrotima
sterling i lira sterlina
steward (on plane) o a-erosinothos
stewardess i a-erosinothos
sticking plaster to lefkoplast
still: I'm still waiting akoma perimeno
is he still there? ineh akoma eki?
keep still! stasoo akinitos!
sting: I've been stung by... meh tsibiseh...

stockings i na-ilon kaltses

stomach to stomakhi

stomach ache o ponos sto stomakhi, o stomakhoponos

stone (rock) i petra

stop stamatao

  please, stop here (to taxi driver etc) parakalo, stamatisteh etho

  do you stop near…? stamatateh konda…?

  stop doing that! stamata na to kanis afto!

stopover i stasi

storm i THi-ela

straight: it's straight ahead ineh olo efrHia

  a straight whisky ena sketo whisky

straightaway amesos

strange (odd) paraxenos

stranger (*male/female*) o xenos/ i xeni

  I'm a stranger here imeh xenos etho

strap to loori

strawberry i fraoola

stream to rema, to potamaki

street o thromos

  on the street sto thromo

streetmap o othikos khartis

string (cord) o spangos

  (guitar etc) i khorthi

strong thinatos

stuck frakarismenos

  the key's stuck koliseh to klithi

student o fititis, i fititria

stupid vlakas

suburb ta pro-astia

subway (US: railway) o ipo-yios

suddenly xafnika

suede to kastori

sugar i zakhari

suit (man's) to koostoomi

  (woman's) to ta-yer

  it doesn't suit me (jacket etc) then moo pa-i

  it suits you soo pa-i

suitcase i valitsa

summer to kalokeri

  in the summer to kalokeri

sun o ilios

  in the sun ston ilio

  out of the sun sti skia

sunbathe kano ilioτHerapia

sunblock (cream) to andiliako

sunburn to kapsimo apo ton ilio

sunburnt kamenos apo ton ilio

Sunday i Kiriaki

sunglasses ta yalia ilioo

sun lounger i shez long

sunny: it's sunny ekhi liakatha

sun roof (in car) i tzamenia skepi

sunset i thisi too ilioo

sunshade i ombrela ilioo

sunshine i liakatha

sunstroke i ili-asi

suntan to mavrisma

suntan lotion to lathi
  mavrismatos

suntanned iliokamenos

suntan oil to lathi mavrismatos

super katapliktikos

supermarket to supermarket

supper to thipno

supplement (extra charge)
  epipleon, to prosτHeto

sure: are you sure?
  iseh sigooros?

  sure! veveos!

surname to epiτHeto

swearword i vrisia

sweater to poolover

sweatshirt i fanela

Sweden i Soo-ithia

Swedish (adj) Soo-ithikos

sweet (taste) glikos

  (dessert) to gliko

sweets i karameles

swelling to priximo

swim kolimbao

  I'm going for a swim
  pao ya kolibi

  let's go for a swim
  pameh ya kolibi

swimming costume to ma-yo

swimming pool i pisina

swimming trunks to ma-yo

switch o thiakoptis

switch off (engine) svino

  (TV, lights) klino

switch on (engine) anavo

  (TV, lights) anigo

swollen prismenos

T

table to trapezi

  a table for two
  ena trapezi ya thio

tablecloth to trapezomandilo

table tennis to ping-pong

table wine to epitrapezio krasi

tailback (of traffic) i oora

tailor o raftis

take (lead) perno

  (accept) thekhomeh

  **can you take me to the
  airport?** boriteh na meh pateh
  sto a-erothromio?

do you take credit cards?
thekhesteh pistotikes kartes?

fine, I'll take it endaxi тнa to
paro

can I take this? (leaflet etc)
boro na paro afto?

how long does it take?
posi ora тнa pari?

it takes three hours
perni tris ores

is this seat taken?
ineh piasmeni i тнesi?

hamburger to take away
khamboorger ya to spiti

**can you take a little off
here?** (to hairdresser) boriteh na
pareteh ligo apo etho?

talcum powder i poothra talk

talk (*verb*) milo

tall psilos

tampons ta tampax, ta tabon

tan to mavrisma

to get a tan mavrizo

tank (of car) to depozito

tap i vrisi

tape (cassette) i kaseta
(sticky) i tenia

tape measure to metro

tape recorder to magnitofono

taste i yefsi

can I taste it? boro na to
thokimaso?

taxi to taxi

will you get me a taxi?
тнa moo kaleseteh ena taxi?

where can I find a taxi?
poo boro na vro ena taxi?

DIALOGUE

**to the airport/to the
Hilton Hotel please**
sto a-erothromio/sto
xenothokhio Khilton,
parakalo

how much will it be?
poso тнa stikhisi?

35 euros trianda-pendeh
evro

**that's fine, right here,
thanks** endaxi, etho pera
ineh, efkharisto

taxi-driver o taxidzis

taxi rank o staтнmos taxi

tea to tsa-i

tea for one/two please
tsa-i ya enan/thio parakalo

teabags ta fakelakia tsa-i

teach: could you teach me?
boris na meh maтнis?

teacher (*male/female*)
o thaskalos/i thaskala

team i omatha

teaspoon to kootalaki

tea towel i petseta koozinas

teenager o neos, i nea

telephone to tilefono

television i tileorasi

tell: could you tell him...?
boriteh na too piteh...?

temperature (weather)
i тнermokrasia
(fever) o piretos

temple (church) o na-os

tennis to tennis

tennis ball i bala too tennis

tennis court to yipetho tennis

tennis racket i raketa tennis

tent i skini

term (at university, school)
i s-kholiki periothos

terminus (rail) to terma

terrible foveros

terrific exeretikos

text (*verb*) stelno minima seh

text (message) to minima sto
kinito

than apo

  smaller than
  mikroteros apo

thanks, thank you
efkharisto

  thank you very much
  efkharisto para poli

  thanks for the lift efkharisto
  poo meh pirateh

  no thanks okhi efkharisto

  thanks efkharisto
  that's OK, don't mention it
  parakalo, then kani tipoteh

that ekinos, ekini, ekino

  that one ekino

  I hope that... elpizo oti...

  that's nice ti orea!

  is that...? afto ineh...?

  that's it (that's right) akrivos

the o, i, to; (*plural*) i, i, ta

theatre to THeatro

their o/i/to... toos

theirs thiki toos

them toos, tis, ta

for them ya ekinoos

with them maftoos

I gave it to them
to ethosa saftoos

  who? – them pi-i? – afti

then (at that time) toteh

  (after that) katopin

there eki

  over there eki pera

  up there eki pano

  is there...? iparkhi...?

  are there...? iparkhoon...?

  there is... iparkhi...

  there are... iparkhoon...

  there you are (giving
  something) oristeh

thermometer to THermometro

Thermos flask to THermos

these afti, aftes, afta

  can I have these?
  boro na ekho afta?

Thessaly i THesalia

they afti, aftes, afta

thick pakhis

  (stupid) khazos

thief (*male/female*) o kleftis/
i kleftra

thigh to booti

thin leptos

  (person) athinatos

thing to pragma

  my things ta pragmata moo

think skeptomeh

  (believe) nomizo

  I think so etsi nomizo

  I don't think so then nomizo

I'll think about it THa to skepto

third party insurance asfalia ya
khrisi apo tritoos

thirsty: I'm thirsty thipso

this aftos, afti, afto

  this one afto etho

  this is my wife apo etho i
yineka moo

  is this…? ineh…?

those ekini, ekines, ekina

  which ones? – those
pi-a? – afta

Thrace i THraki

thread i klosti

throat o lemos

throat pastilles pastili-es
lemoo

through thiamesoo

  does it go through…?
(train, bus) perna-i apo to…?

throw (verb) rikhno

throw away (verb) peto

thumb o andikhiras

thunderstorm i kateyitha

Thursday i Pempti

ticket to isitirio

DIALOGUE

a return to Athens ena
isitirio epistrofis ya tin
ATHina

coming back when?
poteh ineh i epistrofi?

today/next Tuesday
simera/tin epomeni Triti

that will be 45 euros
saranda-pendeh evro,
parakalo

---

ticket office (bus, rail) i THiritha

tide i paliri-a

tie (necktie) i gravata

tight (clothes etc) stenos

  it's too tight ineh poli steno

tights to kalson

till mekhri

time o khronos

  (occasion) i fora

  what's the time?
ti ora ineh?

  this time afti ti fora

  last time tin perasmeni fora

  next time tin epomeni fora

  four times teseris fores

timetable to programa

tin (can) i konserva

tinfoil to asimokharto

tin-opener to anikhtiri

tiny mikroskopikos

tip (to waiter etc) to filothorima

tired koorasmenos

  I'm tired imeh koorasmenos

tissues ta khartomandila

to: to Salonica/London
ya tin THesaloniki/to Lonthino

  to Greece/England
ya tin Elatha/Anglia

  to the post office
sto takhithromio

toast (bread) to tost

today simera

toe to thakhtilo too pothioo

together mazi

  we're together (in shop etc)
imasteh mazi

can we pay together?
boroomeh na plirosoomeh mazi?

toilet i too-aleta

where is the toilet?
poo ineh i too-aleta?

I have to go to the toilet
prepi na pao stin too-aleta

toilet paper kharti iyias

tomato i domata

tomato juice to domatozoomo,
o domatokhimos

tomato ketchup to ketsap

tomorrow avrio

tomorrow morning avrio to
pro-i

the day after tomorrow
methavrio

toner (cosmetic) to tonotiko

tongue i glosa

tonic (water) to tonik

tonight apopseh

tonsillitis i amigthalititha

too (excessively) poli

(also) episis

too hot poli kafto

too much para poli

me too kego episis

tooth to thondi

toothache o ponothondos

toothbrush i othondovoortsa

toothpaste i othondokrema

top: on top of... pano apo...

at the top stin korifi

top floor to retire

topless yimnostiti

torch o fakos

total to sinolo

tour i peri-iyisi, i xenayisi

is there a tour of...?
iparkhi peri-iyisi ya...?

tour guide o/i xenagos

tourist (*male/female*) o tooristas/
i tooristria

tourist information office
Grafio Pliroforion E-OT

tour operator to taxithiotiko
grafio

towards pros

towel i petseta

town i poli

in town stin poli

just out of town akrivos exo
apo tin poli

town centre to kendro
tis polis

town hall to thimarkhio

toy to pekh-nithi

track (US) i platforma
see **platform**

tracksuit i athlitiki forma

traditional parathosiakos

traffic i kikloforia

traffic jam i kikloforiaki
simforisi

traffic lights ta fanaria tis
trokheas

trailer (for carrying tent etc)
i rimoolka

(caravan) to trokhospito

trailer park topotHesia ya
trokhospita

train to treno

by train meh treno

is this the train for...?
afto ineh to treno ya...?

sure neh

**no, you want that platform
there** okhi, THa pateh seh
ekini tin platforma eki

trainers (shoes) ta aTHlitika
papootsia

train station o sithiro-thromikos
staTHmos

tram to tram

translate metafrazo

could you translate that?
boriteh na metafraseteh afto?

translation i metafrasi

translator o/i metafrastis

trashcan o skoopithodenekes

travel taxithevo

**we're travelling
around** taxithevoomeh
triyiro

travel agent's
to taxithiotiko grafio

traveller's cheque
i taxithiotiki epitayi

tray o thiskos

tree to thendro

tremendous tromeros

trendy modernos

trim: just a trim please
(to hairdresser) ligo konditera,
parakalo

trip (excursion) to taxithi

I'd like to go on a trip to...
THa iTHela na pao ena taxithi
stin...

trolley to trolley, to karotsaki

trolleybus to trolley

trouble o belas

I'm having trouble with...
ekho provlimata meh...

sorry to trouble you
meh sinkhoriteh poo sas
vazo seh mbela

trousers to pandaloni

true aliTHinos

that's not true
then ineh aliTHia

trunk (of car) to port-bagaz

trunks (swimming) to mayo

try prospatho, thokimazo

can I have a try?
boro na thokimaso?

try on provaro

can I try it on? boro na to
thokimaso pano moo?

T-shirt to bloozaki

Tuesday i Triti

tuna o tonos

tunnel i siraga

Turkey i Toorkia

Turkish (adj) Toorkikos

Turkish coffee Toorkikos kafes,
Elinikos kafes

Turkish-Cypriot (adj)
Toorkiko-Kipriakos

turn: turn left/right
stripseh aristera/thexia

where do I turn off?
poo strivo?

**turn off: can you turn the
heating off?** boris na klisis ti
THermansi/to kalorifer?

turn on: can you turn the heating on? boris na anixis ti THermansi/to kalorifer?

turning (in road) i strofi

TV i tileorasi

tweezers to tsimbithaki

twice thio fores

twice as much ta thipla

twin beds thio krevatia

twin room to thomatio meh thio krevatia

twist: I've twisted my ankle stramboolixa ton astragalo moo

type to ithos

a different type of… ena alo ithos apo…

typical kharaktiristikos

tyre to lastikho

U

ugly askhimos

UK to Inomeno Vasili-o

ulcer to elkos

umbrella i ombrela

uncle o THios

unconscious anesTHitos

under apo kato

(less than) ligotero apo

underdone (meat) misop-simenos

underground (railway) o ipo-yios

underpants to sovrako, to slip

understand: I understand katalaveno

I don't understand then katalaveno

do you understand? katalavenis?

unemployed anergos

United States i Inomenes Politi-es

university to panepistimio

unleaded petrol i amolivthi venzini

unlimited mileage aperiorista khiliometra

unlock xeklithono

unpack anigo tis valitses

until mekhri

unusual asiniTHistos

up pano

(upwards) pros ta pano

up there eki pano

he's not up yet (not out of bed) then sikoTHikeh akomi

what's up? (what's wrong?) ti yineteh?

upmarket (restaurant etc) akrivos

upset stomach o stomakhoponos

upside down ta pano kato

upstairs pano

urgent epigon

us mas

with us meh mas

for us ya mas

use khrisimopi-o

may I use…? boro na khrisimopi-iso…?

useful khrisimos

usual siniTHismenos

the usual (drink etc) to siniTHismeno

V

vacancy: do you have any vacancies? (hotel) ekheteh elefrHera thomatia?

vacation i thiakopes *see* **holiday**

vaccination o emvoliasmos

vacuum cleaner i ilektriki skoopa

valid (ticket etc) engiros

  how long is it valid for? ya poso is-khi-i?

valley i kilatha

valuable (*adj*) politimos

  can I leave my valuables here? boro na afiso ta timalfi moo etho?

value i axia

van to trokhospito

vanilla i vanilia

  a vanilla ice cream ena pagoto vanilia

vary: it varies metavaleteh

vase to vazo

veal to moskhari

vegetables ta lakhanika

vegetarian o/i khortofagos

vending machine o aftomatos politis

very poli

  very little for me poli ligo ya mena

  I like it very much moo aresi para poli

vest (under shirt) to fanelaki

via thia mesoo

video (film) i video-tenia

view i THea

villa i vila

village to khorio

vinegar to xithi

vineyard to ambeli

visa i viza

visit (*verb*) episkeptomeh

  I'd like to visit… THa iTHela na episkefto…

vital: it's vital that… ineh vasiko na…

vodka i votka

voice i foni

volleyball to volley-ball, i khirosferisi

voltage i tasis

vomit (*verb*) kano emeto

W

waist i mesi

waistcoat to yileko

wait perimeno

  wait for me perimeneh meh!

  don't wait for me mi meh perimenis

  can I wait until my wife gets here? boro na paragilo otan elTHi i yineka moo?

  can you do it while I wait? na perimeno na to kaneteh?

  could you wait here for me? boriteh na meh perimeneteh na yiriso?

waiter o servitoros

  waiter! garson!

waitress i garsona, i servitora

waitress! sas parakalo!

wake: can you wake me up at 5.30? boriteh na meh xipniseteh stis pendeh keh misi?

wake-up call tilefonima ya xipnima

Wales i Oo-alia

walk: is it a long walk? ineh poli perpatima?

it's only a short walk ekhi ligo perpatima

I'll walk THa perpatiso

I'm going for a walk pao ena peripato

wall o tikhos

wallet to portofoli

wander: I like just wandering around moo aresi na khazevo triyiro

want: I want a... THelo ena...

I don't want any...

then THelo...

I want to go home THelo na pao spiti moo

I don't want to then THelo

he wants to... THeli na...

what do you want? ti THelis?

ward (in hospital) o THalamos

warm zestos

I'm so warm zestenomeh arketa

was: I was... imoon...

he/she/it was... itan...

wash (verb) pleno

(oneself) plenomeh

can you wash these? boriteh na plineteh afta?

washer (for bolt etc) i rothela

washhand basin o niptiras

washing (clothes) i boogatha

washing machine to plindirio

washing powder i skoni

plindirioo, to aporipandiko

washing-up liquid
to sapooni piaton

wasp i sfinga

watch (wristwatch) to rolo-i

**will you watch my
things for me?** boriteh na
prosekheteh ta pragmata moo?

watch out! prosekheh!

watch strap to looraki roloyioo

water to nero

may I have some water?
moo thineteh ligo nero?

waterproof (*adj*) athi-avrokhos

waterskiing to THalasio ski

wave (in sea) to kima

**way: could you tell me the
way to…?** boriteh na moo
piteh pos THa pa-o sto ..?

it's this way apo etho ineh

it's that way apo eki ineh

is it a long way to…?
ineh makri-a ya to…?

no way! apokli-eteh!

**could you tell me the way
to…?** boriteh na moo
thixeteh to thromo ya…?

**go straight on until you
reach the traffic lights**
piyeneteh olo isia mekhri
na ftaseteh sta fanaria

turn left stripsteh aristera

take the first on the right
parteh ton proto thromo
sta thexia

see **where**

we emis

weak athinatos

weather o keros

**what's the weather
forecast?** ti ipeh to theltio
keroo?

it's going to be fine THa
ineh kalos keros

it's going to rain THa vrexi

it'll brighten up later THa
anixi o keros argotera

website i istoselitha

wedding o gamos

wedding ring i vera

Wednesday i Tetarti

week i evthomatha

a week (from) today
seh mia evthomatha apo simera

a week (from) tomorrow
seh mia evthomatha apo avrio

weekend to Savatokiriako

at the weekend
to Savatokiriako

weight to varos

weird paraxenos

weirdo o trelaras

welcome: welcome to…
kalos ilthateh sto…

you're welcome (don't mention
it) parakalo

well: I don't feel well
then esthanomeh kala

she's not well
ekini then ineh kala

you speak English very well

milateh poli kala Anglika
well done! bravo
this one as well ki afto episis
well well! (surprise) ya thes!

DIALOGUE

how are you? ti kanis?
very well, thanks poli kala, efkharisto
and you? ki esi?

well-done (meat) kalopsimenos
Welsh Oo-alos
  I'm Welsh (*male/female*)
  imeh Oo-alos/Oo-ali
were: we were imasteh
  you were isasteh/isteh
  they were itan
west thitikos
  in the west sta thitika
West Indian (*adj*) apo tis thitikes
  Inthi-es
wet vregmenos
what? ti?
  what's that? ti ineh ekino?
  what should I do?
  ti prepi na kano?
  what a view! ti THea!
  what bus do I take?
  ti leoforio prepi na paro?
wheel i rotha
wheelchair i anapiriki politHrona
when? poteh?
  when we get back
  otan yirisoomeh
  when's the train/ferry?
  poteh fevyi to treno/to karavi?
where? poo?

I don't know where it is
then xero poo ineh

DIALOGUE

where is the cathedral?
  poo ineh o katHethrikos
  naos?
it's over there ineh eki pera
could you show me where it is on the map? boriteh
  na moo thixeteh sto kharti
  poo ineh?
it's just here ineh akrivos etho
see **way**

which: which bus?
  pio leoforio?

DIALOGUE

which one? pio?
that one ekino
this one? afto?
no, that one okhi, ekino

while: while I'm here oso imeh
  etho
whisky to whisky
white aspros
white wine to aspro krasi
who? pios?
  who is it? pios ineh?
  the man who... o antHropos
  poo...
whole: the whole week
  oli tin evthomatha
  the whole lot ola
whose: whose is this?
  pianoo ineh afto?
why? yati?
  why not? yati okhi?

wide platis

wife: my wife i sizigos moo

Wi-Fi to wi-fi

will: will you do it for me?
THa moo to kanis afto?

wind o anemos

window to paraTHiro

  near the window konda sto
paraTHiro

  in the window (of shop)
sti vitrina

window seat i THesi sto
paraTHiro

windscreen to parbriz

windscreen wiper
o ialokaTHaristiras

windsurfing to windsurfing

windy: it's so windy
ekhi poli a-era

wine to krasi

  **can we have some
more wine?** boroomeh na
ekhoomeh ligo krasi akoma?

wine list o katalogos ton krasion

winter o khimonas

  in the winter ton khimona

winter holiday i khimerines
thiakopes

wire to sirma

  (electric) to ilektriko kalothio

wish: best wishes
poles efkhes

with meh

  I'm staying with…
meno meh…

without khoris

witness o/i martiras

**will you be a witness for
me?** THa iseh martiras moo?

woman i yineka

wonderful THavmasios

won't: it won't start
then THa xekinisi

wood (material) to xilo

woods (forest) to thasos

wool to mali

word i lexi

work i thoolia

  it's not working
then thoolevi

  I work in… ergazomeh seh…

world o kosmos

worry: I'm worried
stenokhori-emeh

worry beads to kombolo-i

worse: it's worse ineh khirotera

worst o khiroteros

worth: is it worth a visit?
axizi mia episkepsi?

**would: would you give this
to…?** boriteh na thoseteh afto
ston…?

wrap: could you wrap it up?
boriteh na to tilixeteh?

wrapping paper to kharti
peritiligmatos

  (for presents) kharti ya thora

wrist o karpos

write grafo

  could you write it down?
boriteh na moo to
grapseteh?

  how do you write it?
pos to grafeteh?

writing paper
to kharti alilografias

wrong: it's the wrong key
afto ineh laтнos klithi

  the bill's wrong o logariasmos
  ineh laтнos

  sorry, wrong number
  signomi, laтнos noomero

  sorry, wrong room
  signomi, laтнos thomatio

  **there's something wrong
  with...** iparkhi kapio laтнos
  meh...

  what's wrong? ti simveni?

X

X-ray i aktinografia

Y

yacht to yot

yard i yartha
(courtyard, backyard) i avli

year o khronos

yellow kitrinos

yes neh

yesterday kh-тнеs

yesterday morning
kh-тнеs to pro-i

  the day before yesterday
  prokh-тнеs

yet akomi

has it arrived yet? akomi then eftaseh?	DIALOGUE
no, not yet okhi, okhi akomi	
you'll have to wait a little longer yet тнa prepi na perimeneteh akomi ligo	

yoghurt to ya-**oo**rti

you (*familiar*) esi
(*plural or polite*) esis

  I'll see you later
  тнa seh tho argotera

  this is for you afto ineh ya sas

  with you mazi sas

young neos

your (*familiar*) o/i/to... soo
(*plural or polite*) o/i/to... sas

  your camera i fotografiki
  mikhani soo/sas

yours (*familiar*) thiko soo
(*plural or polite*) thiko sas

youth hostel o xenonas neon

Z

zero mithen

zip to fermoo-ar

  could you put a new zip in?
  boriteh na valeteh ena kenooryio fermoo-ar?

zip code o takhithromikos
kothikos

zoo o zo-oloyikos kipos

GREEK
→ ENGLISH

Colloquialisms

The following are words and expressions you might well hear. You shouldn't be tempted to use any of the stronger ones unless you are sure of your audience.

άντε γαμήσου andeh gamisoo
  fuck off!
βλάκα vlaka idiot, blockhead
βρωμο... vromo bloody...
γαμώ το! gamo to fuck!
γκόμενα gomena bird, chick
γουστάρω goostaro I feel like it
δεν πειράζει den pirazi
  it doesn't matter
είσαι; iseh do you want to?
έλα ela come on!, move!
θαυμάσια! THavmasia great!
in in fashionable
καμάκι kamaki stud, Don Juan

κερατάς keratas bastard
μαλάκας malakas wanker
μου τα'πρηξες moo taprixes
  you're getting on my tits,
  you're getting up my nose
μπάτσος batsos cop
Παναγία μου Panayia moo
  my God!
πούστης poostis faggot, poofter
πουτάνα pootana whore
πώ πώ! po po bloody hell!
ρε Κώστα reh Kosta Kostas, my
  old pal
ρε μαλάκα reh malaka you stupid
  wanker
σκάσε! skaseh shut up!
σκατά! skata shit!
στ'αρχίδια μου starkhidia moo
  I don't give a fuck
τζάμπα tzamba dirt cheap
τί γίνεται; ti yineteh
  how is it going?
τί νά κάνουμε; ti na kanoomeh
  what can you do?
τύφλα στο μεθύσι tifla sto meTHisi
  pissed (drunk)

> **Travel tip** Any sort of disrespect towards the Greek state or Orthodox Church in general, or Greek civil servants in particular, may be actionable, so best keep your comments to yourself. This is a culture where verbal injuries matter, where libel laws greatly favour plaintiffs, and the alleged public utterance of *malakas* (wanker) can result in a court case.

A

αγάπη (η) agapi (i) love

αγαπημένος agapimenos favourite

αγαπώ agapo love (*verb*)

αγγίζω angizo touch (*verb*)

ΑΓΓΛΙΑ Αγγλία (η) Anglia (i)
England

Αγγλίδα (η) Anglitha (i)
Englishwoman

ΑΓΓΛΙΚΑ Αγγλικά (τα) Anglika
(ta) English

ΑΓΓΛΙΚΟΣ Αγγλικός Anglikos
English

άγγλος (ο) Anglos (o) Englishman

αγελάδα (η) ayelatha (i) cow

αγενής ayenis rude

άγκυρα (η) angira (i) anchor

αγκώνας (ο) angonas (o) elbow

ΑΓΝΟ ΠΑΡΘΕΝΟ ΜΑΛΛΙ
αγνό παρθένο μαλλί
pure new wool

ΑΓΟΡΑ αγορά (η) agora (i)
market

αγοράζω agorazo buy (*verb*)

αγόρι (το) agori (to) boy

άγριος agrios wild, fierce

αγρόκτημα (το) agroktima (to)
farm

αγρότης (ο) agrotis (o) farmer

αγώνας (ο) agonas (o) fight,
struggle; game

άδεια (η) athia (i) licence;
permission

άδεια οδηγήσεως (η) athia
othiyiseos (i) driving licence

άδειος athios empty, vacant

αδελφή (η) athelfi (i) sister

ΑΔΕΛΦΟΙ αδελφοί brothers

αδελφός (ο) athelfos (o) brother

ΑΔΙΕΞΟΔΟ αδιέξοδο
cul-de-sac, dead end

αδύνατος athinatos impossible;
weak

Α.Ε. public limited company

ΑΕΡΑΝΤΛΙΑ αεραντλία (η)
air pump

αέρας (ο) aeras (o) air; wind;
choke

ΑΕΡΟΔΡΟΜΙΟ αεροδρόμιο (το)
aerothromio (to) airport

ΑΕΡΟΛΙΜΗΝ αερολιμήν (ο)
aerolimin (o) airport

αεροπλάνο (το) aeroplano (to)
plane

αεροπορική εταιρεία (η)
aeroporiki eteria (i) airline

ΑΕΡΟΠΟΡΙΚΩΣ αεροπορικώς
aeroporikos by air; by air mail

ΑΕΡΟΣΥΝΟΔΟΣ αεροσυνοδός
(ο/η) aerosinothos (o/i)
steward, stewardess

ΑΘΗΝΑ Αθήνα (η) ATHina (i)
Athens

αθλητής (ο) aTHlitis (o) athlete

ΑΘΛΗΤΙΚΑ αθλητικά (τα)
aTHlitika (ta) sports shop

αθλητικά παπούτσια (τα) aTHlitika
papootsia (ta) trainers

ΑΘΛΗΤΙΚΕΣ ΕΓΚΑΤΑΣΤΑΣΕΙΣ
αθλητικές εγκαταστάσεις
sporting facilities

αθλητική φόρμα (η) aTHlitiki forma
(i) tracksuit

ΑΘΛΗΤΙΚΟ ΚΕΝΤΡΟ αθλητικό

A
B
Γ
Δ
E
Z
H
Θ
I
K
Λ
M
N
Ξ
O
Π
P
Σ
T
Y
Φ
X
Ψ
Ω

κέντρο (το) aΤΗlitiko kendro (to)
sports centre

αθώος aΤΗoos innocent

ΑΙΓΑΙΟ Αιγαίο (το) E-yeo (to)
Aegean

**ΑΙΘΟΥΣΑ ΤΡΑΝΖΙΤ αίθουσα
τράνζιτ** transit lounge

αίμα (το) ema (to) blood

αιμορραγώ emorago bleed

αισθάνομαι esΤΗanomeh feel (*verb*)

ΑΙΤΗΣΗ αίτηση (η) etisi (i)
application form; application

αιτία (η) etia (i) cause; reason

εξ αιτίας… exetias…
because of…

αιώνας (ο) eonas (o) century

ΑΚΑΤΑΛΛΗΛΟ ακατάλληλο
adults only

Α΄ ΚΑΤΗΓΟΡΙΑΣ
Α΄ κατηγορίας first class

ακολουθώ akolooΤΗo
follow

ακόμα, ακόμη akoma, akomi
still, yet; even; also

ακουστικά (τα) akoostika (ta)
hearing aid; headphones

ΑΚΟΥΣΤΙΚΟ ακουστικό (το)
akoostiko (to) receiver

ακούω akoo-o hear; listen

άκρη (η) akri (i) edge; end; tip

**ΑΚΡΙΒΕΣ ΑΝΤΙΤΙΜΟ ΜΟΝΟ
ακριβές αντίτιμο μόνο**
exact fare only

ακριβός akrivos expensive

ακροατήριο (το) akroatirio (to)
audience

ΑΚΡΥΛΙΚΟ ακρυλικό akriliko
acrylic

ΑΚΤΗ ακτή (η) akti (i) beach;
coast, shore

ακυρώνω akirono cancel

ΑΛΒΑΝΙΑ Αλβανία (η) Alvania (i) Albania

αληθινός aliTHinos true; real

αλλά alla but

ΑΛΛΑΓΗ ΛΑΔΙΩΝ αλλαγή λαδιών oil change

αλλάζω allazo change (*verb*)

αλλάζω ρούχα allazo rookha change one's clothes

ΑΛΛΕΡΓΙΑ αλλεργία (η) alleryia (i) allergy

ΑΛΛΕΡΓΙΑ ΣΤΗ ΓΥΡΗ αλλεργία στη γύρη alleryia sti yiri hay fever

αλλεργικός σε alleryikos seh allergic to

άλλη ali other; else

άλλη μία ali mia another

άλλο alo other; else; another

  όχι άλλο okhi alo no more

άλλο ένα alo ena another

άλλος alos other; else

άλλος ένας alos enas another

αλλού aloo elsewhere

αλμυρός almiros salty

άλογο (το) alogo (to) horse

ΑΛΟΙΦΗ αλοιφή (η) alifi (i) ointment

αλουμινόχαρτο (το) aloominokharto (to) aluminium foil

ΑΛΣΟΣ άλσος (το) alsos (to) wooded park, grove

αλτ! alt! stop!

αλυσίδα (η) alisitha (i) chain

ΑΜΑΞΑ άμαξα (η) amaxa (i) coach, car (**on train**)

ΑΜΑΞΙ αμάξι (το) amaxi (to) car (**on train**)

ΑΜΑΞΟΣΤΟΙΧΙΑ αμαξοστοιχία (η) amaxostikhia (i) train

Αμερικανίδα (η) Amerikanitha (i) American (**woman**)

Αμερικανικός Amerikanikos American (*adj*)

Αμερικανός (ο) Amerikanos (o) American (**man**)

ΑΜΕΡΙΚΗ Αμερική (η) Ameriki (i) America

ΑΜΕΣΟΣ ΔΡΑΣΙΣ άμεσος δράσις emergencies

αμέσως amesos immediately

αμμόλοφοι (οι) amolofi (i) sand dunes

άμμος (η) amos (i) sand

αμορτισέρ (το) amortiser (to) shock-absorber

αμπέλι (το) ambeli (to) vineyard

αμπέρ (το) amper amp

ΑΜΠΟΥΛΕΣ αμπούλες ampoules

αν an if

ΑΝΑΒΡΑΖΟΝΤΑ ΔΙΣΚΙΑ αναβράζοντα δισκία effervescent tablets

ανάβω anavo light (*verb*)

αναγκαίος anangeos necessary

ανάγκη anangi need

αναγνωρίζω anagnorizo recognize, acknowledge, admit

ανακατεύω anakatevo mix (*verb*)

ΑΝΑΚΟΙΝΩΣΗ ανακοίνωση (η) anakinosi (i) announcement

ΑΝΑΚΛΗΣΙΣ ανάκλησις (η) anaklisis (i) withdrawal

A
B
Γ
Δ
E
Z
H
Θ
I
K
Λ
M
N
Ξ
O
Π
P
Σ
T
Y
Φ
X
Ψ
Ω

ΑΝΑΛΗΨΗ ανάληψη
withdrawal(s) (of money)

αναμείνατε στο ακουστικό
anaminateh sto akoostiko
hold the line please

ανάμεσα anamesa among;
between

αναπαύομαι anapavomeh
rest, relax

ανάπαυση (η) anapafsi (i) rest

αναπαυτικός anapaftikos
comfortable

αναπηρική πολυθρόνα (η) anapiriki
poliτHrona (i) wheelchair

ανάπηρος anapiros disabled

αναπνέω anapneo breathe

αναποδογυρίζω anapothoyirizo
knock over

αναπτήρας (ο) anaptiras (o) lighter

αναπτύσσω anaptiso develop;
explain

ανατολή (η) anatoli (i) east; dawn

ανατολή του ήλιου (η) anatoli too
ilioo (i) sunrise

ΑΝΑΧΩΡΕΙ ΚΑΘΗΜΕΡΙΝΑ
ΓΙΑ… αναχωρεί καθημερινά
γιά… departs daily to…

ΑΝΑΧΩΡΗΣΕΙΣ αναχωρήσεις
departures

ΑΝΑΧΩΡΗΣΗ αναχώρηση (η)
anakhorisi (i) departure

ΑΝΑΨΥΚΤΗΡΙΟ αναψυκτήριο
refreshments

άνδρας (ο) anthras (o) man

ΑΝΔΡΙΚΑ ανδρικά (τα) anthrika
(ta) menswear

ΑΝΔΡΙΚΑ ΕΙΔΗ ΚΑΙ
ΑΞΕΣΟΥΑΡ ανδρικά είδη και
αξεσουάρ men's fashions and
accessories

ΑΝΔΡΙΚΑ ΕΝΔΥΜΑΤΑ ανδρικά
ενδύματα anthrika enthimata
menswear

ΑΝΔΡΙΚΑ ΕΣΩΡΟΥΧΑ ανδρικά
εσώρουχα anthrika esorookha
men's underwear

ΑΝΔΡΙΚΑΙ ΚΟΜΜΩΣΕΙΣ
ανδρικαί κομμώσεις anthrikeh
komosis men's hairdresser

ΑΝΔΡΙΚΑ ΥΠΟΔΗΜΑΤΑ
ανδρικά υποδήματα anthrika
ipothimata men's footwear

ΑΝΔΡΙΚΑ ΥΠΟΚΑΜΙΣΑ
ανδρικά υποκάμισα anthrika
ipokamisa men's shirts

ΑΝΔΡΩΝ ανδρών gents' (toilet),
men's room

ανεβαίνω aneveno get in (car);
get up; go up

ΑΝΕΛΚΥΣΤΗΡΑΣ
ανελκυστήρας (ο) anelkistiras (o)
lift, elevator

ΑΝΕΜΙΣΤΗΡΑΣ ανεμιστήρας
(ο) anemistiras (o) fan

άνεμος (ο) anemos (o) wind

ΑΝΕΞΑΡΤΗΤΟ ΔΙΑΜΕΡΙΣΜΑ
ανεξάρτητο διαμέρισμα (το)
anexartito thiamerisma (to)
self-catering apartment

ανεξάρτητος anexartitos
independent

άνεργος anergos unemployed

ανήκω aniko belong

ανησυχώ anisikho be anxious,
be worried

ανησυχώ για anisikho ya
worry about

ανηψιά (η) anipsia (i) niece

ανηψιός (ο) anipsios (o) nephew

ΑΝΘΟΠΩΛΕΙΟ ανθοπωλείο
(το) anTHopolio (to) florist's

άνθρωποι (οι) anTHropi (i) people

αν και an keh although

ΑΝΟΔΟΣ άνοδος (η) anothos (i)
ascent, way up

ανοίγω anigo open (verb);
switch on

ανοίγω τις βαλίτσες anigo tis
valitses unpack

ΑΝΟΙΚΤΑ ανοικτά anikta open

ΑΝΟΙΚΤΟ ΑΠΟ... ΩΣ...
ανοικτό από... ως,... anikto
apo... os... open from... to...

ΑΝΟΙΚΤΟΝ ανοικτόν anikton
open (adj)

ανοικτός aniktos open (adj); on
(light)

άνοιξη (η) anixi (i) spring (season)

ανοιχτήρι (το) anikhtiri (to)
tin opener; corkscrew

ΑΝΟΙΧΤΟ ανοιχτό anikhto
open; light (colour)

ΑΝΤΑΛΛΑΚΤΙΚΑ
ανταλλακτικά (τα) spare parts

ΑΝΤΑΛΛΑΚΤΙΚΑ
ΑΥΤΟΚΙΝΗΤΩΝ
ανταλλακτικά αυτοκινήτων
(τα) auto spares

ανταλλάσω andalaso exchange
(verb)

άντε! andeh! come on!

αντέχω andekho endure, tolerate

αντί andi instead of

ΑΝΤΙΒΙΟΤΙΚΟ αντιβιοτικό (το)
andiviotiko (to) antibiotic

ΑΝΤΙ-ΙΣΤΑΜΙΝΙΚΟ ΦΑΡΜΑΚΟ
αντι-ισταμινικό φάρμακο (το)
andi-istaminiko farmako (to)
antihistamine

αντίκα (η) andika (i) antique

ΑΝΤΙΚΕΣ αντίκες andikes
antiques

αντίο andio goodbye

αντιπαθητικός andipaTHitikos
obnoxious

ΑΝΤΙΠΡΟΣΩΠΕΙΑ
ΑΥΤΟΚΙΝΗΤΩΝ
αντιπροσωπεία αυτοκινήτων
(η) andiprosopia aftokiniton (i)
car dealer

ΑΝΤΙΠΡΟΣΩΠΟΣ
αντιπρόσωπος (ο) andiprosopos
(o) agent

αντιπυρετικό andipiretiko
anti-fever

ΑΝΤΙΣΗΠΤΙΚΟ αντισηπτικό
(το) andisiptiko (to) antiseptic

ΑΝΤΙΣΥΛΛΗΠΤΙΚΟ
αντισυλληπτικό (το)
andisiliptiko (to) contraceptive

ΑΝΤΙΣΥΛΛΗΠΤΙΚΟ ΧΑΠΙ
αντισυλληπτικό χάπι
(το) andisiliptiko khapi (to)
contraceptive pill

ΑΝΤΙΤΙΜΟ (ΔΙΑΔΡΟΜΗΣ)
αντίτιμο (διαδρομής) (το)
anditimo (thiathromis) (to) fare

ΑΝΤΙΦΛΕΓΜΩΔΕΣ
αντιφλεγμώδες
anti-inflammation

αντλία (η) andlia (i) pump

ΑΝΤΛΙΑ ΒΕΝΖΙΝΗΣ αντλία
βενζίνης petrol/gas pump

ΑΝΤΛΙΑ ΝΤΙΖΕΛ αντλία ντίζελ

A
B
Γ
Δ
E
Z
H
Θ
I
K
Λ
M
N
Ξ
O
Π
P
Σ
T
Y
Φ
X
Ψ
Ω

diesel pump

ΑΝΩ άνω ano up

ΑΞΕΣΟΥΑΡ ΑΥΤΟΚΙΝΗΤΩΝ
αξεσουάρ αυτοκινήτων (τα)
auto accessories

άξονας (ο) axonas (o) axle

ΑΠΑΓΟΡΕΥΕΤΑΙ απαγορεύεται
it is prohibited

ΑΠΑΓΟΡΕΥΕΤΑΙ Η ΕΙΣΟΔΟΣ
απαγορεύεται η είσοδος
no entry, no admission

ΑΠΑΓΟΡΕΥΕΤΑΙ Η
ΚΑΤΑΠΟΣΙΣ απαγορεύεται η
κατάποσις do not swallow

ΑΠΑΓΟΡΕΥΕΤΑΙ Η
ΚΑΤΑΣΚΗΝΩΣΗ
απαγορεύεται η κατασκήνωση
no camping

ΑΠΑΓΟΡΕΥΕΤΑΙ Η
ΚΟΛΥΜΒΗΣΗ
απαγορεύεται η κολύμβηση
no swimming

ΑΠΑΓΟΡΕΥΕΤΑΙ Η ΛΗΨΙΣ
ΔΙΑ ΤΟΥ ΣΤΟΜΑΤΟΣ
απαγορεύεται η λήψις διά
του στόματος not to be taken
orally

ΑΠΑΓΟΡΕΥΕΤΑΙ Η
ΣΤΑΘΜΕΥΣΗ απαγορεύεται η
στάθμευση no parking

ΑΠΑΓΟΡΕΥΕΤΑΙ Η ΣΤΑΣΗ
απαγορεύεται η στάση
no waiting, no stopping

ΑΠΑΓΟΡΕΥΕΤΑΙ Η
ΧΟΡΗΓΗΣΗ ΑΝΕΥ
ΣΥΝΤΑΓΗΣ ΙΑΤΡΟΥ
απαγορεύεται η χορήγηση άνευ
συνταγής ιατρού
available on prescription only

ΑΠΑΓΟΡΕΥΕΤΑΙ Ο
ΓΥΜΝΙΣΜΟΣ απαγορεύεται ο
γυμνισμός nudism prohibited

ΑΠΑΓΟΡΕΥΟΝΤΑΙ ΟΙ
ΚΑΤΑΔΥΣΕΙΣ απαγορεύονται
οι καταδύσεις no diving

ΑΠΑΓΟΡΕΥΕΤΑΙ ΤΟ
ΚΑΜΠΙΝΓΚ απαγορεύεται το
κάμπινγκ no camping

ΑΠΑΓΟΡΕΥΕΤΑΙ ΤΟ
ΚΑΠΝΙΖΕΙΝ απαγορεύεται το
καπνίζειν no smoking

ΑΠΑΓΟΡΕΥΕΤΑΙ ΤΟ
ΚΑΠΝΙΣΜΑ απαγορεύεται το
κάπνισμα no smoking

ΑΠΑΓΟΡΕΥΕΤΑΙ ΤΟ ΚΥΝΗΓΙ
απαγορεύεται το κυνήγι
no hunting

ΑΠΑΓΟΡΕΥΕΤΑΙ ΤΟ
ΠΡΟΣΠΕΡΑΣΜΑ
απαγορεύεται το
προσπέρασμα no overtaking,
no passing

ΑΠΑΓΟΡΕΥΕΤΑΙ ΤΟ ΨΑΡΕΜΑ
απαγορεύεται το ψάρεμα
no fishing

ΑΠΑΓΟΡΕΥΜΕΝΗ ΠΕΡΙΟΧΗ
απαγορευμένη περιοχή
restricted area

απαγορευμένος apagorevmenos
forbidden

απαίσιος apesios appalling

απαιτώ apeto demand (verb)

απαλός apalos soft

απαντάω apandao answer (verb)

απάντηση (η) apandisi (i) answer

απένταρος apendaros broke

απίθανος apithanos incredible

ΑΠΛΗ ΒΕΝΖΙΝΗ απλή βενζίνη
(η) apli venzini (i) two-star
petrol/gas

ΑΠΛΗ ΔΙΑΔΡΟΜΗ απλή
διαδρομή (η) apli thiathromi (i)
single/one-way fare

ΑΠΛΟ ΕΙΣΙΤΗΡΙΟ απλό
εισιτήριο (το) aplo isitirio (to)
single/one-way ticket

απλός aplos simple

απλώνω aplono stretch (*verb*)

από apo from; since; than

από το... στο... apo to... sto...
from... to...

από κάτω apo kato below, under

από πάνω apo pano over, above

αποβιβάζομαι apovivazomeh
land (*verb*)

απογειώνομαι apoyionomeh
take off (*verb*)

απόγευμα (το) apoyevma (to)
afternoon

το απόγευμα to apoyevma
in the afternoon

ΑΠΟΓΕΥΜΑΤΙΝΗ
ΠΑΡΑΣΤΑΣΗ απογευματινή
παράσταση (η) apoyevmatini
parastasi (i) matinee

απογοητευμένος apogo-itevmenos
disappointed

ΑΠΟΔΕΙΞΗ απόδειξη **(η)** apothixi
(i) receipt, evidence

ΑΠΟ ΔΕΥΤΕΡΟ ΧΕΡΙ από
δεύτερο χέρι apo theftero kheri
second-hand

ΑΠΟΛΥΜΑΝΤΙΚΟ
απολυμαντικό (το) apolimandiko
(to) disinfectant

ΑΠΟΣΚΕΥΕΣ αποσκευές **(οι)**
aposkeves (i) luggage, baggage

ΑΠΟΣΜΗΤΙΚΟ αποσμητικό
(το) aposmitiko (to) deodorant

ΑΠΟΣΤΟΛΕΑΣ αποστολέας
apostoleas sender

απότομος apotomos steep

απότομος βράχος (ο) apotomos
vrakhos (o) cliff

αποφασίζω apofasizo decide

απόψε apopseh tonight

ΑΠΡΙΛΙΟΣ Απρίλιος (ο) Aprilios
(o) April

Α΄ ΠΡΟΒΟΛΗΣ α΄ προβολής
major cinema/movie theater

απρόσμενος aprosmenos
surprising

ΑΠΩΛΕΣΘΕΝΤΑ
ΑΝΤΙΚΕΙΜΕΝΑ απωλεσθέντα
αντικείμενα apolesTHenda
adikimena
lost property

αράχνη (η) arakhni (i) spider

αργά arga late; slowly

αργίες (οι) aryies (i) public
holidays

αργός argos slow

αργότερα argotera later

αργώ argo arrive late; go slowly

ΑΡΙΘΜΟΣ αριθμός (ο) ariTHmos
(o) number

ΑΡΙΘΜΟΣ ΘΕΣΕΩΣ αριθμός
θέσεως ariTHmos THeseos
seat number

αριστερά aristera left

αριστερόχειρας aristerokhiras
left-handed

A
B
Γ
Δ
E
Z
H
Θ
I
K
Λ
M
N
Ξ
O
Π
P
Σ
T
Y
Φ
X
Ψ
Ω

αρκετά arketa enough; quite

αρκετοί arketi several

αρνητικό (το) arnitiko (to) negative

αρουραίος (ο) arooreos (o) rat

αρραβωνιασμένος aravoniasmenos engaged (to be married)

αρραβωνιαστικιά (η) aravoniastikia (i) fiancée

αρραβωνιαστικός (ο) aravoniastikos (o) fiancé

αρρενωπός arenopos manly; macho

αρρώστια (η) arostia (i) disease

άρρωστος arostos ill, sick

ΑΡΤΟΠΟΙΕΙΟ αρτοποιείο (το) artopi-io (to) bakery

αρχαιολογία (η) arkheoloyia (i) archaeology

αρχαίος arkheos ancient

αρχαιότητες (οι) arkheotites (i) ruins

αρχάρια (η) arkharia (i) beginner

αρχάριος (ο) arkharios (o) beginner

αρχείο (το) arkhio (to) file

αρχή (η) arkhi (i) beginning

αρχίζω arkhizo begin

αρχιτέκτων (ο/η) arkhitekton (o/i) architect

άρωμα (το) aroma (to) perfume

ΑΣΑΝΣΕΡ ασανσέρ (το) asanser (to) lift, elevator

ασετόν (το) aseton (to) nail varnish remover

ΑΣΗΜΕΝΙΟΣ ασημένιος asimenios silver

ΑΣΗΜΙΚΑ ασημικά (τα) asimika (ta) silver(ware)

ΑΣΘΕΝΟΦΟΡΟ ασθενοφόρο (το) asTHenoforo (to) ambulance

ΑΣΘΜΑ άσθμα (το) asTHma (to) asthma

ΑΣΠΙΡΙΝΗ ασπιρίνη (η) aspirini (i) aspirin

άσπρος aspros white

άστατος astatos changeable

αστείο (το) astio (to) joke

αστείος astios funny, amusing

αστέρι (το) asteri (to) star

αστράγαλος (ο) astragalos (o) ankle

ΑΣΤΥΝΟΜΙΑ αστυνομία (η) astinomia (i) police

ΑΣΤΥΝΟΜΙΚΟ ΤΜΗΜΑ αστυνομικό τμήμα (το) astinomiko tmima (to) police station

αστυφύλακας (ο) astifilakas (o) policeman

αστυνομικός (η) astinomikos (i) policewoman

ΑΣΦΑΛΕΙΑ ασφάλεια (η) asfalia (i) fuse; insurance

ΑΣΦΑΛΕΙΑΙ ασφάλειαι asfali-eh insurance

ασφαλής asfalis safe

άσχημα askhima badly

άσχημος askhimos ugly

ατζέντα (η) atzenda (i) address book

ατμόπλοιο (το) atmoplio (to) steamer

άτομο (το) atomo (to) person

ΑΥΓΟΥΣΤΟΣ Αύγουστος (ο) Avgoostos (o) August

αυθεντικός afTHendikos genuine

αύριο avrio tomorrow

Αυστραλέζα (η) Afstraleza (i) Australian (**woman**)

Αυστραλέζικος Afstralezikos Australian (*adj*)

ΑΥΣΤΡΑΛΙΑ Αυστραλία (η) Afstralia (i) Australia

Αυστραλός (ο) Afstralos (o) Australian (**man**)

αυτά, αυτές afta, aftes these; they; them

αυτή afti she; this (one)

αυτής aftis of her

αυτί (το) afti (to) ear

αυτό afto it; this

   αυτό εδώ afto etho this one

αυτοί afti these; they

ΑΥΤΟΚΙΝΗΤΟ αυτοκίνητο (το) aftokinito (to) car

αυτόματος aftomatos automatic (*adj*)

αυτό που afto poo what

αυτός aftos he; this (one)

αυτός ο ίδιος aftos o ithios himself

αυτού aftoo of him, of it

αυτούς aftoos them

ΑΥΤ/ΤΟ aut/to car

αυτών afton of them

αφεντικό (το) afendiko (to) boss

ΑΦΕΤΗΡΙΑ αφετηρία (η) afetiria (i) terminus

αφήνω afino leave (*verb*)

ΑΦΙΞΕΙΣ αφίξεις arrivals

ΑΦΙΞΗ άφιξη (η) afixi (i) arrival

αφίσα (η) afisa (i) poster

ΑΦΟΙ. αφοί. bros.

ΑΦΟΡΟΛΟΓΗΤΑ αφορολόγητα
(τα) aforoloyita (ta) duty-free

αφροδίσιο νόσημα (το) afrothisio nosima (to) VD

ΑΦΡΟΣ ΞΥΡΙΣΜΑΤΟΣ αφρός ξυρίσματος (ο) afros xirismatos (o) shaving foam

αφρός (ο) afros (o) surf

αχθοφόρος (ο) akhthoforos (o) doorman

αχινός (ο) akhinos (o) sea urchin

> **Travel tip** If you're unlucky enough to step on one of the black, spiky sea urchins that infest rocky shorelines all year round, a sterilized sewing needle and some olive oil are effective for removing the spines. If you don't extract them they'll fester, and walking on the wound pushes them in further.

B

ΒΑΓΟΝΙ βαγόνι (το) vagoni (to) coach, car (**train**)

ΒΑΓΚΟΝ-ΛΙ βαγκόν-λι vagon-li sleeper, sleeping car

βάζο (το) vazo (to) vase

βάζω vazo put

ΒΑΘΙΑ ΝΕΡΑ βαθιά νερά deep water

βάθος: στο βάθος sto vaTHos in the background; at the bottom

βαθύς vaTHis deep

βαλβίδα (η) valvitha (i) valve

βαλίτσα (η) valitsa (i) bag, suitcase

Α Β Γ Δ Ε Ζ Η Θ Ι Κ Λ Μ Ν Ξ Ο Π Ρ Σ Τ Υ Φ Χ Ψ Ω

ВАМВАКЕРО βαμβακερό (το)
vamvakero (to) cotton

βαρετός varetos boring

ВАРКА βάρκα (η) varka (i)
small boat; dinghy

βάρκα με κουπιά varka meh koopia
rowing boat

βάρκα με μηχανή varka meh
mikhani motorboat

ВАРОΣ βάρος (το) varos (to)
weight

βαρύς varis heavy; rich (food)

βασιλιάς (ο) vasilias (ο) king

βασίλισσα (η) vasilisa (i) queen

ВАФН βαφή (η) vafi (i) hair dye

βάφω vafo paint; tint (*verb*)

βγάζω φωτογραφία vgazo
fotografia photograph (*verb*)

βγαίνω vgeno go out

ВГАΛТЕ ТНΝ КАРТА βγάλτε
την κάρτα remove the card

βέβαια veveh-a of course

βελόνα (η) velona (i) needle

βελτιώνω veltiono improve

ВΕΝΖΙΝΑΔΙΚΟ βενζινάδικο (το)
venzinathiko (to) petrol station,
gas station

ВΕΝΖΙΝΗ βενζίνη (η) venzini (i)
petrol, gas

βεντιλατέρ (το) vendilater (to)
fan belt

ВΕΡΝΙΚΙ ПАПОΥТΣΙΩΝ
βερνίκι παπουτσιών (το) verniki
papootsion (to) shoe polish

ВНХАΣ βήχας (ο) vikhas (ο) cough

βήχω vikho cough (*verb*)

βιάζομαι viazomeh hurry (*verb*)

βιάσου! viasoo! hurry up!

βιασμός (ο) viasmos (ο) rape

βιβλίο (το) vivlio (to) book

βιβλίο διαλόγων vivlio thialogon
phrasebook

ВΙΒΛΙΟΘΗΚΗ βιβλιοθήκη (η)
vivlioTHiki (i) library

ΒΙΒΛΙΟΠΩΛΕΙΟ βιβλιοπωλείο
(το) vivliopolio (to) bookshop,
bookstore

ΒΙΔΑ βίδα (η) vitha (i) screw

ΒΙΖΑ βίζα (η) viza (i) visa

βίλλα (η) vila (i) villa

βίντεο (το) video (to) video

ΒΙΤΑΜΙΝΕΣ βιταμίνες (οι)
vitamines (i) vitamins

Β΄ ΚΑΤΗΓΟΡΙΑΣ
Β΄ κατηγορίας second class

βλάβη (η) vlavi (i) breakdown (car)

βλάκας (ο) vlakas (o) idiot; stupid

βλέπω vlepo see

βοήθεια (η) voiTHia (i) help

βοηθώ vo-iTHo help (verb)

βόμβα (η) vomva (i) bomb

Βόρειος Ιρλανδία (η) vorios
Irlanthia (i) Northern Ireland

ΒΟΥΛΓΑΡΙΑ Βουλγαρία (η)
voolgaria (i) Bulgaria

Βουλγαρικός voolgarikos Bulgarian
(adj)

βουλιάζω vooliazo sink (verb)

ΒΟΥΛΚΑΝΙΖΑΤΕΡ
βουλκανιζατέρ voolkanizater
tyre repairs

βουνό (το) voono (to) mountain

βούρτσα (η) voortsa (i) brush

βουτάω vootao dive (verb)

Β΄ ΠΡΟΒΟΛΗΣ β΄ προβολής
local cinema/movie theater

βράδυ (το) vrathi (to) evening
το βράδυ to vrathi in the evening

βραδυά (η) vrathia (i) evening

ΒΡΑΔΥΝΗ ΠΑΡΑΣΤΑΣΗ
βραδυνή παράσταση
evening performance

βράζω vrazo boil (verb)

βράχια (τα) vrakhia (ta) rocks;
cliffs

βραχιόλι (το) vrakhioli (to) bracelet

βράχος (ο) vrakhos (o) rock

ΒΡΕΤΑΝΝΙΑ Βρεταννία (η)
vretania (i) Britain

Βρεταννίδα (η) vretanitha (i) Briton
(woman)

Βρεταννικός vretanikos British

Βρεταννός (ο) vretanos (o) Briton
(man)

βρέχει vrekhi it's raining

βρίσκω vrisko find (verb)

βροντή (η) vrondi (i) thunder

βροχή (η) vrokhi (i) rain

βρύση (η) vrisi (i) tap, faucet

βρώμικος vromikos dirty

βυζαίνω vizeno breastfeed

βυθός (ο) vithos (o) bottom (of sea)

Γ

γάιδαρος (ο) gaitharos (o) donkey

ΓΑΛΑΚΤΟΠΩΛΕΙΟ
γαλακτοπωλείο (το) galaktopolio
(to) shop/take-away café selling
dairy products

ΓΑΛΑΚΤΩΜΑ ΚΑΘΑΡΙΣΜΟΥ
γαλάκτωμα καθαρισμού (το)
galaktoma kaTHarismoo (to)
cleansing lotion

ΓΑΛΛΙΑ Γαλλία (η) galia (i)
France

Γαλλικός galikos French (adj)

γάμος (ο) gamos (o) wedding

A
B
Γ
Δ
E
Z
H
Θ
I
K
Λ
M
N
Ξ
O
Π
P
Σ
T
Y
Φ
X
Ψ
Ω

γαμπρός (ο) gambros (ο)
bridegroom; son-in-law;
brother-in-law

γάντια (τα) gandia (ta) gloves

γάτα (η) gata (i) cat

γειά σου! yia soo! hello!; bless
you!; cheers!

γείτονας (ο) yitonas (ο) neighbour

γελοίο yelio ridiculous

γελώ yelo laugh (verb)

γεμάτος yematos full

γεμίζω yemizo fill (verb)

γενέθλια (τα) yeneтHlia (ta)
birthday

γένια (τα) yenia (ta) beard

γενναίος yeneos brave

ΓΕΡΜΑΝΙΑ Γερμανία (η)
Yermania (i) Germany

Γερμανικός Yermanikos German
(adj)

γέρος yeros old (person)

ΓΕΥΜΑ γεύμα (το) yevma (to)
meal

γεύση (η) yefsi (i) flavour; taste

ΓΕΦΥΡΑ γέφυρα (η) yefira (i)
bridge

ΓΗΠΕΔΟ γήπεδο (το) yipetho (to)
football pitch

ΓΗΠΕΔΟ ΤΕΝΝΙΣ γήπεδο
τέννις yipetho tenis tennis court

για ya for

για μένα ya mena for me

γιαγιά (η) yaya (i) grandmother

ΓΙΑ ΕΞΩΤΕΡΙΚΗ ΧΡΗΣΗ
ΜΟΝΟΝ για εξωτερική χρήση
μόνον for external use only

ΓΙΑ ΕΣΩΤΕΡΙΚΗ ΧΡΗΣΗ

ΜΟΝΟΝ για εσωτερική χρήση
μόνον for internal use only

γιακάς (ο) yakas (ο) collar

γιατί; yati? why?

ΓΙΑ ΤΟ ΣΠΙΤΙ για το σπίτι ya to
spiti to take away, to go (food)

ΓΙΑΤΡΟΣ γιατρός (ο/η) yatros
(ο/i) doctor

γίνομαι yinomeh become; happen
τι γίνεται; ti yineteh?
what's happening?

ΓΙΟΡΤΗ ΚΡΑΣΙΟΥ γιορτή
κρασιού (η) yorti krasioo (i)
wine festival

γιός (ο) yos (ο) son

γιώτ (το) yot (to) yacht

γκάζι (το) gazi (to) gas;
accelerator

ΓΚΑΛΕΡΙ γκαλερί (η) galeri (i)
art gallery

ΓΚΑΡΑΖ γκαράζ (το) garaz (to)
garage (for parking/repairs)

ΓΚΑΡΝΤΑΡΟΜΠΑ
γκαρνταρόμπα (η) gardaroba (i)
cloakroom (for coats)

Γ΄ ΚΑΤΗΓΟΡΙΑΣ
Γ΄ κατηγορίας third class

γκολφ (το) golf (to) golf

γκρίζος grizos grey

γκρουπ (το) groop (to) group

γλάρος (ο) glaros (ο) seagull

ΓΛΙΦΙΤΖΟΥΡΙ γλιφιτζούρι (το)
glifidzoori (to) lollipop

ΓΛΥΚΟ γλυκό (το) gliko (to)
sweet, candy

γλυκός glikos sweet (adj)

γλυστερός glisteros slippery

γλυστράω glistrao skid (*verb*)

γλώσσα (η) glosa (i) language; tongue

γνωρίζω gnorizo know

δεν γνωρίζω then gnorizo I don't know

γόνατο (το) gonato (to) knee

γονείς (οι) gonis (i) parents

γουίντσερφ (το) gooindserf (to) sailboard

ΓΟΥΝΑΡΙΚΑ γουναρικά (τα) goonarika (ta) furrier

ΓΟΥΝΕΣ γούνες goones furs

γουρούνι (το) goorooni (to) pig

γοφός (ο) gofos (o) hip

γραβάτα (η) gravata (i) tie, necktie

γράμμα (το) grama (to) letter

γράμματα (τα) gramata (ta) post, mail

γραμματική (η) gramatiki (i) grammar

ΓΡΑΜΜΑΤΟΚΙΒΩΤΙΟ γραμματοκιβώτιο (το) gramatokivotio (to) letterbox, mailbox

γραμματόσημο (το) gramatosimo (to) stamp

ΓΡΑΜΜΕΣ ΤΡΑΙΝΟΥ γραμμές traίνου railway crosses road

ΓΡΑΜΜΗ γραμμή (η) grami (i) route, line

γρασίδι (το) grasithi (to) lawn

γραφείο (το) grafio (to) office

ΓΡΑΦΕΙΟ ΤΑΞΙΔΙΩΝ γραφείο ταξιδίων grafio taxithion travel agency

γραφομηχανή (η) grafomikhani (i) typewriter

γράφω grafo write

γρήγορα grigora quick; quickly

γρήγορος grigoros fast

ΓΡΙΠΠΗ γρίππη (η) gripi (i) flu

γρύλλος (ο) grilos (o) jack

γυαλί (το) yali (to) glass (material)

ΓΥΑΛΙΑ γυαλιά (τα) yalia (ta) glasses, eyeglasses

ΓΥΑΛΙΑ ΗΛΙΟΥ γυαλιά ηλίου yalia ilioo sunglasses

ΓΥΜΝΑΣΙΟ γυμνάσιο (το) yimnasio (to) secondary school

γυμνασμένος yimnasmenos fit (healthy)

ΓΥΜΝΑΣΤΗΡΙΟ γυμναστήριο (το) yimnastirio (to) gym

γυμνός yimnos naked

γυναίκα (η) yineka (i) woman; wife

ΓΥΝΑΙΚΕΙΑ γυναικεία (τα) yinekia (ta) ladies' wear

ΓΥΝΑΙΚΕΙΑΙ ΚΟΜΜΩΣΕΙΣ γυναικείαι κομμώσεις (οι) yinekieh komosis (i) ladies' salon

ΓΥΝΑΙΚΕΙΑ ΦΟΡΕΜΑΤΑ γυναικεία φορέματα yinekia foremata ladies' dresses

ΓΥΝΑΙΚΕΙΕΣ ΚΑΛΤΣΕΣ - ΚΑΛΣΟΝ γυναικείες κάλτσες - καλσόν yinekies kaltses - kalson ladies' socks - stockings

ΓΥΝΑΙΚΩΝ γυναικών ladies' (toilet), ladies' room

γυρνώ yirno turn (*verb*)

γυρνώ πίσω yirno piso arrive back, return; take back

γυρνώ σπίτι yirno spiti return home

A
B
Γ
Δ
E
Z
H
Θ
I
K
Λ
M
N
Ξ
O
Π
P
Σ
T
Y
Φ
X
Ψ
Ω

δακτυλίδι (το) thaktilíthi (to) ring
(on finger)

δανείζομαι thanízomeh borrow

δανείζω thanízo lend

δασκάλα (η) thaskala (i) instructor;
teacher

δάσκαλος (ο) thaskalos (o)
instructor; teacher

δάσος (το) thasos (to) forest

δάχτυλο (το) thakhtilo (to) finger

δάχτυλο του ποδιού thakhtilo too
pothioo toe

δε theh not

Δ.Ε.Η. public electricity company

δείκτης (ο) thiktis (o) gauge; index
finger

ΔΕΙΠΝΟ δείπνο (το) thipno (to)
evening meal

δείχνω thikhno show (*verb*)

δέκα theka ten

δεκαεννιά theka-enia nineteen

δεκαέξι theka-exi sixteen

δεκαεπτά theka-epta seventeen

δεκαοχτώ theka-okhto eighteen

δεκαπενθήμερο thekapenTHimero
fortnight

δεκαπέντε thekapendeh fifteen

δεκατέσσερα thekatesera fourteen

δέκατος thekatos tenth

δεκατρία thekatria thirteen

ΔΕΚΕΜΒΡΙΟΣ Δεκέμβριος (ο)
Thekemvrios (o) December

δέμα (το) thema (to) parcel

ΔΕΜΑΤΑ δέματα parcels,
packages

δεν then not

δένδρο (το) thenthro (to) tree

**ΔΕΝ ΛΕΙΤΟΥΡΓΕΙ δεν
λειτουργεί** then litooryi
out of order

**ΔΕΝ ΣΙΔΕΡΩΝΕΤΑΙ δεν
σιδερώνεται** do not iron

δεξιός, δεξιά thexios, thexia
right (side)

δεξίωση (η) thexiosi (i)
reception (party)

ΔΕΡΜΑ δέρμα (το) therma (to)
skin; leather

ΔΕΡΜΑΤΑ δέρματα (τα) thermata
(ta) leather goods

ΔΕΣΠΟΙΝΙΔΑ δεσποινίδα (η)
thespinitha (i) young woman;
Miss; Ms

ΔΕΣΠΟΙΝΙΣ δεσποινίς thespinis
Miss; Ms

ΔΕΥΤΕΡΑ Δευτέρα (η) theftera (i)
Monday

ΔΕΥΤΕΡΗ ΘΕΣΗ δεύτερη θέση
second class

δευτερόλεπτο (το) thefterolepto
(to) second

δεύτερος thefteros second (*adj*)

ΔΕΥΤΕΡΟ ΧΕΡΙ δεύτερο χέρι
theftero kheri second-hand

δέχομαι thekhomeh accept; receive

δηλητηρίαση (η) thilitiriasi (i)
poisoning

δηλητήριο (το) thilitirio (to) poison

ΔΗΜΑΡΧΕΙΟ δημαρχείο (το)
thimarkhio (to) town hall

**ΔΗΜΟΣΙΑ ΛΟΥΤΡΑ δημόσια
λουτρά (τα)** thimosia lootra (ta)

public baths

δημόσιος thimosios public

δημοσιογράφος (ο/η)
thimosiografos (o/i) reporter

δημοτική μουσική (η) thimotiki
moosiki (i) folk music

διαβάζω thiavazo read

ΔΙΑΒΑΣΗ ΠΕΖΩΝ διάβαση
πεζών **(η)** pedestrian crossing

ΔΙΑΒΑΤΗΡΙΟ διαβατήριο **(το)**
thiavatirio (to) passport

διαβητικός (ο) thiavitikos (o)
diabetic

διαβητική (η) thiavitiki (i) diabetic

**ΔΙΑΔΡΟΜΗ ΜΕΤ'
ΕΠΙΣΤΡΟΦΗΣ** διαδρομή
μετ' επιστροφής **(η)** thiathromi
met' epistrofis (i) return/round
trip fare

διάδρομος (ο) thiathromos (o)
corridor

διάθεση (η) thiaτhesi (i) mood

δίαιτα (η) thieta (i) diet

διακοπές (οι) thiakopes (i)
holiday, vacation

διακοπή (η) thiakopi (i)
interruption; power cut

διακόπτης (ο) thiakoptis (o) switch

διακόπτω thiakopto interrupt

διακόσια thiakosia two hundred

διαλέγω thialego choose

ΔΙΑΛΕΙΜΜΑ διάλειμμα **(το)**
thialima (to) interval, intermission

διάλεκτος (η) thialektos (i) dialect

ΔΙΑΛΥΜΑ διάλυμα **(το)** thialima
(to) solution

διαμάντι (το) thiamandi (to)
diamond

Διαμαρτυρόμενος (ο)
thiamartiromenos (o) Protestant

ΔΙΑΜΕΡΙΣΜΑ διαμέρισμα **(το)**
thiamerisma (to) apartment, flat

διά μέσου thia mesoo through

διαμονή (η) thiamoni (i)
accommodation; stay

ΔΙΑΝΥΚΤΕΡΕΥΟΝ
διανυκτερεύον open all night

διάρκεια (η) thiarkia (i) duration

ΔΙΑΡΚΕΙΑ ΠΤΗΣΕΩΣ
διάρκεια πτήσεως
thiarkia ptiseos flight time

διαρροή (η) thiaroi (i) leak

ΔΙΑΡΡΟΙΑ διάρροια **(η)** thiaria (i)
diarrhoea

διάσημος thiasimos famous

ΔΙΑΣΤΑΥΡΩΣΗ διασταύρωση
(η) thiastavrosi (i) junction,
crossroads, intersection

διασχίζω thiaskhizo go through

ΔΙΑΤΗΡΕΙΤΑΙ ΣΕ ΨΥΓΕΙΟ
διατηρείται σε ψυγείο
keep refrigerated

διαφημιστικό (το) thiafimistiko (to)
leaflet; advertisements **(on TV)**;
trailer **(cinema)**

διαφορετικά thiaforetika otherwise

διαφορετικός thiaforetikos
different

διάφραγμα (το) thiafragma (to)
shutter **(in camera)**

διαχειριστής (ο) thiakhiristis (o)
manager

διαχειρίστρια (η) thiakhiristria (i)
manageress

διδάσκω thithasko teach

δίδυμοι (οι) thithimi (i) twins

A
B
Γ
Δ
E
Z
H
Θ
I
K
Λ
M
N
Ξ
O
Π
P
Σ
T
Y
Φ
X
Ψ
Ω

ΔΙΕΥΘΥΝΣΗ διεύθυνση (η)
thiefτHinsi (i) address

δίκαιος thikeos fair, just

δικά μας thika mas ours

δικά μου thika moo mine

δικά σας, δικά σου thika sas, thika soo yours

ΔΙΚΑΣΤΗΡΙΟ δικαστήριο (το)
thikastirio (to) law court

δικά της thika tis hers

δικά του thika too his, its

δικά τους thika toos theirs

δικηγόρος (ο/η) thikigoros (o/i) lawyer

δική μας thiki mas ours

δική μου thiki moo mine

δική σας, δική σου thiki sas, thiki soo yours

δική του thiki too his

δική τους thiki toos theirs

ΔΙΚΛΙΝΟ ΔΩΜΑΤΙΟ δίκλινο δωμάτιο (το) thiklino thomatio (to) double room

δικό μας thiko mas ours

δικό μου thiko moo mine

δικό σας, δικό σου thiko sas, thiko soo yours

δικό τους thiko toos theirs

δικό της thiko tis hers

δικό του thiko too his; its

δικός μας thikos mas ours

δικός μου thikos moo mine

δικός σας, δικός σου thikos sas, thikos soo yours

δικός του thikos too his

δικός τους thikos toos theirs

δίνω thino give

ΔΙΟΔΙΑ διόδια (τα) thiothia (ta) toll

διορθώνω thiorτΗono mend, correct

ΔΙΠΛΗ ΤΑΡΙΦΑ διπλή ταρίφα (η) double tariff

διπλό thiplo double

ΔΙΠΛΟ ΔΩΜΑΤΙΟ διπλό δωμάτιο (το) thiplo thomatio (to) double room

διπλό κρεβάτι (το) thiplo krevati (to) double bed

ΔΙΣ. δις. Miss

ΔΙΣΚΑΔΙΚΟ δισκάδικο (το) thiskathiko (to) record shop

δίσκος (ο) thiskos (o) record; tray

Δ´ ΚΑΤΗΓΟΡΙΑΣ
Δ´ κατηγορίας fourth class

δοκιμάζω thokimazo taste (*verb*); try (on)

ΔΟΛΛΑΡΙΟ δολλάριο (το) tholario (to) dollar

δόντι (το) thondi (to) tooth

ΔΟΣΟΛΟΓΙΑ ΕΝΗΛΙΚΩΝ δοσολογία ενηλίκων adult dosage

ΔΟΣΟΛΟΓΙΑ ΠΑΙΔΩΝ δοσολογία παίδων children's dosage

δουλειά (η) thoolia (i) job; work

δουλειές (οι) thoolies (i) business

δουλεύω thoolevo work (*verb*)

δεν δουλεύει then thoolevi it's not working

ΔΡΟΜΟΛΟΓΙΑ δρομολόγια (τα) thromoloyia (ta) timetable, schedule

δρόμος (ο) thromos (o) road; street

δροσερός throser**os** cool

δυνατός thinat**os** loud; possible; strong

δύο thi**o** two

ΔΥΟ ΠΑΡΑΣΤΑΣΕΙΣ δύο παραστάσεις two shows

δυσάρεστος this**a**restos unpleasant

δύση του ήλιου (η) thi**s**i too **i**lioo (i) sunset

ΔΥΣΚΟΙΛΙΑ δυσκοίλια (η) thisk**i**lia (i) constipation

δύσκολος this**k**olos difficult

ΔΥΣΠΕΨΙΑ δυσπεψία (η) thispeps**i**a (i) indigestion

δυστύχημα (το) thist**i**khima (to) accident

δυστυχώς thistikh**os** unfortunately

δώδεκα thoth**e**ka twelve

ΔΩΔΕΚΑΔΑ δωδεκάδα (η) thothek**a**tha (i) dozen

ΔΩΜΑΤΙΟ δωμάτιο (το) thom**a**tio (to) room

ΔΩΡΑ δώρα gifts

ΔΩΡΕΑΝ δωρεάν thore**a**n free (of charge)

δώρο (το) th**o**ro (to) gift

ΔΩΡΟ ΠΑΣΧΑ Δώρο Πάσχα th**o**ro Paskha Easter supplement paid to taxi drivers

ΔΩΡΟ ΧΡΙΣΤΟΥΓΕΝΝΩΝ Δώρο Χριστουγέννων th**o**ro khristooy**e**non Christmas supplement paid to taxi drivers

E

Ε.Α.Σ. Athens Public Transport Corporation

εβδομάδα (η) evthom**a**tha (i) week

εβδομήντα evthom**i**nda seventy

έβδομος **e**vthomos seventh

A
B
Γ
Δ
E
Z
H
Θ
I
K
Λ
M
N
Ξ
O
Π
P
Σ
T
Y
Φ
X
Ψ
Ω

Εβραίος Evreos Jewish

έγγραφο (το) engrafo (to) document

εγγύηση (η) egi-isi (i) guarantee

έγινε! eyineh! OK, coming up!

εγκαίρως engeros on time

έγκαυμα από τον ήλιο (το) engavma apo ton ilio (to) sunburn

έγκυος engios pregnant

έγκυρος engiros valid

έγχρωμο φιλμ (το) enkhromo film (to) colour film

εγώ ego I

εγώ ο ίδιος ego o ithios myself

εδώ etho here

έθιμο (το) eTHimo (to) custom

ΕΘΝΙΚΗ ΟΔΟΣ εθνική οδός (η) eTHniki othos (i) motorway, highway, freeway

ΕΘΝΙΚΗ ΠΙΝΑΚΟΘΗΚΗ Εθνική Πινακοθήκη ETHniki PinakoTHiki National Art Gallery

ΕΘΝΙΚΟΤΗΤΑ εθνικότητα (η) eTHnikotita (i) nationality

ΕΙΔΗ είδη (τα) ithi (ta) goods

ΕΙΔΗ ΑΥΤΟΚΙΝΗΤΟΥ είδη αυτοκινήτου auto accessories

ΕΙΔΗ ΔΩΡΩΝ είδη δώρων gifts

ΕΙΔΗ ΜΠΕΜΠΕ είδη μπεμπέ ithi bebeh babywear

ΕΙΔΗ ΡΟΥΧΙΣΜΟΥ είδη ρουχισμού ithi roukhismoo clothes

ΕΙΔΗ ΣΠΟΡ είδη σπορ ithi spor sports equipment, sportswear

ΕΙΔΗ ΧΑΡΤΟΠΩΛΕΙΟΥ είδη χαρτοπωλείου ithi khartopolioo stationery

ΕΙΔΙΚΗ ΠΡΟΣΦΟΡΑ ειδική προσφορά special price, special offer

ειδικώς ithikos especially

είχες ikhes you had

είκοσι ikosi twenty

ειλικρινής ilikrinis sincere

είμαι imeh I am

είμαστε imasteh we are

είναι ineh he/she/it is; they are

είστε isteh you are

ΕΙΣΑΓΩΓΗΣ εισαγωγής imported

είσαι iseh you are

ΕΙΣΙΤΗΡΙΟ εισιτήριο (το) isitirio (to) ticket

ΕΙΣΙΤΗΡΙΟ ΜΕ ΕΠΙΣΤΡΟΦΗ εισιτήριο με επιστροφή isitirio meh epistrofi return/round trip ticket

ΕΙΣΟΔΟΣ είσοδος (η) isothos (i) entrance, way in

ΕΙΣΟΔΟΣ ΕΛΕΥΘΕΡΑ είσοδος ελευθέρα admission free

ΕΙΣΟΔΟΣ ΠΡΑΤΗΡΙΟΥ είσοδος πρατηρίου entrance to petrol/ gas station

ΕΙΣΠΡΑΚΤΩΡ εισπράκτωρ (ο) ticket collector

είχα ikha I had

είχαμε ikhameh we had

είχαν ikhan they had

είχατε ikhateh you had

είχε ikheh he/she/it had

είχες ikhes you had

Ε′ ΚΑΤΗΓΟΡΙΑΣ Ε′ κατηγορίας fifth class

εκατό ekato hundred

εκατομμύριο: ένα εκατομμύριο ena ekatomirio one million

ΕΚΔΟΣΗ ΕΙΣΙΤΗΡΙΩΝ έκδοση εισιτηρίων ekthosi isitirion ticket office

εκεί eki there, over there

εκεί κάτω eki kato down there

εκείνα, εκείνες ekina, ekines those

εκείνη, εκείνο ekini, ekino that

εκείνοι ekini those

εκείνος ekinos that

ΕΚΘΕΣΗ έκθεση (η) ekτHesi (i) exhibition, showroom

ΕΚΚΛΗΣΙΑ εκκλησία (η) eklisia (i) church

Ε.Κ.Ο. Greek state petrol company

εκπληκτικός ekpliktikos surprising

έκπληξη (η) ekplixi (i) surprise

ΕΚΠΤΩΣΕΙΣ εκπτώσεις (οι) sales

ΕΚΤΑΚΤΗ ΑΝΑΓΚΗ έκτακτη ανάγκη (η) ektakti anangi (i) emergency

εκτός ektos except

έκτος ektos sixth

έλα! ela! you don't say!; come on!, hurry up!

ΕΛ.ΑΣ. Greek police

ΕΛΑΣΤΙΚΑ ελαστικά tyres

ελαστικός elastikos elastic

ελατήριο (το) elatirio (to) spring (in seat etc)

ελαττωματικός elatomatikos faulty

ΕΛΑΤΤΩΣΑΤΕ ΤΑΧΥΤΗΤΑ ελαττώσατε ταχύτητα reduce speed

ελαφρός elafros light (not heavy)

ελάχιστος elakhistos smallest; few

ελεγκτής (ο) elenktis (o) inspector (bus)

ΕΛΕΓΧΟΣ έλεγχος (ο) elenkhos (o) check, inspection

ΕΛΕΓΧΟΣ ΑΠΟΣΚΕΥΩΝ έλεγχος αποσκευών baggage control

ΕΛΕΓΧΟΣ ΔΙΑΒΑΤΗΡΙΩΝ έλεγχος διαβατηρίων passport control

ΕΛΕΓΧΟΣ ΕΙΣΙΤΗΡΙΩΝ έλεγχος εισιτηρίων ticket inspection

ΕΛΕΓΧΟΣ ΕΠΙΒΑΤΩΝ έλεγχος επιβατών passenger control

ΕΛΕΥΘΕΡΑ ΕΙΣΟΔΟΣ ελευθέρα είσοδος elefτHera isothos admission free

ΕΛΕΥΘΕΡΟΝ ελεύθερον elefτHeron free; for hire (taxi)

ελεύθερος elefτHeros free; single (unmarried)

ελιά (η) elia (i) olive; spot (blemish)

ελικόπτερο (το) elikoptero (to) helicopter

ελκυστικός elkistikos attractive

ΕΛΛΑΔΑ Ελλάδα (η) Elatha (i) Greece

Έλληνας (ο) Elinas (o) Greek (man)

Ελληνίδα (η) Elinitha (i) Greek (woman)

ΕΛΛΗΝΙΚΑ Ελληνικά (τα) Elinika (ta) Greek (language)

ΕΛΛΗΝΙΚΗ ΑΣΤΥΝΟΜΙΑ Ελληνική Αστυνομία (η) Greek police

A
B
Γ
Δ
E
Z
H
Θ
I
K
Λ
M
N
Ξ
O
Π
P
Σ
T
Υ
Φ
X
Ψ
Ω

ΕΛΛΗΝΙΚΗ ΡΑΔΙΟΦΩΝΙΑ
Ελληνική Ραδιοφωνία
Greek radio

ΕΛΛΗΝΙΚΗ ΤΗΛΕΟΡΑΣΗ
Ελληνική Τηλεόραση
Greek television

ΕΛΛΗΝΙΚΗΣ ΚΑΤΑΣΚΕΥΗΣ
Ελληνικής κατασκευής
made in Greece

ΕΛΛΗΝΙΚΟ ΠΡΟΙΟΝ Ελληνικό
προιόν
produce of Greece

ΕΛΛΗΝΙΚΟΣ Ελληνικός Elinikos
Greek (*adj*)

Ε.Λ.Π.Α. E.L.P.A. Greek motoring
organization

ελπίζω elpizo hope (*verb*)

ΕΛ.ΤΑ. Greek Post Office

εμάς emas us

εμβολιασμός (ο) emvoliasmos (o)
vaccination

εμβόλιο (το) emvolio (to) vaccine

εμείς emis we

εμένα emena me

ΕΜΠΟΡΙΚΟ ΚΕΝΤΡΟ εμπορικό
κέντρο (το) emboriko kendro (to)
shopping centre

εμπρός ebros come in; hello
(response on phone)

ένα(ν) ena(n) a; one

εναντίον enandion against

ένας enas a; one

ένατος enatos ninth

ενδιαφέρον enthiaferon interesting

ενενήντα eneninda ninety

ένεση (η) enesi (i) injection

ενήλικη (η) eniliki (i) adult

ΕΝΗΛΙΚΟΣ ενήλικος (ο)
enilikos (o) adult

ΕΝΘΥΜΙΟ ενθύμιο (το) enTHimio
(to) souvenir

εννιά enia nine

εννοώ enoo mean (*verb*)

ΕΝΟΙΚΙΑΖΟΝΤΑΙ ενοικιάζονται
enikiazondeh
for hire, to rent

ΕΝΟΙΚΙΑΖΟΝΤΑΙ
ΑΥΤΟΚΙΝΗΤΑ ενοικιάζονται
αυτοκίνητα car rental

ΕΝΟΙΚΙΑΖΟΝΤΑΙ ΒΑΡΚΕΣ
ενοικιάζονται βάρκες
boats for hire

ΕΝΟΙΚΙΑΖΟΝΤΑΙ ΔΩΜΑΤΙΑ
ενοικιάζονται δωμάτια
rooms to let

ΕΝΟΙΚΙΑΣΗ ΑΥΤΟΚΙΝΗΤΩΝ
ενοίκιαση αυτοκινήτων
car rental

Travel tip Cars have obvious
advantages for reaching inac-
cessible corners of the country, but Greece has one of the
highest fatal accident rates in
Europe. Local driving habits
can be atrocious: overtaking
is erratic and tailgating wide-
spread, lane lines go unheed-
ed, turn signals go unused
and motorbikes hog the road.
And matters are made worse
by poor road conditions and
absent signposting.

ενοίκιο (το) enikio (to) rent

ενός enos of a

ενοχλητικός enokhlitikos annoying

ενοχλώ enokhlo disturb

εντάξει endaxi that's all right; OK

έντεκα endeka eleven

έντομο (το) endomo (to) insect

ΕΝΤΥΠΑ έντυπα
printed matter

ενώ eno while

εξαιρετικός exeretikos terrific

εξ αιτίας ex etias because of

εξαρτάται exartateh it depends

ΕΞΑΤΜΙΣΗ εξάτμιση (η)
exatmisi (i) exhaust

εξαφανίζομαι exafanizomeh
disappear

ΕΞΕΤΑΣΕΙΣ εξετάσεις (οι)
exetasis (i) check-up; exams

εξηγώ exigo explain

εξήντα exinda sixty

έξι exi six

ΕΞΟΔΟΣ έξοδος (η) exothos (i)
exit; gate (at airport); door

ΕΞΟΔΟΣ ΑΥΤ/ΤΩΝ έξοδος αυτ/
των vehicle exit

ΕΞΟΔΟΣ ΚΙΝΔΥΝΟΥ έξοδος
κινδύνου emergency exit

εξοχή (η) exokhi (i) countryside

έξοχος exokhos excellent

ΕΞΠΡΕΣ εξπρές expres
special delivery; express

εξυπηρετώ exipireto serve (verb),
assist

έξυπνος exipnos clever, intelligent

έξω! exo! get out!

ΕΞΩΣΤΗΣ εξώστης exostis circle
(in theatre)

εξωτερικός exoterikos external

στο εξωτερικό sto exoteriko
abroad

ΕΞΩΤΕΡΙΚΟΥ εξωτερικού
postage abroad

εξωφρενικός exofrenikos shocking

Ε.Ο.Κ. E.O.K. EEC, EU

Ε.Ο.Τ. E.O.T. National Tourist
Agency

επαληθεύω epaliTHevo check (verb),
verify

επαναλαμβάνω epanalamvano
repeat

επαφή: έρχομαι σε επαφή
erkhomeh seh epafi contact (verb)

Ε.Π.Ε. Ltd

επείγον epigon urgent

επειδή epithi because

επέκταση (η) epektasi (i)
extension lead

επέτειος (η) epetios (i) anniversary

ΕΠΙΒΑΤΗΣ επιβάτης (ο/η)
epivatis (o/i) passenger

επιβεβαιώνω epiveveono confirm

επίδεσμος (ο) epithesmos (o)
bandage

επίθεση (η) epiTHesi (i) attack
(noun)

επιθετικός epiTHetikos aggressive

ΕΠΙΘΕΤΟ επίθετο (το) epiTHeto
(to) surname

επικίνδυνος epikinthinos
dangerous

ΕΠΙΛΕΞΑΤΕ ΤΟΝ ΑΡΙΘΜΟ
επιλέξατε τον αριθμό
dial the number

επίπεδος epipethos flat (even)

έπιπλα (τα) epipla (ta) furniture

ΕΠΙΠΛΩΜΕΝΑ ΔΩΜΑΤΙΑ
επιπλωμένα δωμάτια
furnished rooms

A
B
Γ
Δ
E
Z
H
Θ
I
K
Λ
M
N
Ξ
O
Π
P
Σ
T
Υ
Φ
X
Ψ
Ω

επίσης epísis too, also

επισκέπτομαι episkeptomeh visit (*verb*)

ΕΠΙΣΚΕΥΑΖΟΝΤΑΙ ΥΠΟΔΗΜΑΤΑ επισκευάζονται υποδήματα shoe repairs

επισκευή (η) episkevi (i) repair

επίσκεψη (η) episkepsi (i) visit

επιστήμη (η) epistimi (i) science

ΕΠΙΣΤΟΛΕΣ επιστολές letters

επιστρέφω epistrefo give back; arrive back .

ΕΠΙΣΤΡΕΦΩ ΣΕ 5´ επιστρέφω σε 5´ back in 5 minutes

ΕΠΙΤΑΓΗ επιταγή (η) epitayi (i) cheque, (US) check

επιτέλους epiteloos at last

επίτηδες epitithes deliberately

επιτρέπω epitrepo let (allow)

επιτρέπεται epitrepeteh it is permitted

επιτυχία (η) epitikhia (i) success

επόμενος (ο) epomenos (o) next

εποχή (η) epokhi (i) season

επτά epta seven

E.P.A. Greek radio

ΕΡΓΑ έργα roadworks

ΕΡΓΑ ΕΠΙ ΤΗΣ ΟΔΟΥ ΣΕ ΜΗΚΟΣ… ΧΙΛ. έργα επί της οδού σε μήκος… χιλ. roadworks for… km

εργάζομαι ergazomeh work (*verb*)

ΕΡΓΑΛΕΙΑ ΠΥΡΑΣΦΑΛΕΙΑΣ εργαλεία πυρασφάλειας fire-fighting equipment

εργαλείο (το) ergalio (to) tool

ΕΡΓΑΣΤΗΡΙΟ ΗΛΕΚΤΡΟΝΙΚΩΝ εργαστήριο ηλεκτρονικών electronics

εργένης (ο) eryenis (o) bachelor

εργοστάσιο (το) ergostasio (to) factory

ερυθρά (η) eriTHra (i) German measles

έρχομαι erkhomeh come

έρωτας (ο) erotas (o) love

κάνω έρωτα kano erota make love

ερώτηση (η) erotisi (i) question

εσάς, εσείς, εσένα esas, esis, esena you

ΕΣΤΙΑΤΟΡΙΟ εστιατόριο (το) estiatorio (to) restaurant

εσύ esi you

Ε.Σ.Υ. National Health Service

εσώρουχα (τα) esorookha (ta) underwear

ΕΣΩΡΟΥΧΑ ΓΥΝΑΙΚΕΙΑ εσώρουχα γυναικεία esorookha yinekia ladies' underwear

ΕΣΩΤΕΡΙΚΟΥ εσωτερικού inland postage

E.T. Greek television

εταιρεία (η) eteria (i) company

ετικέτα (η) etiketa (i) label

ΕΤΟΙΜΑ ΓΥΝΑΙΚΕΙΑ έτοιμα γυναικεία ladies' clothing

ετοιμάζω etimazo prepare

ΕΤΟΙΜΑ ΠΑΙΔΙΚΑ έτοιμα παιδικά children's clothing

έτοιμος etimos ready

έτσι etsi so; like this

έτσι κι έτσι etsi ki etsi so-so

ευαίσθητος evesTHitos sensitive
ευγενικός evyenikos kind; polite
ευγνώμων evgnomon grateful
ΕΥΚΑΙΡΙΑ ευκαιρία (η) efkeria (i) bargain
ΕΥΚΑΙΡΙΕΣ ευκαιρίες bargains
εύκολος efkolos easy
ΕΥΡΩΠΑΪΚΟΣ Ευρωπαϊκός Evropa-ikos European
ΕΥΡΩΠΗ Ευρώπη (η) Evropi (i) Europe
ευτυχισμένος eftikhismenos happy
ευτυχώς eftikhos fortunately
ευχαριστημένος efkharistimenos glad; pleased
ευχάριστος efkharistos pleasant
ευχαριστώ efkharisto thank you
ΕΦΗΜΕΡΙΔΑ εφημερίδα (η) efimeritha (i) newspaper
εφημεριδοπώλης (ο) efimerithopolis (o) newsagent

ΕΦΟΡΙΑ εφορία (η) tax office
έχει ekhi he/she/it has
έχεις ekhis you have
έχεις…; ekhis…? do you have…?
έχετε ekheteh you have
έχετε…; ekheteh…? do you have…?
έχουμε ekhoomeh we have
έχουν ekhoon they have
έχω ekho I have

Z

ζακέτα (η) zaketa (i) cardigan
ΖΑΧΑΡΟΠΛΑΣΤΕΙΟ ζαχαροπλαστείο (το) zakharoplastio (to) cake shop or café selling cakes and soft drinks

ζέστη (η) zesti (i) heat
  κάνει ζέστη kani zesti it's warm
ΖΕΣΤΟ ζεστό zesto hot
ΖΕΣΤΟ ΝΕΡΟ ζεστό νερό zesto
  nero hot water
ζεστός zestos hot; warm
ζευγάρι (το) zevgari (to) pair
ζηλιάρης ziliaris jealous
ζημιά (η) zimia (i) damage
ζημιές: κάνω ζημιές kano zimies
  break (verb)
ζητάω συγγνώμη zitao signomi
  apologize
ζω zo live (verb)
ζωγραφίζω zografizo paint
  (verb: pictures)
ζωγραφική (η) zografiki (i) painting
ζωή (η) zoï (i) life
ζώνη (η) zoni (i) belt
ζώνη ασφαλείας (η) zoni asfalias
  (i) seat belt
ζωντανός zondanos alive
ζώο (το) zo-o (to) animal
ΖΩΟΛΟΓΙΚΟΣ ΚΗΠΟΣ
  ζωολογικός κήπος (ο)
  zo-oloyikos kipos (o) zoo

H

η i the
ή i or
  ή... ή... i... i... either... or...
ήδη ithi already
ήθελα: θα ήθελα τΗa ithela
  I would like
ηθοποιός (ο/η) iτHopios (o/i)

actor, actress
ΗΛ/ΓΕΙΟ ηλ/γειο
  electrical goods
ΗΛΕΚΤΡΙΚΑ ΕΙΔΗ ηλεκτρικά
  είδη ilektrika ithi
  electrical goods
ηλεκτρική σκούπα (η) ilektriki
  skoopa (i) vacuum cleaner
ηλεκτρικό ρεύμα (το) ilektriko
  revma (to) electricity
ΗΛΕΚΤΡΙΚΟΣ ηλεκτρικός (ο)
  ilektrikos (o) underground,
  (US) subway
ηλεκτρικό σίδερο (το) ilektriko
  sithero (to) iron (for ironing)
ηλεκτρικός ilektrikos electric
ΗΛΕΚΤΡΟΛΟΓΟΣ
  ηλεκτρολόγος (ο) ilektrologos (o)
  electrician
ηλίαση (η) iliasi (i) sunstroke
ηλικία (η) ilikia (i) age
ηλιοθεραπεία: κάνω
  ηλιοθεραπεία kano ilioτHerapia
  sunbathe
ηλιόλουστος ilioloostos sunny
ήλιος (ο) ilios (o) sun
ήμαστε imasteh we were
ημέρα (η) imera (i) day
ημερολόγιο (το) imeroloyio (to)
  calendar, diary
ημερομηνία (η) imerominia (i)
  date (time)
ΗΜΕΡΟΜΗΝΙΑ ΛΗΞΗΣ
  ημερομηνία λήξης
  best before
ΗΜΕΡΟΜΗΝΙΑ ΠΑΡΑΣΚΕΥΗΣ
  ημερομηνία παρασκευής
  date of manufacture

ΗΜΙΔΙΑΤΡΟΦΗ ημιδιατροφή (η) imithiatrofí (i) half board

ΗΜΙΣΚΛΗΡΟΙ ΦΑΚΟΙ ΕΠΑΦΗΣ ημίσκληροι φακοί επαφής (οι) imiskliri faki epafis (i) gas permeable lenses

ήμουν ímoon I was

ΗΝΩΜΕΝΕΣ ΠΟΛΙΤΕΙΕΣ ΑΜΕΡΙΚΗΣ Ηνωμένες Πολιτείες Αμερικής (οι) Inomenes Polities Amerikis (i) United States of America

Η.Π.Α. (οι) I.P.A. (i) USA

ηρεμώ iremó calm down

ΗΡΩΩΝ ηρώων (το) iro-on (to) war memorial

ήσουν, ήστε ísoon, ísteh you were

ΗΣΥΧΙΑ ησυχία isikhía quiet

> **Travel tip** The hours between 3 and 5pm, the midday siesta, are sacrosanct; it's not acceptable to make phone calls to strangers – unless you're booking a room – or any sort of noise (especially with motorcycles) at this time. Quiet is also legally mandated between midnight and 8am in residential areas.

ήσυχος ísikhos quiet

ήταν ítan he/she/it was; they were

θάλασσα (η) THalasa (i) sea

ΘΑΛΑΣΣΙΑ ΣΠΟΡ θαλάσσια σπορ water sports

ΘΑΛΑΣΣΙΟ ΣΚΙ θαλάσσιο σκι (το) THalasio ski (to) waterskiing

θάνατος (ο) THanatos (o) death

θα σε δω! THa seh tho! see you!

θαυμάσιος THavmasios wonderful

θεά (η) THea (i) goddess

θέα (η) THea (i) view

ΘΕΑΤΡΙΚΟ ΕΡΓΟ θεατρικό έργο (το) THeh-atriko ergo (to) play (theatre)

ΘΕΑΤΡΟ θέατρο (το) THeatro (to) theatre

θεία (η) THía (i) aunt

θείος (ο) THíos (o) uncle

θέλετε...; THeleteh...? do you want...?

θέλω THelo want (*verb*)

θεός (ο) THeos (o) God

ΘΕΡΙΝΟΣ θερινός (ο) open-air cinema/movie theater

θέρμανση (η) THermansi (i) heating

θερμοκρασία (η) THermokrasia (i) temperature

θερμόμετρο (το) THermometro (to) thermometer

θερμός (το) THermos (to) Thermos flask

ΘΕΣΕΙΣ θέσεις THesis seats

ΘΕΣΕΙΣ ΚΑΘΗΜΕΝΩΝ θέσεις καθημένων seats

ΘΕΣΕΙΣ ΟΡΘΙΩΝ θέσεις ορθίων standing room

θέση (η) THesi (i) seat

κλείνω θέση klino THesi book a seat

ΘΕΩΡΕΙΑ θεωρεία THeoria boxes (in theatre)

A
B
Γ
Δ
E
Z
H
Θ
I
K
Λ
M
N
Ξ
O
Π
P
Σ
T
Y
Φ
X
Ψ
Ω

θλιμμένος THlimenos depressed; sad

θορυβώδης THorivothis noisy

θρησκεία (η) THriskia (i) religion

θύελλα (η) THiela (i) storm; thunderstorm

θυμάμαι THimameh remember

θυμωμένος THimomenos angry

θυρωρός (ο) THiroros (o) doorman; caretaker

I

ΙΑΜΑΤΙΚΕΣ ΠΗΓΕΣ
ιαματικές πηγές iamatikes piyes spa

ΙΑΝΟΥΑΡΙΟΣ Ιανουάριος (ο) Ianooarios (o) January

ιδέα (η) ithea (i) idea

ιδιοκτήτης (ο) ithioktitis (o) owner

ιδιοκτήτρια (η) ithioktitria (i) owner

ΙΔΙΟΚΤΗΤΟ ΠΑΡΚΙΝΓΚ
ιδιόκτητο πάρκινγκ
private parking

ίδιος ithios same

ΙΔΙΩΤΙΚΗ/ΚΡΑΤΙΚΗ
ΙΔΙΟΚΤΗΣΙΑ ιδιωτική/
κρατική ιδιοκτησία
private/state property

ΙΔΙΩΤΙΚΗ ΠΙΝΑΚΟΘΗΚΗ
ιδιωτική πινακοθήκη
private art gallery

ΙΔΙΩΤΙΚΟΣ ιδιωτικός ithiotikos
private

ΙΔΙΩΤΙΚΟΣ ΔΡΟΜΟΣ
ιδιωτικός δρόμος private road

ιδρώνω ithrono sweat (*verb*)

ιλαρά (η) ilara (i) measles

ΙΝΣΤΙΤΟΥΤΟ ΑΙΣΘΗΤΙΚΗΣ
ινστιτούτο αισθητικής (το)
institooto esTHitikis (to)
beauty salon

ΙΟΥΛΙΟΣ Ιούλιος (ο) Ioolios (o)
July

ΙΟΥΝΙΟΣ Ιούνιος (ο) Ioonios (o)
June

ιππασία (η) ipasia (i) horse-riding

ΙΠΠΟΔΡΟΜΟΣ ιππόδρομος (ο)
ipothromos (o) race course (for horses)

Ιρλανδέζα (η) Irlantheza (i)
Irishwoman

ΙΡΛΑΝΔΙΑ Ιρλανδία (η) Irlanthia
(i) Ireland

Ιρλανδικός Irlanthikos Irish

Ιρλανδός (ο) Irlanthos (o) Irishman

ίσια isia straight

ΙΣΟΓΕΙΟ ισόγειο (το) isoyio (to)
ground floor, (US) first floor

ΙΣΟΠΕΔΟΣ ΔΙΑΒΑΣΙΣ ισόπεδος
διάβασις
level crossing

ΙΣΠΑΝΙΑ Ισπανία (η) Ispania
(i) Spain

Ισπανικός Ispanikos Spanish (*adj*)

ιστιοπλοΐα (η) istioploia (i) sailing

ιστιοπλοϊκό σκάφος (το) istioplo-iko skafos (to) sailing boat

ΙΣΤΙΟΦΟΡΟ ιστιοφόρο (το)
istioforo (to) sailing boat

ιστορία (η) istoria (i) story; history

ιστοσελίδα (η) istoselitha (i)
website

ίσως isos maybe, perhaps

ΙΤΑΛΙΑ Ιταλία (η) Italia (i) Italy

Ιταλικός Italikos Italian (*adj*)

ΙΧΘΥΟΠΩΛΕΙΟ ιχθυοπωλείο (το) ikhTHiopolio (to) fishmonger's

K

Κ. κ. Mr

ΚΑ. κα. Mrs

ΚΑΖΙΝΟ καζίνο (το) kazino (to) casino

καθαρίζω kaTHarizo clean

ΚΑΘΑΡΙΣΤΗΡΙΟ καθαριστήριο (το) kaTHaristirio (to) laundry and dry cleaner's

ΚΑΘΑΡΙΣΤΙΚΟ ΔΕΡΜΑΤΟΣ καθαριστικό δέρματος (το) kaTHaristiko thermatos (to) skin cleanser

ΚΑΘΑΡΟ ΒΑΡΟΣ καθαρό βάρος net weight

καθαρός kaTHaros clean (*adj*)

ΚΑΘΑΡΤΙΚΟ καθαρτικό (το) kaTHartiko (to) laxative

κάθε kaTHeh every

καθεμία, καθένα, καθένας kaTHemia, kaTHena, kaTHenas each

κάθε τι kaTHeh ti everything

καθηγητής (ο) kaTHiyitis (o) teacher, professor

καθηγήτρια (η) kaTHiyitria (i) teacher, professor

ΚΑΘΗΜΕΡΙΝΑ καθημερινά kaTHimerina daily

καθήστε kaTHisteh please sit down

ΚΑΘΟΔΟΣ κάθοδος kaTHothos way down, descent

καθολικός kaTHolikos Catholic (*adj*)

καθόλου kaTHoloo not at all; none; any

κάθομαι kaTHomeh sit down

καθρέφτης (ο) kaTHreftis (o) mirror

καθρέφτης αυτοκινήτου (ο) kaTHreftis aftokinitoo (o) rearview mirror

ΚΑΘΥΣΤΕΡΗΣΗ καθυστέρηση (η) kaTHisterisi (i) delay

καθυστερώ kaTHistero delay (*verb*); be late

και keh and

και εγώ επίσης k ego episis me too

και οι δύο k i thio both of them

ΚΑΙ ΛΟΙΠΑ και λοιπά etc

καινούργιο kenooryio brand-new

ευτυχισμένος ο καινούργιος χρόνος! eftikhismenos o kenooryios khronos! happy New Year!

καιρός (ο) keros (o) weather

καίω keo burn (*verb*)

κακός kakos bad

καλά kala well

καλά! kala! good!

καλάθι (το) kalaTHi (to) basket

καλεί kali it's ringing

ΚΑΛΕΣΑΤΕ καλέσατε dial

ΚΑΛΕΣΤΕ ΤΟΝ ΑΡΙΘΜΟ καλέστε τον αριθμό dial number

καλή διασκέδαση kali thiaskethasi have fun

καλημέρα kalimera good morning

καληνύχτα kalinikhta good night

καλησπέρα kalispera good afternoon; good evening

καλλιτέχνηδα (η) kalitekhnitha (i) artist

καλλιτέχνης (ο) kalitekhnis (o) artist

ΚΑΛΛΥΝΤΙΚΑ καλλυντικά (τα) kalindika (ta) perfume and cosmetics

ΚΑΛΟΚΑΙΡΙ καλοκαίρι (το) kalokeri (to) summer

καλοκαιρινές διακοπές (οι) kalokerines thiakopes (i) summer holidays/vacation

καλοριφέρ (το) kalorifer (to) radiator (heater)

καλός kalos good; kind

καλοψημένος kalopsimenos well-done (meat)

καλσόν (το) kalson (to) tights, pantyhose

κάλτσες (οι) kaltses (i) socks

καλύτερος (ο) kaliteros (o) the best

καλύτερος kaliteros better

   καλύτερος από kaliteros apo better than

καλώς ήλθατε! kalos ilthateh! welcome!

ΚΑΛΩΣ ΩΡΙΣΑΤΕ ΣΤΗΝ... καλώς ωρίσατε στην... welcome to...

καμαριέρα (η) kamari-era (i) chambermaid

καμμία kamia no-one

καμμιά φορά kamia fora sometimes

καμπάνα (η) kabana (i) bell

ΚΑΜΠΙΝΑ καμπίνα (η) kabina (i) cabin (on ship)

ΚΑΜΠΙΝΓΚ κάμπινγκ (το) camping (to) campsite, caravan site, trailer park

ΚΑΜΠΙΝΕΣ καμπίνες kabines changing rooms

ΚΑΝΑΔΑΣ Καναδάς (ο) Kanathas (o) Canada

Καναδή (η) Kanathi (i) Canadian (woman)

Καναδικός Kanathikos Canadian (adj)

Καναδός (ο) Kanathos (o) Canadian (man)

κανάτα (η) kanata (i) jug

κάνει... kani... it is..., it costs...

κάνεις kanis you do

   τι κάνεις; ti kanis? how are you?, how do you do?

κανένα kanena nothing

κανένας kanenas no-one, nobody

κάνετε kaneteh you do

   τι κάνετε; ti kaneteh? how are you?, how do you do?

κανό (το) kano (to) canoe

κάνω kano do; make

καπάκι (το) kapaki (to) lid, cap (of bottle)

καπαρντίνα (η) kapardina (i) raincoat

καπέλο (το) kapelo (to) hat, cap

ΚΑΠΕΤΑΝΙΟΣ καπετάνιος (ο) kapetanios (o) captain (of ship)

ΚΑΠΝΙΖΟΝΤΕΣ καπνίζοντες kapnizondes smoking

καπνίζω kapnizo smoke (verb)

ΚΑΠΝΙΣΤΕΣ καπνιστές kapnistes smokers

ΚΑΠΝΙΣΤΗΡΙΟ καπνιστήριο (το) kapnistirio (to) smoking room

ΚΑΠΝΟΠΩΛΕΙΟ καπνοπωλείο (το) kapnopolio (to) tobacconist's

ΚΑΠΝΟΣ καπνός (ο) kapnos (o) smoke; tobacco

καπό (το) kapo (to) bonnet, (US: of car) hood

κάποιος kapios somebody

κάπου kapoo somewhere

ΚΑΡΑΜΕΛΑ καραμέλα (η) karamela (i) caramel

καρδιά (η) karthia (i) heart

καρδιακή προσβολή (η) karthiaki prosvoli (i) heart attack

καρέκλα (η) karekla (i) chair

καρμπιρατέρ (το) karbirater (to) carburettor

καρνέ επιταγών (τυ) karneh epitagon (to) cheque book, check book

καροτσάκι (το) karotsaki (to) pram; pushchair, buggy

καρπός (ο) karpos (o) wrist

ΚΑΡΤΑ κάρτα (η) karta (i) postcard; business card

κάρτα επιβιβάσεως (η) karta epivivaseos (i) boarding pass

κάρτα επιταγών (η) karta epitagon (i) cheque card, check card

ΚΑΡΤΠΟΣΤΑΛ καρτποστάλ (η) kartpostal (i) postcard

καρφί (το) karfi (to) nail (in wall)

καρφίτσα (η) karfitsa (i) pin; brooch

κασκόλ (το) kaskol (to) scarf (for neck)

καστόρι (το) kastori (to) suede

κάστρο (το) kastro (to) castle

κατά kata against; about

κάταγμα (το) katagma (to) fracture

καταδύσεις (οι) katathisis (i) skin-diving

ΚΑΤΑΘΕΣΗ κατάθεση (η) kataтнesi (i) deposit

καταλαβαίνω katalaveno understand

δεν καταλαβαίνω then katalaveno I don't understand

ΚΑΤΑΛΛΗΛΟ κατάλληλο suitable for all ages

κατάλογος (ο) katalogos (o) list; menu

ΚΑΤΑΝΑΛΩΣΗ ΠΡΙΝ… κατανάλωση πριν… consume before…

καταπίνω katapino swallow (*verb*)

καταρράκτης (ο) kataraktis (o) waterfall

ΚΑΤΑΣΚΕΥΑΖΟΝΤΑΙ ΚΛΕΙΔΙΑ κατασκευάζονται κλειδιά keys cut here

κατασκήνωση (η) kataskinosi (i) camping

ΚΑΤΑΣΤΗΜΑ ΑΦΟΡΟΛΟΓΗΤΩΝ κατάστημα αφορολογήτων (το) katastima aforoloyiton (to) duty-free shop

καταστροφή (η) katastrofi (i) disaster

ΚΑΤΑΣΤΡΩΜΑ κατάστρωμα (το) katastroma (to) deck

A
B
Γ
Δ
E
Z
H
Θ
I
K
Λ
M
N
Ξ
O
Π
P
Σ
T
Υ
Φ
X
Ψ
Ω

κατά τη διάρκεια kata ti thiarkia
while, during

καταψύκτης (ο) katapsiktis (o)
freezer

κατάψυξη (η) katapsixi (i) freezer
compartment

κατεβάζω katevazo download (verb)

κατεβαίνω kateveno get off;
go down

ΚΑΤΕΙΛΗΜΜΕΝΟΣ
κατειλημμένος katilimenos
engaged, occupied

ΚΑΤΕΠΕΙΓΟΝ κατεπείγον
katepigon express

κατευθείαν katefтнian direct

ΚΑΤΕΨΥΓΜΕΝΑ κατεψυγμένα
(τα) katepsigmena (ta)
frozen food

ΚΑΤΕΨΥΓΜΕΝΟ κατεψυγμένο
katepsigmeno frozen (food)

κάτι kati something

  κάτι άλλο kati alo
  something else

ΚΑΤΟΛΙΣΘΗΣΕΙΣ
κατολισθήσεις falling rocks

κατσαβίδι (το) katsavithi (to)
screwdriver

κατσαρόλα (η) katsarola (i)
saucepan

κατσίκα (η) katsika (i) goat

ΚΑΤΩ κάτω kato down;
downstairs

κάτω από kato apo under

καυτερός kafteros spicy, hot

καυτός kaftos hot (to taste)

καφέ kafe brown

ΚΑΦΕΚΟΠΤΕΙΟ καφεκοπτείο
(το) kafekoptio (to) coffee shop

ΚΑΦΕΝΕΙΟ καφενείο (το)
kafenio (to) coffee house, where
Greek coffee is served with
traditional sweets

Travel tip Greek coffee
houses form the pivot of life
in remoter villages, and many
men spend most of their
waking hours there, though
Greek women are rarely seen
in the more traditional estab-
lishments. The chief summer
socializing time is 6–8pm,
immediately after the afternoon nap.

ΚΑΦΕΤΕΡΙΑ καφετέρια (η)
kafeteria (i) café, coffee shop

κάψιμο (το) kapsimo (to) burn

ΚΕΛΣΙΟΥ Κελσίου Kelsioo
centigrade

κέλυφος (το) kelifos (to) shell

ΚΕΝΤΗΜΑΤΑ κεντήματα (τα)
kendimata (ta) embroidery

κεντρική θέρμανση (η) kendriki
тнermansi (i) central heating

ΚΕΝΤΡΟ κέντρο (το) kendro (to)
centre

  κέντρο της πόλης kendro tis
  polis city centre

ΚΕΡΑΜΙΚΑ κεραμικά (τα)
keramika (ta) ceramics

κερδίζω kerthizo earn; win (verb)

κερί (το) keri (to) candle

ΚΕΡΚΥΡΑ Κέρκυρα (η) Kerkira
(i) Corfu

ΚΕΡΜΑ κέρμα (το) kerma (to) coin

ΚΕΡΜΑΤΑ κέρματα kermata
coins

ΚΕΣ. κες. Mrs

κεφάλι (το) kefali (to) head

κηδεία (η) kithia (i) funeral

ΚΗΠΟΘΕΑΤΡΟ κηποθέατρο (το) open-air theatre

ΚΗΠΟΣ κήπος (ο) kipos (o) garden, park

κιβώτιο ταχυτήτων (το) kivotio takhititon (to) gearbox

κιθάρα (η) kithara (i) guitar

ΚΙΛΟ κιλό (το) kilo (to) kilo

ΚΙΝΔΥΝΟΣ κίνδυνος (ο) kinthinos (o) danger; caution

ΚΙΝΔΥΝΟΣ ΠΥΡΚΑΓΙΑΣ κίνδυνος πυρκαγιάς fire risk

κινηματογραφική μηχανή (η) kinimatografiki mikhani (i) camcorder

ΚΙΝΗΜΑΤΟΓΡΑΦΟΣ κινηματογράφος (ο) kinimatografos (o) cinema, movie theater

κινητό (το) kinito (to) mobile phone, cell phone

κίτρινος kitrinos yellow

ΚΚ. κκ. Messrs

κλαίω kleo cry (verb)

κλάξον (το) klaxon (to) horn (of car)

κλέβω klevo steal

κλειδαριά (η) klitharia (i) lock

κλειδί (το) klithi (to) key; spanner, wrench

ΚΛΕΙΔΙΑ κλειδιά keys cut here

κλειδώνω klithono lock (verb)

ΚΛΕΙΝΕΤΕ ΤΗΝ ΠΟΡΤΑ κλείνετε την πόρτα close the door

κλείνω klino close (verb); switch off

ΚΛΕΙΣΤΑ κλειστά klista closed

**ΚΛΕΙΣΤΟ ΑΠΟ... ΩΣ... κλειστό από... ως... ** klisto apo... os... closed from... to...

ΚΛΕΙΣΤΟΝ κλειστόν kliston closed

κλειστός klistos closed; off (lights)

κλέφτης (ο) kleftis (o) thief

κλέφτρα (η) kleftra (i) thief

κλίμα (το) klima (to) climate

ΚΛΙΜΑΤΙΖΟΜΕΝΟΣ κλιματιζόμενος klimatizomenos air-conditioned

ΚΛΙΜΑΤΙΣΜΟΣ κλιματισμός (ο) klimatismos (o) air-conditioning

κλοπή (η) klopi (i) theft

Κ.Λ.Π. κλπ etc

ΚΛΩΣΤΗ κλωστή (η) klosti (i) thread

κόβω kovo cut (verb)

κοιλάδα (η) kilatha (i) valley

κοιμάμαι kimameh sleep (verb); be asleep

ΚΟΙΜΗΤΗΡΙΟ κοιμητήριο (το) kimitirio (to) cemetery

ΚΟΙΝΟΤΙΚΟ ΓΡΑΦΕΙΟ κοινοτικό γραφείο (το) local government office

κοκκαλιάρης kokaliaris skinny

κόκκαλο (το) kokalo (to) bone

κόκκινος kokinos red

κόλλα (η) kola (i) glue

κολλιέ (το) kolie (to) necklace

κόλπος (ο) kolpos (o) vagina; gulf

ΚΟΛΥΜΒΗΤΗΡΙΟ κολυμβητήριο (το) kolimvitirio (to) swimming pool

A
B
Γ
Δ
E
Z
H
Θ
I
K
Λ
M
N
Ξ
O
Π
P
Σ
T
Y
Φ
X
Ψ
Ω

κολυμπάω kolibao swim (*verb*)

κολύμπι (το) kolibi (to) swimming

κολυμπώ kolibo swim (*verb*)

κολώνια (η) kolonia (i) eau de toilette

κολώνια μετά το ξύρισμα kolonia meta to xirisma aftershave

κομμάτι (το) komati (to) piece

ΚΟΜΜΩΣΕΙΣ κομμώσεις (οι) komosis (i) hairdresser's

ΚΟΜΜΩΤΗΡΙΟ κομμωτήριο (το) komotirio (to) hairdresser's

κομμώτρια (η) komotria (i) hairdresser

κομπιουτεράκι (το) kombi-ooteraki (to) calculator

κομπολόι (το) komboloi (to) worry beads

κοντά konda near, close by

κοντέρ (το) konder (to) speedometer

ΚΟΝΤΙΣΙΟΝΕΡ κοντίσιονερ (το) kondisioner (to) conditioner

κοντός kondos short (person)

ΚΟΡΔΟΝΙΑ ΠΑΠΟΥΤΣΙΩΝ κορδόνια παπουτσιών (τα) korthonia papootsion (ta) shoelaces

κόρη (η) kori (i) daughter

κορίτσι (το) koritsi (to) girl

κόρνα (η) korna (i) horn (in car)

κορυφή (η) korifi (i) top

ΚΟΣΜΗΜΑΤΑ κοσμήματα (τα) kosmimata (ta) jewellery

ΚΟΣΜΗΜΑΤΟΠΩΛΕΙΟ κοσμηματοπωλείο (το) kosmimatopolio (to) jeweller's

κόσμος (ο) kosmos (o) world; people, crowd

κοστίζει kostizi it costs

κόστος (το) kostos (to) cost

κουβάς (ο) koovas (o) bucket

κουβέρτα (η) kooverta (i) blanket

κουδούνι (το) koothooni (to) bell (for door)

ΚΟΥΖΙΝΑ κουζίνα (η) koozina (i) cooker; kitchen

ΚΟΥΚΕΤΑ κουκέτα (η) kooketa (i) couchette

κουκέτες (οι) kooketes (i) bunk beds

κούκλα (η) kookla (i) doll

κουμπί (το) koobi (to) button

κουνέλι (το) kooneli (to) rabbit

κούνια (η) koonia (i) cot

κουνούπι (το) koonoopi (to) mosquito

κουπέ (το) koopeh (to) compartment

κουρασμένος koorasmenos tired

ΚΟΥΡΕΑΣ κουρέας (ο) kooreas (o) barber

ΚΟΥΡΕΙΟ κουρείο (το) koorio (to) barber's shop

κούρεμα (το) koorema (to) haircut

κουρτίνα (η) koortina (i) curtain

κουστούμι (το) koostoomi (to) suit

κουτάλι (το) kootali (to) spoon

ΚΟΥΤΑΛΙΕΣ ΓΛΥΚΟΥ κουταλιές γλυκού teaspoonfuls

ΚΟΥΤΑΛΙΕΣ ΣΟΥΠΑΣ κουταλιές σούπας tablespoonfuls

κουτί (το) kooti (to) box; can

κουφός koofos deaf

ΚΡΑΓΙΟΝ κραγιόν (το) krayon (to) lipstick

κράμπα (η) kramba (i) cramp

κρανίο (το) kranio (to) skull

κρατάω kratao hold; keep

ΚΡΑΤΗΣΕΙΣ ΘΕΣΕΩΝ κρατήσεις θέσεων reservations; seat reservations

κράτηση θέσης (η) kratisi THesis (i) reservation

κρεβάτι (το) krevati (to) bed

ΚΡΕΜΑ ΠΡΟΣΩΠΟΥ κρέμα προσώπου (η) krema prosopoo (i) moisturizer

κρεμάστρα (η) kremastra (i) coathanger; peg

ΚΡΕΟΠΩΛΕΙΟ κρεοπωλείο (το) kreopolio (to) butcher's

κρίμα: είναι κρίμα ineh krima it's a pity

κρουαζιέρα (η) kroo-aziera (i) cruise

κρύβομαι krivomeh hide (oneself)

κρύβω krivo hide (something)

κρύο (το) krio (to) cold

κάνει κρύο kani krio it's cold

ΚΡΥΟ ΝΕΡΟ κρύο νερό krio nero cold water

κρύος krios cold (adj)

κρύωμα (το) krioma (to) cold (illness)

Κ.Τ.Ε.Λ. long-distance bus station

κτηνίατρος (ο/η) ktiniatros (o/i) vet

κτίριο (το) ktirio (to) building

κυβέρνηση (η) kivernisi (i) government

κυκλοφορία (η) kikloforia (i) traffic

κυκλοφοριακή συμφόρηση (η) kikloforiaki simforisi (i) traffic jam

ΚΥΛΙΚΕΙΟ κυλικείο (το) kilikio (to) snackbar

ΚΥΛΟΤΕΣ κυλότες (οι) kilotes (i) panties; underpants

A
B
Γ
Δ
E
Z
H
Θ
I
K
Λ
M
N
Ξ
O
Π
P
Σ
T
Υ
Φ
X
Ψ
Ω

κύμα (το) kima (to) wave
κυνηγώ kinigo hunt (*verb*), chase
ΚΥΠΡΟΣ Κύπρος (η) Kipros (i)
Cyprus
Kυρία (η) Kiria (i) Mrs; Ms
κυρία (η) kiria (i) lady; madam
ΚΥΡΙΑΚΕΣ ΚΑΙ ΕΟΡΤΕΣ
Κυριακές και Εορτές
Sundays and holidays
ΚΥΡΙΑΚΗ Κυριακή (η) Kiriaki (i)
Sunday
ΚΥΡΙΑΚΗ ΤΟΥ ΠΑΣΧΑ
Κυριακή του Πάσχα (η) Kiriaki
too Paskha (i) Easter Sunday
κύριε kiri-eh sir
ΚΥΡΙΕΣ κυρίες kiries Mrs
ΚΥΡΙΟΙ κύριοι Messrs
ΚΥΡΙΟΣ Κύριος Kirios Mr
κύριος (ο) kirios (o) gentleman
κύριος kirios main
κύστη (η) kisti (i) bladder
κυττάζω kitazo look (*verb*)
ΚΩΔΙΚΟΣ κωδικός (ο)
kothikos (o) code
ΚΩΔΙΚΟΣ ΑΡΙΘΜΟΣ κωδικός
αριθμός kothikos ariтHmos
dialling code
ΚΩΔΙΚΟΣ ΠΡΟΣΒΑΣΗΣ,
κωδικός πρόσβασης (ο) kothikos
prosvasis (o) password

ΛΑΔΙ λάδι (το) lathi (to) oil
ΛΑΔΙΑ λάδια (τα) lathia (ta)
engine oil
ΛΑΔΙ ΜΑΥΡΙΣΜΑΤΟΣ λάδι

μαυρίσματος lathi mavrismatos
suntan oil
λάθος (το) laтHos (to) mistake
λάθος laтHos wrong
λάθος νούμερο laтHos noomero
wrong number
λαιμός (ο) lemos (o) neck; throat
λακ (η) lak (i) hairspray
λάμπα (η) lamba (i) light bulb;
lamp
λαστιχάκι (το) lastikhaki (to)
rubber band
λάστιχο (το) lastikho (to) rubber
(material); tyre
λεβιές ταχυτήτων (ο) levies
takhititon (o) gear lever
λείπω lipo be missing; be out;
be away
λειτουργία (η) litooryia (i) mass
(church)
λεκές (ο) lekes (o) stain
ΛΕΜΒΟΣ λέμβος (η) lemvos (i)
lifeboat
λένε: λένε ότι lene oti
they say that
  με λένε… meh leneh…
  my name is…
  πως σε λένε; pos seh leneh?
  what's your name?
λέξη (η) lexi (i) word
λεξικό (το) lexiko (to) dictionary
λεπτό (το) lepto (to) minute
λεπτός leptos slim
λέσχη (η) leskhi (i) club
λευκοπλάστ (το) lefkoplast (to)
plaster, Bandaid
ΛΕΦΤΑ λεφτά (τα) lefta (ta)
money

λέω leo say

ΛΕΩΦΟΡΕΙΟ λεωφορείο (το) leoforio (to) bus

ΛΕΩΦΟΡΕΙΟ ΥΠ᾽ ΑΡΙΘΜ... λεωφορείο υπ᾽ αριθμ... bus number...

ΛΕΩΦΟΡΟΣ λεωφόρος (η) leoforos (i) avenue

ΛΗΓΕΙ ΤΗΝ... λήγει την... expires on...

λιακάδα (η) liakatha (i) sunshine

λίγα liga a few

λίγο ligo a little bit

ΣΕ ΛΙΓΟ σε λίγο seh ligo in a little while

λίγος ligos little, short

λιγότερος ligoteros fewer

λιγότερο ligotero less

ΛΙΜΑΝΙ λιμάνι (το) limani (to) harbour

λίμα νυχιών (η) lima nikhion (i) nailfile

ΛΙΜΕΝΑΡΧΕΙΟ λιμεναρχείο (το) port authorities

ΛΙΜΕΝΑΡΧΗΣ λιμενάρχης (ο) harbour master

ΛΙΜΕΝΙΚΗ ΑΣΤΥΝΟΜΙΑ Λιμενική Αστυνομία (η) limeniki Astinomia (i) harbour police

ΛΙΜΗΝ λιμήν (ο) limin (o) port

λίμνη (η) limni (i) lake

λιμνούλα (η) limnoola (i) pond

λίμπρα (η) libra (i) pound (weight)

λιπαρός liparos greasy

λιποθυμώ lipoTHimo faint (verb)

ΛΙΡΑ ΑΓΓΛΙΑΣ λίρα Αγγλίας (η)

lira Anglias (i) pound sterling

ΛΙΤΑΝΕΙΑ λιτανεία (η) litany

ΛΙΤΡΟ λίτρο (το) litro (to) litre

ΛΟΓΑΡΙΑΣΜΟΣ λογαριασμός (ο) logariasmos (o) bill, (US) check

λογικός loyikos sensible

ΛΟΓΙΣΤΗΡΙΟ λογιστήριο (το) loyistirio (to) purser's office

ΛΟΝΔΙΝΟ Λονδίνο (το) Lonthino (to) London

λόξυγγας (ο) loxingas (o) hiccups

λουλούδι (το) looloothi (to) flower

λούσιμο (το) loosimo (to) wash

ΛΟΥΤΡΟ λουτρό (το) lootro (to) bathroom

λόφος (ο) lofos (o) hill

λυπάμαι lipameh I'm sorry

λυπημένος lipimenos sad

ΛΥΡΙΚΗ ΣΚΗΝΗ λυρική σκηνή (η) liriki skini (i) opera house

M

μαγαζί (το) magazi (to) shop

μαγειρεύω mayirevo cook (verb)

μαγειρικά σκεύη (τα) mayirika skevi (ta) cooking utensils

μαγείρισσα (η) mayirisa (i) cook

μάγειρος (ο) mayiros (o) cook

μάγκας (ο) mangas (o) streetwise/ smart person

μαγιό (το) mayo (to) swimming trunks

μάγουλο (το) magoolo (to) chin

μαζί mazi together

μαζί με mazi meh with, together with

μαθαίνω maτHeno learn

μάθημα (το) maτHima (to) lesson

κάνω μάθημα kano maτHima
teach; take a lesson

ΜΑΘΗΜΑΤΑ ΣΚΙ μαθήματα σκι
maτHimata ski skiing lessons

ΜΑΙΟΣ Μάιος (ο) Maios (o) May

μακριά makria far, at a distance

μαλάκας (ο) malakas (o) arsehole,
wanker

μακρύς makris long

ΜΑΛΑΚΟΙ ΦΑΚΟΙ μαλακοί
φακοί (οι) malaki faki (i)
soft lenses

μάλιστα malista yes, certainly

μάλιστα! malista! well!

ΜΑΛΛΙ μαλλί (το) mali (to) wool

μαλλιά (τα) malia (ta) hair

ΜΑΛΛΙΝΟ μάλλινο malino wool

μάλλον malon rather; probably

μαλώνω malono fight (verb)

μαμά (η) mama (i) mum

ΜΑΝΑΒΗΣ μανάβης (ο)
manavis (o) greengrocer's

ΜΑΝΟ μανό (το) mano (to)
nail polish

μανταλάκι (το) mandalaki (to)
clothes peg

μαντήλι (το) mandili (to)
handkerchief; headscarf

μαξιλάρι (το) maxilari (to) pillow

μαραγκός (ο) marangos (o)
carpenter

ΜΑΡΙΝΑ μαρίνα (η) marina (i)
marina

μαρκαδόρος (ο) markathoros (o)
felt-tip pen

ΜΑΡΤΙΟΣ Μάρτιος (ο) Martios
(o) March

μάρτυρας (ο) martiras (o) witness

μασέλα (η) masela (i) dentures

μας mas us; our

μάτι (το) mati (to) eye; ring
(on cooker)

ματς (το) mats (to) match (sport)

μαυρίζω mavrizo tan (verb)

μαύρισμα (το) mavrisma (to)
tan (colour)

μαύρισμα από τον ήλιο mavrisma
apo ton ilio suntan

μαύρος mavros black

μαχαίρι (το) makheri (to) knife

μαχαιροπήρουνα (τα)
makheropiroona (ta) cutlery

με meh with; by; me

με αυτοκίνητο meh aftokinito
by car

ΜΕΓΑΛΗ ΒΡΕΤΑΝΝΙΑ Μεγάλη
Βρεταννία (η) Megali Vretania (i)
Great Britain

Μεγάλη Παρασκευή (η) Megali
Paraskevi (i) Good Friday

μεγάλος megalos big

μεγαλύτερος megaliteros bigger

ΜΕΓΕΘΟΣ μέγεθος (το)
meyeτHos (to) size

μεγέθυνση (η) meyeτHinsi (i)
enlargement

ΜΕΓΙΣΤΟ ΒΑΡΟΣ μέγιστο
βάρος maximum permitted
weight

μέγιστος (ο) meyistos (o) biggest

μεζ (η) mez (i) highlights (in hair)

μεθαύριο meτHavrio the day after
tomorrow

μεθυσμένος meThismenos drunk

μέικ απ (το) meik ap (to) make-up

μελανιά (η) melania (i) bruise

μέλλον (το) melon (to) future

ΜΕ ΜΠΑΝΙΟ με μπάνιο meh banio with bathroom

ΜΕ ΝΤΟΥΣ με ντους meh doos with shower

μένω meno live (in town etc); stay (in hotel etc)

μέρα (η) mera (i) day

μερίδα (η) meriTha (i) portion

μερικά, μερικές, μερικοί merika, merikes, meriki some

μέρος (το) meros (to) part, place; WC

μέσα mesa in; inside

μεσάνυχτα (τα) mesanikhta (ta) midnight

μέση (η) mesi (i) middle; waist

μεσημέρι (το) mesimeri (to) midday

Μεσόγειος (η) Mesoyios (i) Mediterranean

μετά meta after; afterwards

μετά από σας meta apo sas after you

μετά μεσημβρίας meta mesimvrias pm

μετακινούμαι metakinoomeh move (verb)

μέταλλο (το) metalo (to) metal

ΜΕΤΑΞΙ μετάξι (το) metaxi (to) silk

μεταξύ metaxi between

μεταφέρω metafero carry

μεταφράζω metafrazo translate

μετεωρολογικό δελτίο (το) meteoroloyiko theltio (to) weather forecast

ΜΕΤΡΗΤΑ μετρητά metrita cash

ΤΟΙΣ ΜΕΤΡΗΤΟΙΣ τοις μετρητοίς tis metritis in cash

μετρητής βενζίνης (ο) metritis venzinis (o) fuel gauge

μέτριο μέγεθος metrio meyeThos medium-sized

ΜΕΤΡΙΟΣ μέτριος metrios medium; average

ΜΕΤΡΟ μέτρο (το) metro (to) metre

μέτωπο (το) metopo (to) forehead

μέχρι mekhri until

ΜΗ μη do not

ΜΗ ΒΓΑΖΕΤΕ ΤΗΝ ΚΑΡΤΑ μη βγάζετε την κάρτα do not remove the card yet

μηδέν mithen zero

ΜΗΝ ΚΑΠΝΙΖΕΤΕ μην καπνίζετε no smoking

ΜΗ ΚΑΠΝΙΖΟΝΤΕΣ μη καπνίζοντες mi kapnizondes non-smoking

ΜΗ ΚΑΠΝΙΣΤΕΣ μη καπνιστές mi kapnistes non-smokers

μήκος (το) mikos (to) length

μήνας (ο) minas (o) month

μήνας του μέλιτος minas too melitos honeymoon

ΜΗΝ ΕΝΟΧΛΕΙΤΕ μην ενοχλείτε do not disturb

μήνυμα (το) minima (to) text

ΜΗΝ ΟΜΙΛΕΙΤΕ ΣΤΟΝ ΟΔΗΓΟ μην ομιλείτε στον οδηγό do not speak to the driver

A
B
Γ
Δ
E
Z
H
Θ
I
K
Λ
M
N
Ξ
O
Π
P
Σ
T
Y
Φ
X
Ψ
Ω

ΜΗΝ ΠΑΤΑΤΕ ΤΟ ΧΟΡΤΟ
μην πατάτε το χόρτο
keep off the grass

ΜΗ ΠΟΣΙΜΟ (ΝΕΡΟ) μη
πόσιμο (νερό) not for drinking
(water)

μητέρα (η) mitera (i) mother

ΜΗ ΤΟΞΙΚΟ μη τοξικό
non-toxic

μητρόπολη (η) mitropoli (i)
cathedral

μηχανάκι (το) mikhanaki (to)
moped

μηχανή (η) mikhani (i) engine

μηχανικός (ο) mikhanikos (o)
mechanic; engineer

μία mia a; one

μία φορά mia fora once

μιάς mias of a

μίζα (η) miza (i) ignition

ΜΙΚΡΟ ΟΝΟΜΑ μικρό όνομα
(το) mikro onoma (to)
Christian name

ΜΙΚΡΟΣ μικρός mikros
little, small

ΜΙΚΤΟ ΒΑΡΟΣ μικτό βάρος
gross weight

μικρότερος mikroteros smaller

ΜΙΛΑΕΙ μιλάει milai engaged,
occupied

μιλάω milao speak

μιλάτε…; milateh…?
do you speak…?

μισός misos half

ΜΙΣΟΤΙΜΗΣ μισοτιμής
half-price

μισώ miso hate (verb)

μ.μ. m.m. pm

μνημείο (το) mnimio (to)
monument

μόδα (η) motha (i) fashion

της μόδας tis mothas
fashionable

ΜΟΔΕΣ μόδες fashions

μοιάζει miazi it looks/seems

μοιράζομαι mirazomeh share (verb)

μοκέτα (η) moketa (i) carpet

μολύβι (το) molivi (to) pencil

μόλυνση (η) molinsi (i) infection

ΜΟΛΥΣΜΕΝΑ ΥΔΑΤΑ
μολυσμένα ύδατα
polluted water

μολυσμένος molismenos polluted

ΜΟΝΑΔΕΣ μονάδες units

ΜΟΝΑΔΙΚΗ ΕΥΚΑΙΡΙΑ
μοναδική ευκαιρία (η)
special offer

μονή moni monastery

Travel tip Most monasteries
impose a fairly strict dress
code for visitors: no shorts,
and women are expected to
cover their arms and wear
skirts (though most Greek
women will be in trousers);
the necessary wraps are
sometimes provided on
the spot.

μόνο mono only

ΜΟΝΟΔΡΟΜΟΣ μονόδρομος
one-way street

ΜΟΝΟ ΔΩΜΑΤΙΟ μονό
δωμάτιο (το) mono thomatio (to)
single room

ΜΟΝΟΚΛΙΝΟ ΔΩΜΑΤΙΟ
μονόκλινο δωμάτιο (το)

monoklino thomatio (to)
single room

μονό κρεβάτι mono krevati
single bed

μονοπάτι (το) monopati (to) path

μόνος monos alone

μοντέρνος mondernos modern

μορφή MP3 (η) morfi MP3 (i)
MP3 format

μοτοσυκλέτα (η) motosikleta (i)
motorbike

μου moo my

ΜΟΥΣΕΙΟ μουσείο (το) moosio
(to) museum

ΜΟΥΣΙΚΑ ΟΡΓΑΝΑ μουσικά
όργανα moosika organa
musical instruments

μουσική (η) moosiki (i) music

μουσική ποπ (η) moosiki pop (i)
pop music

μουστάκι (το) moostaki (to)
moustache

μπαίνω beno go in, enter

ΜΠΑΚΑΛΙΚΟ μπακάλικο (το)
bakaliko (to) grocer's

μπαλκόνι (το) balkoni (to)
balcony

μπάλλα (η) bala (i) ball (large)

μπαλλάκι (το) balaki (to) ball
(small)

μπαμπάς (ο) babas (o) dad

μπανιέρα (η) baniera (i) bathtub

ΜΠΑΝΙΟ μπάνιο (το) banio (to)
bath

κάνω μπάνιο kano banio swim
(verb); have a bath

πάω για μπάνιο pao ya banio
go swimming

ΜΠΑΡ μπαρ (το) bar (to) bar

μπάρμαν (ο) barman (o) barman

μπάρ γούμαν (η) bar goúman (i)
bar woman (i)
barmaid

μπαταρία (η) bataria (i) battery

μπεζ bez beige

μπέιμπι-σίττερ (η) baby-sitter (i)
babysitter

μπερδεμένος berthemenos
complicated

μπικίνι (το) bikini (to) bikini

μπλε bleh blue

μπλούζα (η) blooza (i) blouse

μπλουζάκι (το) bloozaki (to)
T-shirt

μπόρα (η) bora (i) shower (rain)

μπορείς boris you can

μπορείς να…; boris na…?
can you…?

μπορείτε boriteh you can

μπορείτε να…; boriteh na…?
can you…?

μπρος bros forwards; in front of

βάζω μπρος vazo bros switch on
(engine)

μπορώ boro I can

μπότα (η) bota (i) boot (shoe)

μπουγάδα (η) boogatha (i) washing

βάζω μπουγάδα vazo boogatha
do the washing

μπουζί (το) boozi (to) spark plug

ΜΠΟΥΖΟΥΚΙΑ μπουζούκια
(τα) boozookia (ta) club with
bouzouki music

μπουκάλι (το) bookali (to) bottle

μπουκιά (η) bookia (i) bite

μπούτι (το) booti (to) thigh

A
B
Γ
Δ
E
Z
H
Θ
I
K
Λ
M
N
Ξ
O
Π
P
Σ
T
Y
Φ
X
Ψ
Ω

ΜΠΟΥΤΙΚ μπουτίκ **(η)** bootik (i) boutique

μπροστινό μέρος (το) brostino meros (to) front (part)

ΜΠΥΡΑ μπύρα bira beer, lager

μπωλ (το) bol (to) bowl

μύγα (η) miga (i) fly

μυθιστόρημα (το) miTHistorima (to) novel

μυρίζω mirizo smell (*verb*)

μυρμήγκι (το) mirmingi (to) ant

μυρωδιά (η) mirothia (i) smell

μυστικός mistikos secret

μυς (ο) mis (o) muscle

μύτη (η) miti (i) nose

μύωπας miopas shortsighted

μωβ mov purple

μωρό (το) moro (to) baby

N

να na here is/are

ναι neh yes

ναι, ναι! neh neh! oh yes I do!

νάιτκλαμπ (το) nightclub (to) nightclub

ΝΑ ΛΑΜΒΑΝΕΤΑΙ ΜΟΝΟΝ ΑΠΟ ΤΟ ΣΤΟΜΑ να λαμβάνεται μόνον από το στόμα to be taken orally only

ΝΑ ΛΑΜΒΑΝΕΤΑΙ... ΦΟΡΕΣ ΗΜΕΡΗΣΙΩΣ να λαμβάνεται... φορές ημερησίως to be taken... times daily

ναρκωτικά (τα) narkotika (ta) drugs (narcotics)

ΝΑ ΦΥΛΑΣΣΕΤΑΙ ΜΑΚΡΙΑ

ΑΠΟ ΠΑΙΔΙΑ να φυλάσσεται μακριά από παιδιά keep out of reach of children

νέα (η) nea (i) teenager

νέα (τα) nea (ta) news

ΝΕΑ ΖΗΛΑΝΔΙΑ Νέα Ζηλανδία **(η)** Nea Zilanthia (i) New Zealand

ΝΕΚΡΟΤΑΦΕΙΟ νεκροταφείο **(το)** nekrotafio (to) cemetery

Νέο Έτος (το) Neo Etos (to) New Year

ΝΕΟΖΗΛΑΝΔΕΖΑ Νεοζηλανδέζα **(η)** Neozilantheza (i) New Zealander

ΝΕΟΖΗΛΑΝΔΟΣ Νεοζηλανδός **(ο)** Neozilanthos (o) New Zealander

νέοι (οι) nei (i) young people

νέος (ο) neos (o) teenager

νέος neos new; young

ΝΕΡΟ νερό **(το)** nero (to) water

νεροχύτης (ο) nerokhitis (o) sink

νευρικός nevrikos nervous

νεφρά (τα) nefra (ta) kidneys

νησί (το) nisi (to) island

νιπτήρας (ο) niptiras (o) washbasin

νιώθω nioTHo feel

ΝΟΕΜΒΡΙΟΣ Νοέμβριος **(ο)** Noemvrios (o) November

νοικιάζω nikiazo rent (*verb*)

ΝΟΜΑΡΧΙΑ νομαρχία **(η)** local government office

νομίζω nomizo think

ΝΟΜΟΣ νομός **(ο)** county

νόμος (ο) nomos (o) law

ΝΟΣΟΚΟΜΕΙΟ νοσοκομείο **(το)** nosokomio (to) hospital

νόστιμο nostimo tasty

νοστιμώτατο nostimotato delicious

ΝΟΥΜΕΡΟ νούμερο (το)
noomero (to) number

ΝΤΕΜΙ ΠΑΝΣΙΟΝ ντεμί
πανσιόν (η) demi pansion (i)
half board

ντεπόζιτο (το) ndepozito (to) tank

ΝΤΗΖΕΛ ντήζελ (το) dizel (to)
diesel

ντισκοτέκ (η) ndiskotek (i) disco

ντιστριμπυτέρ (το) ndistribiter (to)
distributor

ντουλάπι (το) ndoolapi (to) cupboard

ΝΤΟΥΣ ντους (το) doos (to)
shower (in bathroom)

ΝΤΡΑΙΒ - ΙΝ ντραιβ - ιν drive-in

ντροπαλός ndropalos shy

ντύνομαι ndinomeh dress (oneself)

ντύνω ndino dress (verb: someone)

νύφη (η) nifi (i) daughter-in-law;
sister-in-law; bride

νύχι (το) nikhi (to) fingernail

νυχοκόπτης (ο) nikhokoptis (o)
nail clippers

νύχτα (η) nikhta (i) night

ΝΥΧΤΕΡΙΝΟ ΚΕΝΤΡΟ
νυχτερινό κέντρο nikhterino
kendro nightclub

νυχτικό (το) nikhtiko (to) nightdress

νωρίς noris early

ξαδέλφη (η) xathelfi (i) cousin

ξάδελφος (ο) xathelfos (o) cousin

ξανά xana again

ξανθός xanThos blond

ξαπλώνω xaplono lie down

ξαφνικά xafnika suddenly

ξεκουράζομαι xekoorazomeh
relax

ξεναγός (ο/η) xenagos (o/i) guide

ΞΕΝΟΔΟΧΕΙΟ ξενοδοχείο (το)
xenothokhio (to) hotel

ξένος xenos foreign

ΞΕΝΩΝΑΣ ξενώνας (ο) xenonas
(o) guesthouse

ΞΕΝΩΝΑΣ ΝΕΟΤΗΤΑΣ
ξενώνας νεότητας xenonas
neotitas youth hostel

ΞΕΝΩΝΑΣ ΝΕΩΝ ξενώνας νέων
xenonas neon
youth hostel

ΞΕΠΟΥΛΗΜΑ ξεπούλημα
closing-down sale

ξέρω xero know
δεν ξέρω then xero I don't know

ξεφωνίζω xefonizo scream (verb)

ξεχνώ xekhno leave (verb); forget

ξεχωριστά xekhorista separately

ξηρός xiros dry

ξοδεύω xothevo spend

ξύλο (το) xilo (to) wood

ξυνός xinos sour

ξυπνάω xipnao wake up

ξυπνητήρι (το) xipnitiri (to)
alarm clock

ξύπνιος xipnios awake

ξυραφάκι (το) xirafaki (to) razor

ξυρίζομαι xirizomeh shave (verb)

ξύρισμα (το) xirisma (to) shave

ξυριστική μηχανή (η) xiristiki
mikhani (i) electric shaver

O

o o the

O.A. Olympic Airways

O/Γ ferry

ογδόντα ogthonda eighty

όγδοος ogthoos eighth

οδηγάω othigao drive

οδηγός (ο/η) othigos (o/i) driver

ΟΔΙΚΑ ΕΡΓΑ οδικά έργα
roadworks

ΟΔΟΝΤΙΑΤΡΟΣ οδοντίατρος
(ο/η) othondiatros (o/i) dentist

οδοντόβουρτσα (η) othondovoortsa
(i) toothbrush

ΟΔΟΝΤΟΓΙΑΤΡΟΣ
οδοντογιατρός (ο/η)
othondoyatros (o/i) dentist

ΟΔΟΝΤΙΑΤΡΕΙΟ οδοντιατρείο
(το) othondiatrio (to) dentist's

ΟΔΟΝΤΟΚΡΕΜΑ οδοντόκρεμα
(η) othondokrema (i) toothpaste

ΟΔΟΣ οδός (η) othos (i) road,
street

**ΟΔΟΣ ΑΝΕΥ ΣΗΜΑΝΣΕΩΣ ΣΕ
ΜΗΚΟΣ… ΧΙΛ.** οδός άνευ
σημάνσεως σε μήκος… χιλ
no road markings for… km

οδυνηρός othiniros painful

όζα (η) oza (i) nail polish

O.H.E. UN

οι i the

οικογένεια (η) ikoyenia (i) family

ΟΚΤΩΒΡΙΟΣ Οκτώβριος (ο)
Oktovrios (o) October

όλα ola all

όλα καλά ola kala that'll do

nicely, everything's fine

όλα πληρωμένα ola pliromena
all inclusive

όλες, όλη oles, oli all

ΟΛΙΣΘΗΡΟ ΟΔΟΣΤΡΩΜΑ
ολισθηρό οδόστρωμα slippery
road surface

όλο olo amm

όλοι oli everyone; all

ολόκληρος olokliros whole

όλος olos all

Ο.Λ.Π. Piraeus Port Authorities

ΟΛΥΜΠΙΑΚΗ ΑΕΡΟΠΟΡΙΑ
Ολυμπιακή Αεροπορία
Olympic Airways

ομάδα (η) omatha (i) group; team

ομάδα αίματος (η) omatha ematos
(i) blood group

ομίχλη (η) omikhli (i) fog

όμοιος omios similar

όμορφος omorfos fine, beautiful

ομοφυλόφιλος (ο) omofilofilos
(o) gay

ομπρέλλα (η) ombrella (i)
umbrella

όνειρο (το) oniro (to) dream

ΟΝΟΜΑ όνομα (το) onoma (to)
name; first name

οπά! opa! watch it!

ΟΠΕΡΑ όπερα (η) opera (i) opera

όπισθεν (η) opisthen (i)
reverse (gear)

όπλο (το) oplo (to) gun; rifle

ΟΠΤΙΚΑ οπτικά (τα) optika (ta)
optician's

ΟΠΤΙΚΟΣ οπτικός (ο) optikos (o)
optician

ΟΠΩΡΟΠΩΛΕΙΟ οπωροπωλείο
(το) oporopolio (to) grocer's

όπως opos like; as

όπως και νάναι opos keh naneh
anyway

**ΟΡΓΑΝΙΣΜΟΣ ΗΝΩΜΕΝΩΝ
ΕΘΝΩΝ** Οργανισμός
Ηνωμένων Εθνών United
Nations Organization

οργανωμένη εκδρομή (η)
organomeni ekthromi (i)
package tour

οργανώνω organono organize

όρεξη (η) orexi (i) appetite

καλή όρεξη! kali orexi! enjoy
your meal!, bon appetit!

ΟΡΘΙΩΝ orthion standing

ΟΡΙΟ ΤΑΧΥΤΗΤΑΣ όριο
ταχύτητας (το) speed limit

ορίστε; oriste? can I help you?

όροφος (ο) orofos (o) floor, storey

ΟΡΥΚΤΕΛΑΙΟ ορυκτέλαιο (το)
orikteleo (to) engine oil

ορχήστρα (η) orkhistra (i)
orchestra

Ο.Σ.Ε. Greek Railways

όταν otan when

Ο.Τ.Ε. Greek
Telecommunications Company

ότι oti that

οτιδήποτε otithipoteh anything

Ο.Υ. water authorities

Ουαλλή (η) Ooali (i) Welshwoman

ΟΥΑΛΛΙΑ Ουαλλία (η) Ooalia
(i) Wales

Ουαλλικός Ooalikos Welsh (adj)

Ουαλλός (ο) Ooalos (o)

Welshman

ΟΥΖΕΡΙ ουζερί oozeri bar serving
ouzo and beer with snacks or
full meals

ούλο (το) oolo (to) gum (in mouth)

ΟΥΡΑ ουρά (η) oora (i) queue;
tail; queue here

κάνω ουρά kano oora queue
(verb)

ουρανός (ο) ooranos (o) sky

ούτε... ούτε... oote... oote...
neither... nor...

ΟΦΘΑΛΜΙΑΤΡΟΣ
οφθαλμίατρος (ο/η)
eye specialist

όχημα (το) okhima (to) vehicle

ΟΧΙ όχι okhi no; not

όχι άλλο okhi allo no more

ΟΧΙ ΕΠΙΤΑΓΕΣ όχι επιταγές
no cheques/checks

ΟΧΙ ΥΠΕΡΑΣΤΙΚΑ όχι
υπεραστικά no long-distance
calls

οχτώ okhto eight

Π

ΠΑΓΟΣ πάγος (ο) pagos (o) ice

παγωτο παγωτό (το) pagoto (to)
ice cream

**παγωτο ξυλακι παγωτό ξυλάκι
(το)** pagoto xilaki (to)
ice lolly

πάει: πώς πάει; pos pai? how are
things?

ΠΑΖΑΡΙ παζάρι (το) pazari (to)
bazaar

ΠΑΘΟΛΟΓΟΣ παθολόγος (ο/η) paTHologos (o/i) doctor, general practitioner

ΠΑΙΔΙ παιδί (το) pethi (to) child

> **Travel tip** Most domestic ferry-boat companies and airlines offer discounts for children, ranging from fifty to one hundred percent depending on their age; hotels and rooms won't charge extra for infants, and levy modest supplements for extra beds for older children.

ΠΑΙΔΙΑΤΡΟΣ παιδίατρος (ο/η) paediatrician

ΠΑΙΔΙΚΑ παιδικά (τα) pethika (ta) children's wear

ΠΑΙΔΙΚΑ ΕΙΔΗ παιδικά είδη (τα) pethika ithi (ta) children's department

ΠΑΙΔΙΚΑ ΕΣΩΡΟΥΧΑ παιδικά εσώρουχα pethika esorookha children's underwear

ΠΑΙΔΙΚΑ ΦΟΡΜΑΚΙΑ παιδικά φορμάκια pethika formakia babywear, toddlers' clothes

ΠΑΙΔΙΚΟ παιδικό pethiko children's (adj)

παίζω pezo play (verb)

παίρνω perno get; take

παίρνω τηλέφωνο perno tilefono phone (verb)

ΠΑΙΧΝΙΔΙ παιχνίδι (το) pekhnithi (to) game; toy

ΠΑΚΕΤΟ πακέτο (το) paketo (to) package; packet

ΠΑΛΑΙΟΠΩΛΕΙΟ παλαιοπωλείο (το) paleopolio (to) antique shop

παλαιός paleos old, ancient, antique

παλάτι (το) palati (to) palace

παλίρροια (η) paliria (i) tide

παλτό (το) palto (to) coat

πάνα (η) pana (i) nappy, diaper

ΠΑΝΕΠΙΣΤΗΜΙΟ (το) panepistimio (to) university

ΠΑΝΗΓΥΡΙ πανηγύρι (το) paniyiri (to) fair, funfair

πανί (το) pani (to) sail

ΠΑΝ/ΜΙΟ παν/μιο university

ΠΑΝΣΙΟΝ πανσιόν (η) pansion (i) guesthouse

πάντα panda always; still

παντελόνι (το) pandaloni (to) trousers, (US) pants

παντζούρια (τα) pandzooria (ta) shutters

ΠΑΝΤΟΠΩΛΕΙΟ παντοπωλείο (το) pandopolio (to) grocery store

πάντοτε pandoteh always

παντού pandoo everywhere

παντόφλες (οι) pandofles (i) slippers

παντρεμένος pandremenos married

παντρεμένη pandremeni married

πάνω pano on; up; upstairs

πάνω από pano apo above

παξιμάδι (το) paximathi (to) nut (for bolt)

παπάκι (το) papaki (to) at sign

παπάς (ο) papas (o) priest

πάπια (η) papia (i) duck

πάπλωμα (το) paploma (to) quilt

παπούτσι (το) papootsi (to) shoe

παππούς (ο) pappoos (o) grandfather

παραγγελία (η) parangelia (i) message

παραγγέλνω parangelno order (*verb*: in restaurant)

παράδειγμα (το) parathigma (to) example

παραδείγματος χάρι parathigmatos khari for example

παράδοση (η) parathosi (i) tradition

παραδοσιακός parathosiakos traditional

παράθυρο (το) paraThiro (to) window

παρακαλώ parakalo please; excuse me; don't mention it

παρακαλώ; parakalo? can I help you?

ΠΑΡΑΚΑΜΠΤΗΡΙΟΣ παρακαμπτήριος (η) diversion

ΠΑΡΑΛΑΒΗ ΑΠΟΣΚΕΥΩΝ

παραλαβή αποσκευών (η) paralavi aposkevon (i) baggage claim

ΠΑΡΑΛΙΑ παραλία (η) paralia (i) beach

κοντά στην παραλία konda stin paralia at the seaside

παραμάνα (η) paramana (i) safety pin

παραμένω parameno stay (*verb*), remain

παράξενος paraxenos strange

παραπονούμαι paraponoomeh complain

ΠΑΡΑΣΚΕΥΗ Παρασκευή (η) Paraskevi (i) Friday

παρατηρώ paratiro watch (*verb*)

παρατσούκλι (το) paratsookli (to) nickname

παρεξήγηση (η) parexiyisi (i) misunderstanding

παρκάρω parkaro park (*verb*)

ΠΑΡΚΙΝΓΚ πάρκινγκ (το)
parking (to) car park, parking lot

πάρκο (το) parko (to) park

ΠΑΡΟΔΟΣ πάροδος (η) parothos
(i) side street

παρπρίζ (το) parpriz (to)
windscreen

πάρτυ (το) parti (to) party,
celebration

παστίλιες λαιμού (οι) pastili-es
lemoo (i) throat pastilles

Πάσχα (το) Paskha (to) Easter

πατέρας (ο) pateras (o) father

πατερίτσες (οι) pateritses (i)
crutches

πάτωμα (το) patoma (to) floor
(of room)

ΠΑΥΣΙΠΟΝΟ παυσίπονο (το)
pafsipono (to) painkiller

πάχος (το) pakhos (to) fat (on meat)

παχύς pakhis fat; thick

πάω pao go (verb)

πεζοδρόμιο (το) pezothromio (to)
pavement, sidewalk

ΠΕΖΟΔΡΟΜΟΣ πεζόδρομος (ο)
pedestrian precinct

ΠΕΖΟΙ πεζοί pedestrians

πεθαίνω peтнeno die

πεθαμένος peтнamenos dead

πεθερά (η) peтнera (i)
mother-in-law

πεθερός (ο) peтнeros (o)
father-in-law

πειράζει pirazi it matters

  θα σε πείραζε αν...;
  тнa seh pirazeh an...?
  do you mind if I...?

δεν πειράζει then pirazi
it doesn't matter

ΠΕΙΡΑΙΑΣ Πειραιάς Pireas
Piraeus

ΠΕΜΠΤΗ Πέμπτη (η) Pempti (i)
Thursday

πέμπτος pemptos fifth

πενήντα peninda fifty

πενικιλλίνη (η) penikilini (i)
penicillin

πέννα (η) pena (i) pen

πένσα (η) pensa (i) pliers

πέντε pendeh five

πέος (το) peos (to) penis

περάστε perasteh come in;
come back

ΠΕΡΙΕΧΟΜΕΝΟ περιεχόμενο
contains

περίμενε perimeneh wait

περιμένω perimeno wait (for);
expect

ΠΕΡΙΟΔΙΚΟ περιοδικό (το)
periothiko (to) magazine

περίοδος (η) periothos (i) period

περιοχή (η) periokhi (i) area

περίπατος (ο) peripatos (o) walk

  πάω περίπατο pao peripato
  go for a walk

Travel tip If you have the
time and stamina, walking
is probably the best way to
see the quieter islands. The
more accessible island hikes
include the well-organized
Corfu Trail, and Crete
and Evvia have sizeable
mountains and good hiking
routes.

περίπου peripoo about, approximately

ΠΕΡΙΠΤΕΡΟ περίπτερο periptero newspaper kiosk

ΣΕ ΠΕΡΙΠΤΩΣΗ ΑΝΑΓΚΗΣ ΣΠΑΣΤΕ ΤΟ ΤΖΑΜΙ se περίπτωση ανάγκης σπάστε το τζάμι seh periptosi anangis spasteh to tzami in emergency break glass

περισσότερο perisotero more, most (of)

περισσότερος perisoteros more, most (of)

ΠΕΡΜΑΝΑΝΤ περμανάντ (η) permanand (i) perm

περνάω pernao cross, go through

περπατάω perpatao walk (*verb*)

πέρσυ persi last year

πετάλι (το) petali (to) pedal

πετάω petao throw away (*verb*)

πέτρα (η) petra (i) stone

πετσέτα (η) petseta (i) napkin; towel

πετσέτα κουζίνας petseta koozinas tea towel

πετώ peto fly (*verb*)

πέφτω pefto fall (*verb*)

πηγή (η) piyi (i) fountain

πηγούνι (το) pigooni (to) chin

πηδάω pithao jump (*verb*)

πηρούνι (το) pirooni (to) fork

πιάνω piano catch (*verb*)

πιατάκι (το) piataki (to) saucer

πιατικά (τα) piatika (ta) crockery

πιάτο (το) piato (to) dish; plate

ΠΙΕΣΗ ΑΙΜΑΤΟΣ πίεση αίματος (η) blood pressure

πιθανώς piTHanos probably

πικάντικος pikandikos spicy

πικάπ (το) pikap (to) record player

πικνίκ (το) piknik (to) picnic

πικρός pikros bitter

πιλότος (ο) pilotos (o) pilot

πινακίδες (οι) pinakithes (i) number plates

ΠΙΝΑΚΟΘΗΚΗ πινακοθήκη (η) pinakoTHiki (i) art gallery

πινγκ-πονγκ (το) ping-pong (to) table tennis

πινέλο (το) pinelo (to) paintbrush

πινέλο γιά ξύρισμα pinelo ya xirisma shaving brush

πίνω pino drink (*verb*)

πίπα (η) pipa (i) pipe (for smoking)

ΠΙΣΙΝΑ πισίνα (η) pisina (i) swimming pool

πιστεύω pistevo believe

πιστολάκι (το) pistolaki (to) hairdryer

πιστόλι (το) pistoli (to) gun, pistol

πιστοποιητικό (το) pistopi-itiko (to) certificate

ΠΙΣΤΩΤΙΚΗ ΚΑΡΤΑ πιστωτική κάρτα (η) pistotiki karta (i) credit card

πίσω piso back; behind

πίσω φώτα (τα) piso fota (ta) rear lights

ΠΙΤΣΑΡΙΑ πιτσαρία (η) pitsaria (i) pizzeria

πλαστική σακούλα (η) plastiki sakoola (i) plastic bag

πλαστικός plastikos plastic

ΠΛΑΤΕΙΑ πλατεία (η) platia (i) square (in town); stalls (in theatre)

A
B
Γ
Δ
E
Z
H
Θ
I
K
Λ
M
N
Ξ
O
Π
P
Σ
T
Y
Φ
X
Ψ
Ω

πλάτη (η) plati (i) back (of person)

πλατύς platis wide

ΠΛΑΤΦΟΡΜΑ πλατφόρμα (η) platforma (i) platform, (US) track

πλέκω pleko knit

πλένομαι plenomeh wash (oneself)

πλένω pleno wash (*verb*: something)

πλευρά (η) plevra (i) side

πλευρό (το) plevro (to) rib

πληγή (η) pliyi (i) wound

πλήθος (το) pliTHos (to) crowd

ΠΛΗΡΕΣ πλήρες no vacancies, full

ΠΛΗΡΟΦΟΡΙΕΣ πληροφορίες (οι) plirofories (i) information; directory enquiries

ΠΛΗΡΩΜΑ πλήρωμα (το) crew

πληρώνω plirono pay (*verb*)

πλοίο (το) plio (to) boat, ship

πλούσιος ploosios rich

πλυντήριο (το) plindirio (to) washing machine

ΠΛΥΝΤΗΡΙΟ ΑΥΤΟΚΙΝΗΤΩΝ πλυντήριο αυτοκινήτων car wash

ΠΛΥΝΤΗΡΙΟ ΡΟΥΧΩΝ πλυντήριο ρούχων plindirio rookhon launderette, laundromat

ΠΛΥΣΙΜΟ ΜΕ ΤΟ ΧΕΡΙ πλύσιμο με το χέρι handwash only

πλύσιμο των πιάτων (το) plisimo ton piaton (to) washing up

πνεύμονες (οι) pnevmones (i) lungs

ποδηλασία (η) pothilasia (i) cycling

ποδηλάτης (ο/η) pothilatis (o/i) cyclist

ΠΟΔΗΛΑΤΟ ποδήλατο (το) pothilato (to) bicycle

πόδι (το) pothi (to) foot; leg

με τα πόδια meh ta pothia on foot

ποδόσφαιρο (το) pothosfero (to) football

ποιά; pia? who?

ποιανού; pianoo? whose?

ποιό; pio? which?

ποιός; pios? who?

ποιός είναι; pios ineh? who is it?

πόλεμος (ο) polemos (o) war

πόλη (η) poli (i) city, town

πολιτεία (η) politia (i) state

πολιτικά (τα) politika (ta) politics

πολιτικός politikos political; politician

πολλά, πολλές, πολλή, πολλοί pola, poles, poli, poli many, a lot (of)

πολύ poli a lot of; very; too much

πάρα πολύ para poli too much; very much

πολυσύχναστος polisikhnastos busy (place)

πολύς polis a lot (of)

ΠΟΛΥΤΕΛΕΙΑΣ πολυτελείας luxury class, four-star (hotel)

πονάει ponai hurt

πονόδοντος (ο) ponothondos (o) toothache

πονοκέφαλος (ο) ponokefalos (o) headache

πόνος (ο) ponos (o) ache, pain

ποντίκι (το) pondiki (to) mouse

πόνυ (το) poni (to) pony

πορεία (η) poria (i) route

πόρτα (η) porta (i) door

πορτ-μπαγκάζ (το) port-bagaz (to) (of a car) boot, (US) trunk

πορτ-μπε-μπέ (το) port-be-be (to) carrycot

πορτοκαλί portokali orange (colour)

πορτοφολάς (ο) portofolas (o) pickpocket

πορτοφόλι (το) portofoli (to) wallet

πόσα;, πόσες;, posa?, poses? how many?

ΠΟΣΙΜΟ ΝΕΡΟ πόσιμο νερό (το) posimo nero (to) drinking water

πόσο; poso? how much?

πόσοι; posi? how many?

πόστερ (το) poster (to) poster

ΠΟΣΤ ΡΕΣΤΑΝΤ ποστ ρεστάντ post restant poste restante

ποτάμι (το) potami (to) river

ποτέ poteh never

πότε; poteh? when?

έχετε ποτέ...; ekheteh poteh...? have you ever...?

ποτήρι (το) potiri (to) glass

ΠΟΤΟΠΩΛΕΙΟ ποτοπωλείο (το) potopolio (to) off-licence, liquor store

που poo who, which, that

πού; poo? where?

πούδρα ταλκ (η) poothra talk (i) talcum powder

πουθενά pootнena nowhere

πουκάμισο (το) pookamiso (to) shirt

πουλί (το) pooli (to) bird

ΠΟΥΛΜΑΝ πούλμαν (το) poolman (to) bus, coach

πουλόβερ (το) poolover (to) jumper

πουλώ poolo sell

πούρο (το) pooro (to) cigar

πράγμα (το) pragma (to) thing

πραγματικά pragmatika really

πρακτικός praktikos practical

πρακτορείο (το) praktorio (to) agency

ΠΡΑΚΤΟΡΕΙΟ ΕΦΗΜΕΡΙΔΩΝ πρακτορείο εφημερίδων newsagent, news vendor

ΠΡΑΚΤΟΡΕΙΟ ΛΕΩΦΟΡΕΙΩΝ πρακτορείο λεωφορείων praktorio leoforion bus station

πράσινος prasinos green

ΠΡΑΤΗΡΙΟ ΒΕΝΖΙΝΗΣ πρατήριο βενζίνης (το) pratirio venzinis (to) petrol station, gas station

πρέπει να... prepi na... I must...

ΠΡΕΣΒΕΙΑ πρεσβεία (η) presvia (i) embassy

πρησμένος prismenos swollen

πρίγκηπας (ο) pringipas (o) prince

πριγκίπισσα (η) pringipisa (i) princess

πρίζα (η) priza (i) socket; plug

πρίζα ταυ (η) priza taf (i) adaptor

πριν prin before; ago

πριν τρεις μέρες prin tris meres three days ago

προάστια (τα) proastia (ta) suburbs

A
B
Γ
Δ
E
Z
H
Θ
I
K
Λ
M
N
Ξ
O
Π
P
Σ
T
Y
Φ
X
Ψ
Ω

πρόβατο (το) provato (to) sheep

πρόβλημα (το) provlima (to) problem

ΠΡΟΒΛΗΤΑ προβλήτα (η) provlita (i) quay

προβολείς (οι) provolis (i) headlights

ΠΡΟΓΕΥΜΑ πρόγευμα (το) proyevma (to) breakfast

πρόγονος (ο/η) progonos (o/i) ancestor

ΠΡΟΓΡΑΜΜΑ πρόγραμμα (το) programa (to) timetable, schedule; programme

προκαταβάλλω prokatavalo advance (*verb*)

προκαταβολικά prokatavolika in advance

ΠΡΟΞΕΝΕΙΟ προξενείο (το) proxenio (to) consulate

ΠΡΟΟΡΙΣΜΟΣ προορισμός pro- orismos destination

προσβάλλω prosvalo offend

ΠΡΟΣ ΓΚΑΡΑΖ προς γκαράζ to car deck

ΠΡΟΣΔΕΘΗΤΕ προσδεθήτε fasten your seat belt

προσεκτικός prosektikos careful

πρόσεξε! prosexeh! look out!

ΠΡΟΣΕΧΕ! πρόσεξε! prosekheh! look out!

προσέχω prosekho take care of

ΠΡΟΣΕΧΩΣ προσεχώς coming soon

πρόσθετο (το) prostheto (to) supplementary

προσκαλώ proskalo invite

πρόσκληση (η) prosklisi (i) invitation

ΠΡΟΣ ΟΡΟΦΟΥΣ προς ορόφους to all floors

ΠΡΟΣΟΧΗ! προσοχή! caution!

ΠΡΟΣΟΧΗ ΑΡΓΑ προσοχή αργά caution: slow

ΠΡΟΣΟΧΗ ΕΞΟΔΟΣ ΟΧΗΜΑΤΩΝ προσοχή έξοδος οχημάτων caution: vehicle exit

ΠΡΟΣΟΧΗ ΕΥΦΛΕΚΤΟΝ προσοχή εύφλεκτον caution: highly inflammable

ΠΡΟΣΟΧΗ ΚΙΝΔΥΝΟΣ προσοχή κίνδυνος caution: danger

προσοχή παρακαλώ prosokhi parakalo attention please

ΠΡΟΣΟΧΗ ΣΚΥΛΟΣ προσοχή σκύλος beware of the dog

ΠΡΟΣ ΠΑΡΑΣΚΗΝΙΑ προς παρασκήνια to dressing rooms

προσπέκτους (το) prospektoos (to) brochure

προσπερνώ prosperno overtake

προστατεύω prostatevo protect

ΠΡΟΣΤΙΜΟ πρόστιμο (το) prostimo (to) fine

προσφέρω prosfero offer (*verb*); give

ΠΡΟΣΦΟΡΑ προσφορά special bargain

πρόσωπο (το) prosopo (to) face

προς pros towards

προτείνω protino recommend

ΠΡΟΤΕΡΑΙΟΤΗΤΑ προτεραιότητα (η) right of way

προτιμώ protimo prefer

προφανής profanis obvious

προφέρω profero pronounce

προφορά (η) profora (i) accent

προφυλακτήρας (ο) profilaktiras (o) bumper, fender

ΠΡΟΦΥΛΑΚΤΙΚΑ **προφυλακτικά** contraceptives

ΠΡΟΦΥΛΑΚΤΙΚΟ **προφυλακτικό (το)** profilaktiko (to) condom

προχτές prokhtes the day before yesterday

πρωί (το) proi (to) morning

το πρωί to proi in the morning

ΠΡΩΙΝΟ **πρωινό (το)** pro-ino (to) breakfast

πρώτα prota first, firstly

ΠΡΩΤΕΣ ΒΟΗΘΕΙΕΣ **πρώτες βοήθειες (οι)** protes voiTHi-es (i) first aid

ΠΡΩΤΗ ΘΕΣΗ **πρώτη θέση** first class

πρώτο! proto! great!

ΠΡΩΤΟ ΠΑΤΩΜΑ **πρώτο πάτωμα (το)** proto patoma (to) first floor, (US) second floor

πρώτος protos first

ΠΡΩΤΟΣ ΟΡΟΦΟΣ **πρώτος όροφος** protos orofos first floor, (US) second floor

Πρωτοχρονιά (η) Protokhronia (i) New Year's Day

ΠΤΗΣΕΙΣ ΕΞΩΤΕΡΙΚΟΥ **πτήσεις εξωτερικού** international flights

ΠΤΗΣΕΙΣ ΕΣΩΤΕΡΙΚΟΥ **πτήσεις εσωτερικού** domestic flights

ΠΤΗΣΗ **πτήση (η)** ptisi (i) flight

ΠΤΗΣΗ ΤΣΑΡΤΕΡ **πτήση τσάρτερ** charter flight

πυζάμες (οι) pizames (i) pyjamas

πυξίδα (η) pixitha (i) compass

πύργος (ο) pirgos (o) tower

πυρετός (ο) piretos (o) fever

πυρκαγιά (η) pirkaya (i) fire

ΠΥΡΟΣΒΕΣΤΗΡ **πυροσβεστήρ (ο)** fire extinguisher

ΠΥΡΟΣΒΕΣΤΗΡΑΣ **πυροσβεστήρας (ο)** fire extinguisher

ΠΥΡΟΣΒΕΣΤΙΚΗ ΣΩΛΗΝΑ **πυροσβεστική σωλήνα (η)** fire hose

ΠΥΡΟΣΒΕΣΤΙΚΗ (ΥΠΗΡΕΣΙΑ) **πυροσβεστική (υπηρεσία) (η)** pirosvestiki ipiresia (i) fire brigade

πυροτεχνήματα (τα) pirotekhnimata (ta) fireworks

πυτζάμες (οι) pitzames (i) pyjamas

ΠΩΛΕΙΤΑΙ πωλείται for sale

ΠΩΛΗΣΗ **πώληση (η)** sale

πώς; pos? how?; what?

Ρ

ράβω ravo sew

ραδιόφωνο (το) rathiofono (to) radio

ραντεβού (το) randevoo (to) appointment

ράντζο (το) randzo (to) campbed

ΡΑΦΕΙΟ **ραφείο (το)** rafio (to) tailor's

ρεζέρβα (η) rezerva (i) spare tyre

ΡΕΣΕΨΙΟΝ ρεσεψιόν (η)
resepsion (i) reception

ρεσεψιονίστ (ο/η) resepsionist (o/i)
receptionist

ρε συ! reh si! you there!, oi you!

ρεύμα (το) revma (to) current;
draught

ρευματισμοί (οι) revmatismi (i)
rheumatism

ρίχνω rikhno throw (*verb*)

ρόδα (η) rotha (i) wheel

ροζ roz pink

ρόκ (η) rok (i) rock music

ρολόι (το) roloi (to) clock; watch

ρόμπα (η) roba (i) dressing gown

ΡΟΥΦ - ΓΚΑΡΝΤΕΝ Ρουφ -
Γκάρντεν Roof - garden
roof garden

ρούχα (τα) rookha (ta) clothes

ροχαλίζω rokhalizo snore

ρυμούλκα (η) rimoolka (i) trailer
(for car)

ρυμουλκό rimoolko trailer (for car)

ρωτώ roto ask

Σ

ΣΑΒΒΑΤΟ Σάββατο (το) Savato
(to) Saturday

σαββατοκύριακο (το) savatokiriako
(to) weekend

ΣΑΓΙΟΝΑΡΕΣ σαγιονάρες
sayonares beach sandals,
flip-flops

σαγόνι (το) sagoni (to) jaw

σακάκι (το) sakaki (to) jacket

σακβουαγιάζ (το) sakvooayaz (to)

hand luggage, hand baggage

σακίδιο (το) sakithio (to) rucksack

σάκος (ο) sakos (o) backpack,
rucksack

ΣΑΛΟΝΙ σαλόνι (το) saloni (to)
lounge

ΣΑΜΠΟΥΑΝ σαμπουάν (το)
sampooan (to) shampoo

σαμπρέλα (η) sabrela (i) inner tube

σαν san like, as

σανδάλια (τα) santhalia (ta)
sandals

σάουνα (η) saoona (i) sauna

σάπιος sapios rotten

ΣΑΠΟΥΝΙ ΠΙΑΤΩΝ σαπούνι
πιάτων (το) sapooni piaton (to)
washing-up liquid

ΣΑΠΟΥΝΙ σαπούνι (το) sapooni
(to) soap

σαράντα saranda forty

σας sas you; your

σβήνω svino switch off (engine);
put out (fire)

ΣΒΗΣΤΕ ΤΗΝ ΜΗΧΑΝΗ
σβήστε την μηχανή switch off
engine

σβήστρα (η) svistra (i) rubber,
eraser

σγουρά sgoora curly

σε seh you; to; at; in

σεζ λόνγκ (η) sez long (i)
deckchair

ΣΕΙΡΑ σειρά (η) sira (i) row
(of seats)

σελίδα (η) selitha (i) page

ΣΕΛΛΟΤΕΗΠ σέλλοτέηπ (το)
selloteip (to) Sellotape,
Scotch tape

ΣΕΛΦ ΣΕΡΒΙΣ σελφ σέρβις
self servis self-service

σεντόνι (το) sendoni (to) sheet

σέξυ sexi sexy

ΣΕ ΠΕΡΙΠΤΩΣΗ ΑΝΑΓΚΗΣ
ΣΠΑΣΤΕ ΤΟ ΤΖΑΜΙ σε
περίπτωση ανάγκης σπάστε το
τζάμι in emergency break glass

ΣΕΠΤΕΜΒΡΙΟΣ Σεπτέμβριος (ο)
Septemvrios (o) September

ΣΕΡΒΙΕΤΕΣ σερβιέτες (οι)
servietes (i) sanitary towels/
napkins

σερβιτόρα (η) servitora (i) barmaid;
waitress

σερβιτόρος (ο) servitoros (o) waiter

ΣΗΚΩΣΤΕ ΤΟ ΑΚΟΥΣΤΙΚΟ
σηκώστε το ακουστικό
lift receiver

σημαδούρα (η) simathoora (i) buoy

σημαία (η) simea (i) flag

σημειωματάριο (το) simiomatario
(to) notebook

ΣΗΜΕΡΑ σήμερα simera today

ΣΗΜΕΡΟΝ σήμερον
showing today

σήραγγα (η) siranga (i) tunnel

σιγά-σιγά siga-siga slowly;
slow down

σίγουρος sigooros sure

σίδερο (το) sithero (to) iron

σιδερώνω sitherono iron (verb)

ΣΙΔΗΡΟΔΡΟΜΙΚΟΣ ΣΤΑΘΜΟΣ
σιδηροδρομικός σταθμός (ο)
sithirothromikos staTHmos (o)
railway station

σιδηρόδρομος (ο) sithirothromos
(o) railway

ΣΙΔΗΡΟΥΡΓΕΙΟ σιδηρουργείο
(το) sithirooryio (to)
hardware store

ΣΙΝΕΜΑ σινεμά (το) sinema (to)

Α
Β
Γ
Δ
Ε
Ζ
Η
Θ
Ι
Κ
Λ
Μ
Ν
Ξ
Ο
Π
Ρ
Σ
Τ
Υ
Φ
Χ
Ψ
Ω

cinema, movie theater

σιωπή (η) siopi (i) silence

σκάλα (η) skala (i) ladder

ΣΚΑΛΕΣ σκάλες (οι) skales (i) stairs

σκέπτομαι skeptomeh think

ΣΚΗΝΗ σκηνή (η) skini (i) tent

σκιά (η) skia (i) shade, shadow
  στη σκιά sti skia in the shade

ΣΚΙΑ ΜΑΤΙΩΝ σκιά ματιών (η) skia mation (i) eye shadow

ΣΚΛΗΡΟΙ ΦΑΚΟΙ σκληροί φακοί (οι) skliri faki (i) hard lenses

σκληρός skliros hard

ΣΚΟΝΗ ΠΛΥΝΤΗΡΙΟΥ σκόνη πλυντηρίου (η) skoni plindirioo (i) washing powder

σκοτεινός skotinos dark

σκοτώνω skotono kill (verb)

σκουλαρίκια (τα) skoolarikia (ta) earrings

σκούπα skoopa broom

σκουπίδια (τα) skoopithia (ta) rubbish, garbage

σκουπιδοντενεκές (ο) skoopithondenekes (o) dustbin, trashcan

σκύλος (ο) skilos (o) dog

σκωληκοειδίτις (η) skoliko-ithitis (i) appendicitis

ΣΚΩΤΙΑ Σκωτία (η) Skotia (i) Scotland

Σκωτσέζικος Skotsezikos Scottish

σλάιντ (το) slaid (to) slide

σλιπ (το) slip (to) underpants; panties

ΣΛΙΠΙΝΓΚ ΜΠΑΓΚ σλίπινγκ μπαγκ (το) sliping bag (to) sleeping bag

σοβαρός sovaros serious

σοκ (το) sok (to) shock

ΣΟΚΟΛΑΤΑ σοκολάτα (η) sokolata (i) chocolate

ΣΟΚΟΛΑΤΑ ΓΑΛΑΚΤΟΣ σοκολάτα γάλακτος (η) sokolata galaktos (i) milk chocolate

ΣΟΚΟΛΑΤΑΚΙΑ σοκολατάκια (τα) sokolatakia (ta) chocolates

σόλα (η) sola (i) sole (of shoe)

σόμπα (η) soba (i) oil heater

σορτς (το) sorts (to) shorts

σου soo you; your

σουγιάς (ο) sooyas (o) penknife

ΣΟΥΠΕΡ ΒΕΝΖΙΝΗ σούπερ βενζίνη (η) sooper venzini (i) four-star petrol, premium

ΣΟΥΠΕΡΜΑΡΚΕΤ σούπερμάρκετ (το) soopermarket (to) supermarket

σουτιέν (το) sootien (to) bra

ΣΠΑΓΓΟΣ σπάγγος (ο) spangos (o) string

σπασμένος spasmenos broken

σπάω spao break (verb)

σπηλιά (το) spilia (to) cave

σπιράλ (το) spiral (to) spiral; IUD; incense coil (mosquito repellent)

σπίρτα (τα) spirta (ta) matches

σπίτι (το) spiti (to) house
  στο σπίτι sto spiti at home

σπορ (το) spor (to) sport

σπουδαίος spootheos important

σπρώχνω sprokhno push (*verb*)
σταγόνα (η) stagona (i) drop
ΣΤΑΓΟΝΕΣ σταγόνες drops
ΣΤΑΔΙΟ στάδιο (το) stathio (to)
  stadium
ΣΤΑΘΜΟΣ σταθμός (ο) staTHmos
  (o) station
ΣΤΑΘΜΟΣ ΑΝΕΦΟΔΙΑΣΜΟΥ
  ΘΑΛΑΜΗΓΩΝ σταθμός
  ανεφοδιασμού θαλαμηγών
  yacht refuelling station
ΣΤΑΘΜΟΣ ΛΕΩΦΟΡΕΙΩΝ
  σταθμός λεωφορείων staTHmos
  leoforion bus station
ΣΤΑΘΜΟΣ ΠΡΩΤΩΝ
  ΒΟΗΘΕΙΩΝ σταθμός πρώτων
  βοηθειών staTHmos proton
  vo-iTHion first aid post
ΣΤΑΘΜΟΣ ΤΑΞΙ σταθμός ταξί
  staTHmos taxi taxi stand
ΣΤΑΘΜΟΣ ΥΠΕΡΑΣΤΙΚΩΝ
  ΛΕΩΦΟΡΕΙΩΝ σταθμός
  υπεραστικών λεωφορείων
  staTHmos iperastikon leoforion
  bus station (**long distance**)
ΣΤΑΘΜΟΣ ΧΩΡΟΦΥΛΑΚΗΣ
  σταθμός χωροφυλακής
  staTHmos khorofilakis
  police station
σταματάω stamatao stop (*verb*)
ΣΤΑΣΗ στάση (η) stasi (i) stop
  (for bus, train)
ΣΤΑΣΗ ΑΣΤΙΚΩΝ
  ΣΥΓΚΟΙΝΩΝΙΩΝ στάση
  αστικών συγκοινωνιών
  city bus stop
ΣΤΑΣΗ ΛΕΩΦΟΡΕΙΟΥ στάση
  λεωφορείου bus stop
ΣΤΑΣΗ ΤΑΞΙ στάση ταξί stasi

taxi taxi stand
ΣΤΑΣΙΣ στάσις (η) stasis (i)
  bus stop
στέγη (η) steyi (i) roof
ΣΤΕΓΝΟ ΚΑΘΑΡΙΣΜΑ ΜΟΝΟΝ
  στεγνό καθάρισμα μόνον
  dryclean only
ΣΤΕΓΝΟΚΑΘΑΡΙΣΤΗΡΙΟ
  στεγνοκαθαριστήριο (το)
  stegnokaTHaristirio (to)
  dry cleaner's
στεγνός stegnos dry
στεγνώνω stegnono dry (*verb*)
στέλνω stelno send
στενός stenos narrow; tight
στενοχώρια (η) stenokhoria (i)
  worry (*verb*)
στήθος (το) stiTHos (to) breast;
  chest
στην stin at; in; to; on
ΣΤΙΒΟΣ στίβος (ο)
  athletics stadium
στικ μνήμης (το) stik mnimis (to)
  memory stick
στο sto at; in; to
στόμα (το) stoma (to) mouth
στομάχι (το) stomakhi (to) stomach
στον ston at; in; to;
ΣΤΟΠ! στοπ! stop!
στριφτό (το) strifto (to) hand-
  rolled cigarette
στρογγυλός strongilos round
στρόφαλος (ο) strofalos (o)
  crankshaft
στροφή (η) strofi (i) bend
στρώμα (το) stroma (to) mattress
στυλό (το) stilo (to) biro

Α
Β
Γ
Δ
Ε
Ζ
Η
Θ
Ι
Κ
Λ
Μ
Ν
Ξ
Ο
Π
Ρ
Σ
Τ
Υ
Φ
Χ
Ψ
Ω

συγγενείς (οι) singenis (i) relatives

συγγνώμη signomi sorry;
excuse me

συγγνώμη; signomi? pardon
(me)?, sorry?

σύγκρουση (η) singroosi (i) crash

συγχαρητήρια! sinkharitiria!
congratulations!

συγχωρείτε: με συγχωρείτε meh
sinkhoriteh excuse me

σύζυγος (ο) sizigos (o) husband

συκότι (το) sikoti (to) liver

συλλαμβάνω silamvano arrest

συλλογή (η) siloyi (i) collection

συμβαίνω simveno happen

συμβουλεύω simvoolevo advise

ΣΥΜΠΕΡΙΛΑΜΒΑΝΕΤΑΙ
συμπεριλαμβάνεται included

συμπλέκτης (ο) siblektis (o) clutch

συμφωνώ simfono agree

ΣΥΝΑΓΕΡΜΟΣ συναγερμός (ο)
sinayermos (o) alarm

συναίσθημα (το) sinesTHima (to)
feeling

ΣΥΝΑΛΛΑΓΜΑ συνάλλαγμα
(το) sinalagma (to) foreign
exchange

ΣΥΝΑΛΛΑΓΜΑΤΙΚΗ
ΙΣΟΤΙΜΙΑ συναλλαγματική
ισοτιμία (η) sinalagmatiki
isotimia (i) exchange rate

συνάντηση (η) sinandisi (i) meeting

συναντώ sinando meet

συναρπαστικός sinarpastikos
exciting

συναυλία (η) sinavlia (i) concert

ΣΥΝ/ΓΕΙΟ συν/γειο auto repairs

σύνδεση (η) sinthesi (i) connection
(electrical)

ΣΥΝΕΡΓΕΙΟ (ΑΥΤΟΚΙΝΗΤΩΝ)
συνεργείο (αυτοκινήτων) (το)
auto repairs

συνήθεια (η) siniTHia (i) habit

συνηθισμένος siniTHismenos usual

συνήθως siniTHos usually

ΣΥΝΘΕΤΙΚΟ συνθετικό
synthetic

συννεφιασμένος sinefiasmenos
cloudy

σύννεφο (το) sinefo (to) cloud

συνοδεύω sinothevo accompany

ΣΥΝΟΙΚΙΑ συνοικία (η)
sinikia (i) district

συνολικά sinolika altogether

σύνορα (τα) sinora (ta) border

συνταγή (η) sindayi (i)
prescription; recipe

συνταξιούχος (ο/η) sindaxioohos
(o/i) old-age pensioner

ΣΥΝΤΗΡΗΤΙΚΟ ΔΙΑΛΥΜΑ
συντηρητικό διάλυμα (το)
sindiritiko thialima (to)
soaking solution

σύντομα sindoma soon

ΣΥΡΑΤΕ σύρατε pull

σύρμα (το) sirma (to) wire

ΣΥΣΤΑΤΙΚΑ συστατικά
ingredients

ΣΥΣΤΗΜΕΝΑ συστημένα
sistimena registered mail

συστήνω sistino introduce;
recommend

συχνά sikhna often

σφήγγα (η) sfinga (i) wasp

σφράγισμα (το) sfrayisma (to)

filling (in tooth)

σφυρί (το) sfiri (to) hammer

σχάρα αυτοκινήτου (η) skhara
aftokinitoo (i) roof rack

σχέδιο (το) skhethio (to) plan

σχεδόν skhethon almost

σχοινί (το) skhini (to) rope

ΣΧΟΛΕΙΟ σχολείο (το) skholio
(to) school

σωλήνας (ο) solinas (o) pipe (water)

σώμα (το) soma (to) body

ΣΩΣΙΒΙΑ σωσίβια sosivia lifejackets

σωστός sostos correct

T

τα ta the; them

ταβάνι (το) tavani (to) ceiling

ΤΑΒΕΡΝΑ ταβέρνα (η) taverna (i)
restaurant

> **Travel tip** When looking for
> a good place to eat, the best
> strategy is to go where and
> when the Greeks go – and
> they go late: 2 to 3.30pm for
> lunch, 9 to 11pm for dinner.
> You can eat earlier, but you'll
> probably get indifferent serv-
> ice and food if you frequent
> touristy establishments.

τακούνι (το) takooni (to) heel
(of shoe)

ΤΑΜΕΙΟ ταμείο (το) tamio (to)
box office; cash desk, till,
cashier

**ΤΑΜΙΕΥΤΗΡΙΟ ταμιευτήριο
(το)** tami-eftirio (to) savings bank

ΤΑΜΠΛΕΤΑ ταμπλέτα (η) tableta
(i) tablet

ΤΑΜΠΙΟΝ ταμπόν (τα) tampon
(ta) tampons

τάξη (η) taxi (i) class

ΤΑΞΙ ταξί (το) taxi (to) taxi

ταξιδεύω taxithevo travel (*verb*)

ταξίδι (το) taxithi (to) journey, trip

   καλό ταξίδι! kalo taxithi! have a
good journey!, bon voyage!

ταξίδι για δουλειές taxithi ya
thoolies business trip

**ΤΑΞΙΔΙΩΤΙΚΗ ΕΠΙΤΑΓΗ
ταξιδιωτική επιταγή (η)**
taxithiotiki epitayi (i) traveller's
cheque/traveler's check

**ΤΑΞΙΔΙΩΤΙΚΟ ΓΡΑΦΕΙΟ
ταξιδιωτικό γραφείο (το)**
taxithiotiko grafio (to)
travel agent's

τάπα (η) tapa (i) plug (in sink)

ΤΑ ΡΕΣΤΑ ΣΑΣ τα ρέστα σας
your change

ΤΑΡΙΦΑ ταρίφα tarifa taxi tariff

τασάκι (το) tasaki (to) ashtray

ταύρος (ο) tavros (o) bull

ΤΑΥΤΟΤΗΤΑ ταυτότητα (η)
taftotita (i) pass, identity card

**ΤΑΧΥΔΡΟΜΕΙΟ ταχυδρομείο
(το)** takhithromio (to) post office

**ΤΑΧΥΔΡΟΜΙΚΟΣ ΤΟΜΕΥΣ
ταχυδρομικός τομεύς (ο)**
takhithromikos tomefs (o)
postcode, zipcode

ταχυδρόμος (ο) takhithromos (o)
postman

ταχυδρομώ takhithromo post,
mail (*verb*)

ταχύτητα (η) takhitita (i) gear
(of car)

ταχύτητα (η) takhitita (i) speed

τέλειος telios perfect

τελειώνω teliono finish (*verb*)

ΤΕΛΕΥΤΑΙΑ ΠΑΡΑΣΤΑΣΗ
τελευταία παράσταση
last performance

τελευταίος telefteos last

τελεφερίκ (το) teleferik (to)
cable car

ΤΕΛΟΣ τέλος (το) telos (to) end

ΤΕΛΩΝΕΙΟ Τελωνείο (το)
Telonio (to) Customs

τεμπέλης tebelis lazy

τέννις (το) tenis (to) tennis

τέντα (η) tenda (i) tent, marquee

τέσσερα tesera four

ΤΕΤΑΡΤΗ Τετάρτη (η) Tetarti (i)
 Wednesday

τέταρτο (το) tetarto (to) quarter

τέταρτος tetartos fourth

τέχνη (η) tekhni (i) art

τεχνητός tekhnitos artificial

ΤΕΧΝΗΤΟ ΧΡΩΜΑ τεχνητό
χρώμα artificial colouring

τζαζ (η) tzaz (i) jazz

τζηνς (τα) tzins (ta) jeans

τζόγγιγκ (το) tzoging (to) jogging

τη ti the

τηγάνι (το) tigani (to) frying pan

τηγανίζω tiganizo fry

ΤΗΛΕΓΡΑΦΗΜΑ τηλεγράφημα
(το) tilegrafima (to) telegram

ΤΗΛΕΓΡΑΦΗΜΑΤΑ
τηλεγραφήματα telegrams

ΤΗΛΕΓΡΑΦΙΚΗ ΕΝΤΟΛΗ

τηλεγραφική εντολή tilegrafiki
endoli telegram

ΤΗΛΕΚΑΡΤΑ τηλεκάρτα (η)
tilekarta (i) phonecard

ΤΗΛΕΟΡΑΣΗ τηλεόραση (η)
tileorasi (i) television

ΤΗΛΕΦΩΝΗΜΑ τηλεφώνημα
tilefonima call

ΤΗΛΕΦΩΝΗΜΑ ΚΟΛΛΕΚΤ
τηλεφώνημα κολλέκτ (το)
tilefonima kollekt (to)
reverse charge call

ΤΗΛΕΦΩΝΙΚΗ ΕΝΤΟΛΗ
τηλεφωνική εντολή operator-
controlled phone call

ΤΗΛΕΦΩΝΙΚΟΣ ΘΑΛΑΜΟΣ
τηλεφωνικός θάλαμος (ο)
tilefonikos THalamos (o)
phone box

ΤΗΛΕΦΩΝΙΚΟΣ ΚΑΤΑΛΟΓΟΣ
τηλεφωνικός κατάλογος (ο)
tilefonikos katalogos (o)
phone book

ΤΗΛΕΦΩΝΟ τηλέφωνο (το)
tilefono (to) phone

ΤΗΛΕΦΩΝΩ τηλεφωνώ tilefono
ring, phone (*verb*)

την tin her; on; per; the
την εβδομάδα tin evthomatha
per week

της tis her; to her; of her

τι; ti? what?

ΤΙΜΗ τιμή (η) timi (i) price

ΤΙΜΗ ΑΓΟΡΑΣ τιμή αγοράς
buying rate

ΤΙΜΗ ΑΝΕΥ ΠΟΣΟΣΤΩΝ τιμή
άνευ ποσοστών
price exclusive of extras

ΤΙΜΗ ΔΩΜΑΤΙΟΥ τιμή δωματίου room price

ΤΙΜΗ ΚΑΤ᾽ ΑΤΟΜΟ τιμή κατ᾽ άτομο price per person

ΤΙΜΗ ΚΛΙΝΗΣ τιμή κλίνης price per bed

ΤΙΜΗ ΜΕΤΑ ΠΟΣΟΣΤΩΝ τιμή μετά ποσοστών price inclusive of extras

ΤΙΜΗ ΠΩΛΗΣΗΣ τιμή πώλησης selling rate

τίμιος timios honest

τιμόνι (το) timoni (to) steering wheel

τίνος; tinos? whose

τίποτε tipoteh nothing

ΤΙΠΟΤΕ ΠΡΟΣ ΔΗΛΩΣΗ τίποτε προς δήλωση nothing to declare

τις tis them

ΤΜΗΜΑ τμήμα (το) tmima (to) department

το to to in; it; the; per

τοις εκατό tis ekato per cent

ΤΟΙΣ ΜΕΤΡΗΤΟΙΣ τοις μετρητοίς cash only, no credit cards

τοίχος (ο) tikhos (o) wall

ΤΟ ΚΑΤΑΣΤΗΜΑ ΜΕΤΑΦΕΡΘΗΚΕ ΕΙΣ... το κατάστημα μεταφέρθηκε εις... we have moved to...

ΤΟ ΚΟΜΜΑΤΙ το κομμάτι per item

ΤΟΚΟΣ τόκος (ο) tokos (o) interest

τολμάω tolmao dare (*verb*)

τον ton him; the

ΤΟΞΙΚΟ τοξικό toxic

ΤΟΠΙΚΗ ΩΡΑ τοπική ώρα local time

ΤΟΠΙΚΟ (ΤΗΛΕΦΩΝΗΜΑ) τοπικό (τηλεφώνημα) (το) topiko tilefonima (to) local call

τοπίο (το) topio (to) landscape

τόσο toso so (much); that much

τότε toteh then

του too his; its; to him

ΤΟΥΑΛΕΤΑ τουαλέτα (η) tooaleta (i) toilet, rest room

ΤΟΥΑΛΕΤΑ ΤΩΝ ΓΥΝΑΙΚΩΝ τουαλέτα των γυναικών (η) tooaleta ton yinekon (i) ladies' toilet, ladies' room

ΤΟΥΑΛΕΤΕΣ τουαλέτες tooaletes toilets, rest room

τουλάχιστον toolakhiston at least

του οποίου too opioo whose

τουρίστας (ο) tooristas (o) tourist

ΤΟΥΡΙΣΤΙΚΗ ΑΣΤΥΝΟΜΙΑ Τουριστική Αστυνομία (η) Tooristiki Astinomia (i) Tourist Police

τουριστικός οδηγός (ο) tooristikos othigos (o) guidebook

τουρίστρια (η) tooristria (i) tourist

ΤΟΥΡΚΑΛΑ τουρκάλα (η) toorkala (i) Turk

ΤΟΥΡΚΙΑ Τουρκία (η) Toorkia (i) Turkey

Τούρκος (ο) Toorkos (o) Turk

ΤΟΥΡΚΙΚΟΣ Τουρκικός Toorkikos Turkish (*adj*)

τους toos them; to them

τραβάω travao pull (*verb*)

τραγούδι (το) tragoothi (to) song

τραγουδώ tragootho sing

ΤΡΑΠΕΖΑΡΙΑ τραπεζαρία (η)
trapezaria (i) dining room

ΤΡΑΠΕΖΑ τράπεζα (η) trapeza (i)
bank

τραπέζι (το) trapezi (to) table

τραπεζομάντηλο (το)
trapezomandilo (to) tablecloth

τραυματίζομαι travmatizomeh
hurt, injure

τραυματισμένος travmatismenos
injured

τρελλός trelos mad

ΤΡΕΝΟ τρένο (το) treno (to)
train

τρέχω trekho run (verb)

τρία tria three

τριακόσια triakosia
three hundred

τριάντα trianda thirty

τριαντάφυλλο (το) triandafilo (to)
rose

ΤΡΙΚΛΙΝΟ ΔΩΜΑΤΙΟ τρίκλινο
δωμάτιο (το) triklino thomatio (to)
triple room

ΤΡΙΤΗ Τρίτη (η) Triti (i) Tuesday

ΤΡΙΤΗ ΘΕΣΗ τρίτη θέση
third class

τρίτος tritos third

τρόλλεϋ (το) troleh-i (to) trolley,
trolleybus

τρομερός tromeros tremendous

ΤΡΟΦΗ ΓΙΑ ΔΙΑΒΗΤΙΚΟΥΣ
τροφή γιά διαβητικούς trofi ya
thiavitikoos diabetic foods

τροφική δηλητηρίαση (η) trofiki
thilitiriasi (i) food poisoning

ΤΡΟΧΑΙΑ τροχαία (η)
traffic police

τροχονόμος (ο) trokhonomos (o)
traffic warden

τροχόσπιτο (το) trokhospito (to)
caravan, (US) trailer

ΤΡΟΧΟΣΠΙΤΑ τροχόσπιτα (το)
caravans, (US) trailers

τρύπα (η) tripa (i) hole

τρώω troo eat; have dinner

τσαγιέρα (η) tsayera (i) teapot

ΤΣΑΓΚΑΡΗΣ τσαγκάρης (ο)
tsangaris (o) shoe repairer's

τσάντα (η) tsanda (i) bag; handbag,
(US) purse

ΤΣΑΝΤΕΣ ΜΠΑΝΙΟΥ τσάντες
μπάνιου beach bags

τσέπη (η) tsepi (i) pocket

ΤΣΙΓΑΡΟ τσιγάρο (το) tsigaro (to)
cigarette

τσίμπημα (το) tsibima (to)
bite (insect)

τσιμπιδάκι (το) tsibithaki (to)
tweezers

τσιμπώ tsibo sting (verb)

ΤΣΙΠΣ τσιπς (τα) tsips (ta) crisps,
(US) potato chips

ΤΣΙΧΛΑ τσίχλα (η) tsikhla (i)
chewing gum

τσόκ (το) tsok (to) choke (on car)

τσούχτρα (η) tsookhtra (i) jellyfish

τυλίγω tiligo wrap (verb)

τυφλός tiflos blind

τύχη (η) tikhi (i) luck

καλή τύχη! kali tikhi! good luck!

των ton of them

τώρα tora now

Υ

υαλοκαθαριστήρας (ο)
ialokaτHaristiras (o)
windscreen wiper

υγεία: στην υγειά σας/σου! stin iya
sas/soo! your health!, cheers!

υγιής iyi-is healthy

ΥΓΡΑΕΡΙΟ υγραέριο (το) igraerio
(to) camping gas

υγρός igros damp, wet

ΥΔΡΑΥΛΙΚΑ υδραυλικά (τα)
ithravlika (ta) plumber

ΥΔΡΑΥΛΙΚΟΣ υδραυλικός (ο)
ithravlikos (o) plumber

υπάρχει iparkhi there is

υπάρχουν iparkhoon there are

**ΥΠΕΡΑΣΤΙΚΟ
(ΤΗΛΕΦΩΝΗΜΑ)
υπεραστικό (τηλεφώνημα)
(το)** iperastiko tilefonima (to)
long-distance call, international
call

υπερβάλλω ipervallo exaggerate

υπέρβαρο (το) ipervaro (to)
excess baggage

υπερβολικά ipervolika too

υπερήφανος iperifanos proud

**ΥΠΕΡΠΟΛΥΤΕΛΕΙΑΣ
υπερπολυτελειας**
five-star **(hotel)**

υπεύθυνος ipefτHinos responsible

ΥΠΗΡΕΣΙΑ υπηρεσία (η) ipiresia
(i) service

ύπνο: πάω για ύπνο pao ya ipno
go to bed

υπνοδωμάτιο (το) ipnothomatio (to)
bedroom

ύπνος (ο) ipnos (o) sleep

**ΥΠΝΩΤΙΚΟ ΧΑΠΙ υπνωτικό
χάπι (το)** ipnotiko khapi (to)
sleeping pill

ΥΠΟΓΕΙΑ ΔΙΑΒΑΣΗ ΠΕΖΩΝ
υπόγεια διάβαση πεζών (η)
pedestrian subway

ΥΠΟΓΕΙΟ υπόγειο (το) ipo-yio
(to) basement

ΥΠΟΓΕΙΟΣ υπόγειος (ο) ipo-yios
(o) underground, (US) subway

υπογράφω ipografo sign (verb)

ΥΠΟΔΗΜΑΤΑ υποδήματα (τα)
ipothimata (ta) shoes

ΥΠΟΔΗΜΑΤΑ ΓΥΝΑΙΚΕΙΑ
υποδήματα γυναικεία ipothimata
yinekia ladies' shoes

ΥΠΟΔΗΜΑΤΟΠΟΙΕΙΟ
υποδηματοποιείο (το)
ipothimatopi-io (to) shoe shop

υπολογιστής (ο) ipolo-yistis (o)
computer

υπόλοιπο (το) ipolipo (to) rest,
remainder

υπόσχομαι iposkhomeh promise
(verb)

ΥΠΟΥΡΓΕΙΟ υπουργείο (το)
ministry

ύφασμα (το) ifasma (to) material

ΥΦΑΣΜΑΤΑ υφάσματα ifasmata
clothing; cloth, material

Φ

ΦΑΓΗΤΟ φαγητό (το) fayito (to)
food; meal; lunch

φαγούρα (η) fagoora (i) itch

φάκελος (ο) fakelos (o) envelope

ΦΑΚΟΙ ΕΠΑΦΗΣ φακοί επαφής
(οι) faki epafis (i) contact lenses

φακός (ο) fakos (o) lens; torch

φαλακρός falakros bald

φαλλοκράτης (ο) falokratis (o)
male chauvinist

φανάρια τροχαίας (τα) fanaria
trokheas (ta) traffic lights

φανταστικός fandastikos fantastic

ΦΑΡΜΑΚΕΙΟ φαρμακείο
(το) farmakio (to) chemist's,
pharmacy

φάρμακο (το) farmako (to)
medicine

φαρμακοποιός (ο) farmakopios (o)
chemist, pharmacist

φασαρία (η) fasaria (i) noise

ΦΕΒΡΟΥΑΡΙΟΣ Φεβρουάριος
(ο) Fevrooarios (o) February

φεγγάρι (το) fengari (to) moon

φεμινίστρια (η) feministria (i)
feminist

φερμουάρ (το) fermooar (to) zip

φέρνω ferno bring

ΦΕΡΡΥ ΜΠΩΤ φέρρυ μπωτ (το)
feri bot (to) ferry

Travel tip The extensive
network of Aegean ferries,
catamarans and hydrofoils is
inexpensive and indispensable for hopping between the
sixty-plus inhabited islands,
but planes can save literally days of travel for longer
distances: Athens–Rhodes
is just two hours return by
plane, but 28 hours by boat.

φέτα (η) feta (i) slice

φεύγω fevgo go away

φθινόπωρο (το) fThinoporo (to)
autumn, (US) fall

φίδι (το) fíthi (to) snake

φιλενάδα (η) filenatha (i) girlfriend; friend

φιλί (το) filí (to) kiss

ΦΙΛΜ φιλμ (το) film (to) film, movie

ΦΙΛΟΔΩΡΗΜΑ φιλοδώρημα (το) filothorima (to) service charge; tip

φιλοξενία (η) filoxenía (i) hospitality

φιλοξενούμενη (η) filoxenoomeni (i) guest

φιλοξενούμενος (ο) filoxenoomenos (o) guest

φίλος (ο) fílos (o) boyfriend; friend

φιλοφρόνηση (η) filofronisi (i) compliment

φίλτρο (το) fíltro (to) filter

φιλώ filó kiss (verb)

φλας (το) flas (to) flash; indicator

φλέβα (η) fleva (i) vein

φλυτζάνι (το) flitzani (to) cup

φοβάμαι fovameh be afraid

φοβερός foveros terrible

φόβος (ο) fovos (o) fear

φοιτητής (ο) fititis (o) student

ΦΟΙΤΗΤΙΚΑ ΕΙΣΙΤΗΡΙΑ φοιτητικά εισιτήρια fititika isitiria student tickets

φοιτήτρια (η) fititria (i) student

φορά (η) fora (i) time, occasion

φόρεμα (το) forema (to) dress

φορητός υπολογιστής (ο) foritos ipolo-yistis (o) laptop

φορτηγό (το) fortigo (to) lorry

φορτιστής τηλεφώνου (ο) fortistis tilefonoo (o) phone charger

ΦΟΥΑΓΙΕ φουαγιέ (το) fooayeh (to) foyer

ΦΟΥΛ ΠΑΝΣΙΟΝ φουλ πανσιόν (η) fool pansion (i) full board

ΦΟΥΛ-ΣΑΙΖΟΝ φουλ-σαιζόν high season

ΦΟΥΡΝΟΣ φούρνος (ο) foornos (o) baker's; oven

φουσκάλα (η) fooskala (i) blister

φούστα (η) foosta (i) skirt

φρακαρισμένος frakarismenos blocked; stuck

φράκτης (ο) fraktis (o) fence

φρενάρω frenaro brake (verb)

φρένο (το) freno (to) brake

ΦΡΕΣΚΟΣ φρέσκος freskos fresh

φρικτός friktos horrible

φρύδι (το) frithi (to) eyebrow

φτάνει ftani that's enough

φτάνω ftano arrive

φτέρνα (η) fterna (i) heel (of foot)

φτερνίζομαι fternizomeh sneeze (verb)

φτερό (το) ftero (to) wing

ΦΤΗΝΟΣ φτηνός ftinos cheap, inexpensive

φτιάχνω τις βαλίτσες ftiakhno tis valitses pack (verb)

φτυάρι (το) ftiari (to) spade

φτωχός ftokhos poor

φύγε! fiyeh! go away!

φύκια (τα) fikia (ta) seaweed

ΦΥΛΑΚΗ φυλακή (η) filaki (i) prison

ΦΥΛΑΞΗ ΑΠΟΣΚΕΥΩΝ φύλαξη αποσκευών filaxi aposkevon left luggage, baggage check

φύλλο (το) filo (to) leaf

φύλο (το) filo (to) gender

φύση (η) fisi (i) nature

ΦΥΣΙΚΟ ΠΡΟΪΟΝ φυσικό προϊόν natural product

ΦΥΣΙΚΟΣ φυσικός fisikos natural

ΦΥΣΙΚΟ ΧΡΩΜΑ φυσικό χρώμα natural colouring

φυσιολογικός fisioloyikos normal

ΦΥΤΟ φυτό (το) fito (to) plant

φωνάζω fonazo call; shout (*verb*)

φωνή (η) foni (i) voice

ΦΩΣ φως (το) fos (to) light

φώτα (τα) fota (ta) lights (on car)

ΦΩΤΙΑ φωτιά (η) fotia (i) fire

έχεις φωτιά; ekhis fotia? have you got a light?

φωτογραφία (η) fotografia (i) photograph

ΦΩΤΟΓΡΑΦΙΚΑ φωτογραφικά fotografika cameras

φωτογραφική μηχανή (η) fotografiki mikhani (i) camera

φωτόμετρο (το) fotometro (to) light meter

X

χαίρετε khereteh hello

χαλάκι (το) khalaki (to) rug

χαλί (το) khali (to) carpet

χάλια khalia awful

χαμηλά φώτα (τα) khamila fota (ta) sidelights

χαμηλός khamilos low

χαμόγελο (το) khamoyelo (to) smile

χαμογελώ khamoyelo smile (*verb*)

χάνω khano lose; miss

ΧΑΠΙ χάπι (το) khapi (to) pill

χάρηκα! kharika! pleased to meet you!

ΧΑΡΠΙΚ χάρπικ (το) kharpik (to) bleach (for toilet)

ΧΑΡΤΗΣ χάρτης (ο) khartis (o) map

ΧΑΡΤΙ χαρτί (το) kharti (to) paper

χαρτιά (τα) khartia (ta) playing cards

ΧΑΡΤΙ ΑΛΛΗΛΟΓΡΑΦΙΑΣ χαρτί αλληλογραφίας (το) kharti alilografias (to) writing paper

ΧΑΡΤΙΚΑ χαρτικά (τα) khartika (ta) stationery

ΧΑΡΤΙ ΠΕΡΙΤΥΛΙΓΜΑΤΟΣ χαρτί περιτυλίγματος kharti peritiligmatos wrapping paper

ΧΑΡΤΙ ΥΓΕΙΑΣ χαρτί υγείας kharti iyias toilet paper

ΧΑΡΤΟΜΑΝΤΗΛΑ χαρτομάντηλα (τα) khartomandila (ta) tissues, Kleenex

χαρτόνι (το) khartoni (to) cardboard

χαρτονόμισμα khartonomisma banknote, (US) bill

ΧΑΡΤΟΠΩΛΕΙΟ χαρτοπωλείο (το) khartopolio (to) stationer's

χαρτοφύλακας (ο) khartofilakas (o) briefcase

ΧΑΣΑΠΗΣ χασάπης (ο) khasapis (o) butcher's

χείλι (το) khili (to) lip

ΧΕΙΜΕΡΙΝΟΣ χειμερινός khimerinos (winter) cinema/movie theater

χειμώνας (ο) khimonas (o) winter

ΧΕΙΡΟΠΟΙΗΤΟ χειροποίητο khiropi-ito handmade

χειρότερος khiroteros worse

χειρότερος (ο) khiroteros (o) worst

ΧΕΙΡΟΤΕΧΝΙΑ χειροτεχνία (η) crafts

χειρόφρενο (το) khirofreno (to) handbrake

χέρι (το) kheri (to) arm; hand

χερούλι (το) kherooli (to) handle

χήρα (η) khira (i) widow

χήρος (ο) khiros (o) widower

χθες khTHes yesterday

ΧΙΛ. χιλ. thousand, thousands

ΧΙΛΙΑ χίλια khilia thousand, thousands

ΧΙΛΙΑΔΕΣ χιλιάδες khiliathes thousand, thousands

χιλιόμετρο (το) khiliometro (to) kilometre

χιούμορ (το) khioomor (to) humour

χλιαρός khliaros lukewarm; cool

ΧΛΩΡΙΝΗ χλωρίνη (η) khlorini (i) bleach

χόμπυ (το) khobi (to) hobby

ΧΟΝΔΡΙΚΗΣ χονδρικής wholesale

χορεύω khorevo dance (*verb*)

χορός (ο) khoros (o) dance

χορτάρι (το) khortari (to) grass

χορτοφαγικός khortofayikos vegetarian

> **Travel tip** Vegetarians may experience some difficulties in Greece, and will often have to assemble a meal from various appetizers. Many supposed "vegetable" dishes are cooked in stock or have pieces of meat added, but vegetarian restaurants are on the increase in tourist areas.

χορτοφάγος (ο/η) khortofagos (o/i) vegetarian

χρειάζομαι khriazomeh need (*verb*)

ΧΡΗΜΑΤΙΣΤΗΡΙΟ χρηματιστήριο (το) khrimatistirio (to) currency exchange; stock exchange

χρηματοπιστωτική κρίση (η) khrimatopistotiki krisi (i) credit crunch

χρήση (η) khrisi (i) use

χρησιμοποιώ khrisimopio use (*verb*)

χρήσιμος khrisimos useful

Χριστούγεννα (τα) KHristooyena (ta) Christmas

Καλά Χριστούγεννα! Kala KHristooyena! Happy Christmas!

χρονιά (η) khronia (i) year

Χρόνια Πολλά! khronia pola! Happy Birthday!

του χρόνου too khronoo next year

πόσο χρονών είσαι; poso
khron**o**n **i**seh? how old are you?

χρόνος (ο) khr**o**nos (o) time; year

ΧΡΥΣΟΣ χρυσός (ο) khris**o**s (o)
gold

**ΧΡΥΣΟΣ ΟΔΗΓΟΣ χρυσός
οδηγός (ο)** khris**o**s oth**i**gos (o)
yellow pages

ΧΡΥΣΟΧΟΕΙΟ χρυσοχοείο (το)
khrisokho**i**o (to) jeweller's

χρώμα (το) khr**o**ma (to) colour

**ΧΡΩΜΑΤΑ - ΣΙΔΕΡΙΚΑ
χρώματα - σιδερικά**
paint and hardware store

χτένα (η) kht**e**na (i) comb

χτυπώ kht**i**po hit (*verb*)

χώμα (το) kh**o**ma (to) earth

χώρα (η) kh**o**ra (i) country

χωράφι (το) khor**a**fi (to) field

**ΧΩΡΗΤΙΚΟΤΗΤΟΣ...
ΑΤΟΜΩΝ χωρητικότητος...
ατόμων** max load… persons

χωριό (το) khor**i**o (to) village

χωρίς khor**i**s without

**ΧΩΡΙΣ ΕΙΣΠΡΑΚΤΟΡΑ
χωρίς εισπράκτορα**
no ticket collector

χωρισμένος khorism**e**nos divorced

ΧΩΡΙΣ ΜΠΑΝΙΟ χωρίς μπάνιο
khor**i**s b**a**nio without bathroom

ΧΩΡΙΣ ΝΤΟΥΣ χωρίς ντους
khor**i**s doos without shower

**ΧΩΡΙΣ ΣΥΝΤΗΡΗΤΙΚΑ χωρίς
συντηρητικά** no preservatives

χωριστός khorist**o**s separate

ΧΩΡΟΣ ΔΙΑ ΠΟΔΗΛΑΤΕΣ

χώρος διά ποδηλάτες
cycle path

χώρος φύλαξης αποσκευών (ο)
khoros filaxis aposkevon (o)
left luggage, baggage check

ψαλίδι (το) psalithi (to) scissors

ΨΑΡΑΔΙΚΟ ψαράδικο (το)
psarathiko (to) fishmonger's

ψάρεμα (το) psarema (to) fishing

**ΨΑΡΟΤΑΒΕΡΝΑ ψαροταβέρνα
(η)** psarotaverna (i) restaurant
specializing in seafood

ψάχνω psakhno look for

ψέματα: λέω ψέματα leo psemata
lie **(say untruth)**

ψεύτικος pseftikos false

ψήνω psino bake

ΨΗΣΤΑΡΙΑ ψησταριά (η)
psistaria (i) restaurant
specializing in charcoal-grilled
food

ψιλά (τα) psila (ta) small change

ΨΙΛΙΚΑ ψιλικά (τα) psilika (ta)
small shop

ψυγείο (το) psiyio (to) fridge

ψυγείο αυτοκινήτου (το) psiyio
aftokinitoo (to) radiator **(of car)**

ΨΩΜΑΔΙΚΟ ψωμάδικο
psomathiko baker's

ψωμάς (ο) psomas (o) baker

ψηλός psilos high; tall

ψώνια (τα) psonia (ta) shopping
 πάω για ψώνια pao ya psonia
 go shopping

ΩΘΗΣΑΤΕ ωθήσατε push

ώμος (ο) omos (o) shoulder

ώρα (η) ora (i) hour
 τι ώρα είναι; ti ora ineh?
 what time is it?
 σε λίγη ώρα seh liyi ora soon
 στην ώρα του stin ora too
 on time
 ωραίος oreos beautiful;
 handsome; lovely

**ΩΡΕΣ ΕΠΙΣΚΕΨΕΩΣ ώρες
 επισκέψεως** visiting hours

**ΩΡΕΣ ΛΕΙΤΟΥΡΓΕΙΑΣ ώρες
 λειτουργείας** opening hours

ως os as, since

**ΩΤΟΡΙΝΟΛΑΡΥΓΓΟΛΟΓΟΣ
 ωτορινολαρυγγολόγος (ο/η)**
 ear, nose and throat specialist

ωτοστόπ (το) otostop (to)
 hitchhiking

ωτοστόπ: κάνω ωτοστόπ kano
 otostop hitchhike

A
B
Γ
Δ
E
Z
H
Θ
I
K
Λ
M
N
Ξ
O
Π
P
Σ
T
Y
Φ
X
Ψ
Ω

MENU READER

Food

Essential terms

bread to psomi
butter to vootiro
cup to flidzani
dessert to glikisma
fish to psari
fork to pirooni
glass to potiri
knife to makheri
main course to kirio piato
meat to kreas
menu to menoo
pepper to piperi
plate to piato

salad i salata
salt to alati
set menu to tabl-dot
soup i soopa
spoon to kootali
starter to proto piato
table to trapezi

another..., please ali mia...,
    parakalo
excuse me! parakalo
could I have the bill, please?
    boro na ekho ton logariasmo,
    parakalo?

A–Ω

ΑΓΓΙΝΑΡΕΣ ΑΥΓΟΛΕΜΟΝΟ
αγγινάρες αυγολέμονο aginares
avgolemono artichokes in egg
and lemon sauce

ΑΓΓΟΥΡΑΚΙΑ αγγουράκια
agoorakia cucumbers

ΑΓΓΟΥΡΙ αγγούρι agoori
cucumber

ΑΓΓΟΥΡΙΑ ΚΑΙ ΝΤΟΜΑΤΕΣ
ΣΑΛΑΤΑ αγγούρια και
ντομάτες σαλάτα agooria keh
domates salata cucumber and
tomato salad

ΑΚΤΙΝΙΔΙΟ ακτινίδιο aktinithio
kiwi fruit

ΑΛΑΤΙ αλάτι alati salt

ΑΛΕΥΡΙ αλεύρι alevri flour

ΑΛΕΥΡΙ ΚΑΛΑΜΠΟΚΙΟΥ
αλεύρι καλαμποκιού alevri
kalabokioo cornflour

ΑΛΕΥΡΙ ΣΤΑΡΙΟΥ
αλεύρι σταριού alevri starioo
wheat flour

ΑΛΛΑΝΤΙΚΑ αλλαντικά
alandika sausages, salami,
ham etc

ΑΜΥΓΔΑΛΑ αμύγδαλα amigthala
almonds

ΑΜΥΓΔΑΛΩΤΑ αμυγδαλωτά
amigthalota macaroons;
almond pastries

ΑΝΑΝΑΣ ανανάς ananas
pineapple

ΑΝΘΟΤΥΡΟ ανθότυρο
anThotiro type of cottage
cheese

ΑΝΤΖΟΥΓΙΑ ΣΤΟ ΛΑΔΙ
αντζούγια στο λάδι andsoo-yia
sto lathi anchovies in oil

ΑΡΑΚΑΣ αρακάς arakas peas

ΑΡΑΚΑΣ ΛΑΔΕΡΟΣ αρακάς
λαδερός arakas latheros peas
cooked with tomato and oil

ΑΡΑΚΑΣ ΣΩΤΕ αρακάς σωτέ
arakas soteh peas fried in
butter

ΑΡΝΑΚΙ αρνάκι arnaki lamb

ΑΡΝΑΚΙ ΕΞΟΧΙΚΟ
αρνάκι εξοχικό arnaki exokhiko
leg of lamb baked in
greaseproof paper

ΑΡΝΑΚΙ ΜΕ ΜΠΑΜΙΕΣ
αρνάκι με μπάμιες arnaki meh
bami-es lamb and okra stew

ΑΡΝΑΚΙ ΜΕ ΠΑΤΑΤΕΣ ΣΤΟ
ΦΟΥΡΝΟ αρνάκι με πατάτες
στο φούρνο arnaki meh patates
sto foorno roast lamb and
potatoes

ΑΡΝΑΚΙ ΤΑΣ ΚΕΜΠΑΠ
αρνάκι τας κεμπάπ arnaki tas
kebap lamb in tomato sauce

ΑΡΝΑΚΙ ΤΗΣ ΣΟΥΒΛΑΣ
αρνάκι της σούβλας arnaki tis
soovlas spit-roast lamb

ΑΡΝΑΚΙ ΦΡΙΚΑΣΕ
αρνάκι φρικασέ με μαρούλια
arnaki frikaseh meh maroolia
lamb and lettuce in egg and
lemon sauce

ΑΡΝΙ αρνί arni mutton, lamb

ΑΡΝΙ ΓΕΜΙΣΤΟ ΣΤΟ
ΦΟΥΡΝΟ αρνί γεμιστό στο
φούρνο arni yemisto sto foorno
oven-cooked stuffed lamb

ΑΡΝΙ ΕΞΟΧΙΚΟ αρνί εξοχικό
arni exohiko lamb cooked in
greased foil with cheese and
spices

ΑΡΝΙ ΚΟΚΚΙΝΙΣΤΟ
αρνί κοκκινιστό arni kokinisto
lamb in tomato sauce

**ΑΡΝΙ ΛΑΔΟΡΙΓΑΝΗ ΣΤΟ
ΦΟΥΡΝΟ** αρνί λαδορίγανη
στο φούρνο arni lathorigani sto
foorno oven-cooked lamb with
oil and oregano

ΑΡΝΙ ΜΕ ΑΡΑΚΑ αρνί με
αρακά arni meh araka
lamb with peas

**ΑΡΝΙ ΜΕ ΚΟΛΟΚΥΘΑΚΙΑ
ΑΥΓΟΛΕΜΟΝΟ** αρνί με
κολοκυθάκια αυγολέμονο
arni meh kolokiTHakia
avgolemono lamb with
courgettes/zucchini in egg
and lemon sauce

ΑΡΝΙ ΜΕ ΚΡΙΘΑΡΑΚΙ
αρνί με κριθαράκι arni meh
kriTHaraki lamb with pasta

ΑΡΝΙ ΜΕ ΜΑΚΑΡΟΝΙΑ
αρνί με μακαρόνια arni meh
makaronia lamb with spaghetti

ΑΡΝΙ ΜΕ ΜΕΛΙΤΖΑΝΕΣ
αρνί με μελιτζάνες arni
meh melitzanes lamb with
aubergines/eggplants

ΑΡΝΙ ΜΕ ΜΠΑΜΙΕΣ
αρνί με μπάμιες arni meh
bami-es lamb with okra

ΑΡΝΙ ΜΕ ΠΑΤΑΤΕΣ ΡΑΓΟΥ
αρνί με πατάτες ραγού
arni meh patates ragoo
lamb with potatoes cooked in
tomato sauce

**ΑΡΝΙ ΜΕ ΦΑΣΟΛΑΚΙΑ
ΦΡΕΣΚΑ** αρνί με φασολάκια
φρέσκα arni meh fasolakia freska
lamb with runner beans

ΑΡΝΙ ΜΕ ΧΥΛΟΠΙΤΕΣ αρνί
με χυλοπίτες arni meh khilopites
lamb with a type of lasagne

**ΑΡΝΙ ΜΠΟΥΤΙ ΣΤΟ
ΦΟΥΡΝΟ** αρνί μπούτι στο
φούρνο arni booti sto foorno
oven-cooked leg of lamb

ΑΡΝΙ ΜΠΡΙΖΟΛΕΣ
αρνί μπριζόλες arni brizoles
lamb chops

ΑΡΝΙ ΠΑΪΔΑΚΙΑ
αρνί παϊδάκια arni paithakia
grilled lamb chops

ΑΡΝΙ ΤΑΣ ΚΕΜΠΑΠ
αρνί τας κεμπάπ arni tas kebab
chopped lamb kebab with
tomato sauce

**ΑΡΝΙ ΤΗΣ ΚΑΤΣΑΡΟΛΑΣ
ΜΕ ΠΑΤΑΤΕΣ** αρνί της
κατσαρόλας με πατάτες arni
tis katsarolas meh patates
casseroled lamb cooked with
potatoes

ΑΡΝΙ ΤΗΣ ΣΟΥΒΛΑΣ
αρνί της σούβλας arni tis soovlas
spit-roast lamb

ΑΡΝΙ ΦΡΙΚΑΣΕ
αρνί φρικασέ arni frikaseh
lamb fricassee

ΑΣΤΑΚΟΣ αστακός
astakos lobster

**ΑΣΤΑΚΟΣ ΜΕ
ΛΑΔΟΛΕΜΟΝΟ** αστακός
με λαδολέμονο astakos meh
latholemono lobster cooked in
lemon and oil sauce

ΑΣΤΑΚΟΣ ΜΕ ΜΑΓΙΟΝΕΖΑ
αστακός με μαγιονέζα
astakos meh mayoneza
lobster with mayonnaise

ΑΤΖΕΜ ΠΙΛΑΦΙ ατζέμ πιλάφι
atzem pilafi rice pilaf

ΑΥΓΑ αυγά avga eggs

ΑΥΓΑ ΒΡΑΣΤΑ αυγά βραστά
avga vrasta boiled eggs

ΑΥΓΑ ΒΡΑΣΤΑ ΣΦΙΧΤΑ αυγά
βραστά σφιχτά avga vrasta
sfikhta hard-boiled eggs

ΑΥΓΑ ΓΕΜΙΣΤΑ αυγά γεμιστά
avga yemista
stuffed eggs

ΑΥΓΑ ΓΕΜΙΣΤΑ ΜΕ
ΜΑΓΙΟΝΕΖΑ αυγά γεμιστά
με μαγιονέζα avga yemista meh
mayoneza stuffed eggs with
mayonnaise

ΑΥΓΑ ΜΑΤΙΑ αυγά μάτια avga
matia fried eggs

ΑΥΓΑ ΜΕΛΑΤΑ αυγά μελάτα
avga melata soft-boiled eggs

ΑΥΓΑ ΜΕ ΜΑΝΙΤΑΡΙΑ αυγά
με μανιτάρια avga meh manitaria
mushroom omelette

ΑΥΓΑ ΜΕ ΜΠΕΙΚΟΝ
αυγά με μπέικον avga meh bacon
bacon and eggs

ΑΥΓΑ ΜΕ ΝΤΟΜΑΤΕΣ
αυγά με ντομάτες avga meh
domates eggs cooked in
tomato sauce

ΑΥΓΑ ΜΕ ΤΥΡΙ αυγά με τυρί
avga meh tiri cheese omelette

ΑΥΓΑ ΟΜΕΛΕΤΑ
αυγά ομελέτα avga omeleta
plain omelette

ΑΥΓΑ ΟΜΕΛΕΤΑ ΜΕ
ΠΑΤΑΤΕΣ αυγά ομελέτα
με πατάτες avga omeleta meh
patates omelette with chips/
fries

ΑΥΓΑ ΠΟΣΕ αυγά ποσέ
avga poseh poached eggs

ΑΥΓΑ ΣΦΙΧΤΑ αυγά σφιχτά
avga sfikhta hard-boiled eggs

ΑΥΓΑ ΤΗΓΑΝΗΤΑ
αυγά τηγανητά avga tiganita
fried eggs

ΑΥΓΑ Ω ΓΚΡΑΤΕΝ
αυγά ω γκρατέν avga o graten
eggs au gratin

ΑΥΓΟ αυγό avgo egg

ΑΥΓΟΛΕΜΟΝΟ
αυγολέμονο avgolemono
egg and lemon sauce

ΑΥΓΟΛΕΜΟΝΟ ΣΟΥΠΑ
αυγολέμονο σούπα avgolemono
soopa chicken broth with egg
and lemon

ΑΥΓΟΤΑΡΑΧΟ αυγοτάραχο
avgotarakho roe

ΑΧΛΑΔΙ αχλάδι akhlathi pear

ΒΑΝΙΛΙΑ βανίλια vanilia vanilla

ΒΑΤΟΜΟΥΡΟ βατόμουρο
vatomooro blackberry

ΒΕΡΙΚΟΚΟ βερίκοκο
verikoko apricot

ΒΟΔΙΝΟ βοδινό vothino beef

ΒΟΔΙΝΟ ΒΡΑΣΤΟ
βοδινό βραστό vothino vrasto
boiled beef

ΒΟΔΙΝΟ ΡΟΣΜΠΙΦ
βοδινό ροσμπίφ vothino rosbif
roast beef

BOTANA βότανα votana herbs

ΒΟΥΤΥΡΟ βούτυρο vootiro butter

ΒΡΑΣΤΟ βραστό vrasto boiled

ΒΥΣΣΙΝΟ βύσσινο visino
sour cherries

ΓΑΛΑΚΤΟΜΠΟΥΡΕΚΟ
γαλακτομπούρεκο
galaktobooreko cream-filled
sweet filo pastry with honey

ΓΑΛΟΠΟΥΛΑ γαλοπούλα
galopoola turkey

ΓΑΛΟΠΟΥΛΑ ΓΕΜΙΣΤΗ
γαλοπούλα γεμιστή galopoola
yemisti stuffed turkey

ΓΑΛΟΠΟΥΛΑ ΚΟΚΚΙΝΙΣΤΗ
γαλοπούλα κοκκινιστή
galopoola kokinisti turkey
cooked with tomatoes

**ΓΑΛΟΠΟΥΛΑ ΨΗΤΗ ΣΤΟ
ΦΟΥΡΝΟ** γαλοπούλα ψητή
στο φούρνο galopoola psiti sto
foorno roast turkey

ΓΑΡΔΟΥΜΠΑ γαρδούμπα
garthoomba spit-roast rolled
lamb offal

ΓΑΡΙΔΕΣ γαρίδες garithes
prawns

ΓΑΡΙΔΕΣ ΒΡΑΣΤΕΣ
γαρίδες βραστές garithes vrastes
boiled shrimps

ΓΑΡΙΔΕΣ ΚΟΚΤΑΙΗΛ γαρίδες
κοκταίηλ garithes cocktail
shrimp cocktail

ΓΑΡΙΔΕΣ ΠΙΛΑΦΙ γαρίδες
πιλάφι garithes pilafi shrimp pilaf

ΓΑΡΙΔΟΠΙΛΑΦΟ γαριδοπίλαφο
garithopilafo prawns with rice
cooked in butter

ΓΑΡΝΙΤΟΥΡΑ γαρνιτούρα
garnitoora vegetables

ΓΑΡΝΙΤΟΥΡΑ ΚΑΡΟΤΑ ΣΩΤΕ
γαρνιτούρα καρότα σωτέ
garnitoora karota soteh
sautéed carrots

**ΓΑΡΝΙΤΟΥΡΑ ΚΟΥΝΟΥΠΙΔΙ
ΣΩΤΕ** γαρνιτούρα κουνουπίδι
σωτέ garnitoora koonoopithi soteh
sautéed cauliflower

ΓΑΡΝΙΤΟΥΡΑ ΠΑΤΑΤΕΣ
γαρνιτούρα πατάτες
garnitoora patates potatoes

**ΓΑΡΝΙΤΟΥΡΑ ΣΠΑΝΑΚΙ
ΣΩΤΕ** γαρνιτούρα σπανάκι
σωτέ garnitoora spanaki soteh
sautéed spinach

**ΓΑΡΝΙΤΟΥΡΑ ΦΑΣΟΛΙΑ
ΠΡΑΣΙΝΑ ΣΩΤΕ** γαρνιτούρα
φασόλια πράσινα σωτέ
garnitoora fasolia prasina soteh
sautéed runner beans

ΓΕΜΙΣΤΑ γεμιστά yemista
stuffed, usually with rice and/
or minced meat

ΓΕΜΙΣΤΕΣ γεμιστές yemistes
stuffed vegetables

ΓΙΑΛΑΝΤΖΗ ΝΤΟΛΜΑΔΕΣ
γιαλαντζή ντολμάδες
yalantzi dolmathes vine leaves
stuffed with rice

ΓΙΑΟΥΡΤΙ γιαούρτι ya-oorti
yoghurt

ΓΙΓΑΝΤΕΣ γίγαντες
yigandes white haricot beans;
butter beans

ΓΙΟΥΒΑΡΛΑΚΙΑ γιουβαρλάκια
yoovarlakia meatballs, rice and
seasoning in a sauce

ΓΙΟΥΒΑΡΛΑΚΙΑ ΑΥΓΟΛΕΜΟΝΟ
γιουβαρλάκια αυγολέμονο
yoovarlakia avgolemono
meatballs with egg and lemon
sauce

ΓΙΟΥΒΑΡΛΑΚΙΑ ΜΕ ΣΑΛΤΣΑ ΝΤΟΜΑΤΑΣ
γιουβαρλάκια με σάλτσα
ντομάτας yoovarlakia meh saltsa
domatas meatballs with rice
cooked with tomatoes

ΓΙΟΥΒΕΤΣΙ γιουβέτσι yoovetsi
oven-roasted lamb with pasta

ΓΚΡΕΙΠΦΡΟΥΤ γκρέιπφρουτ
grapefruit grapefruit

ΓΛΥΚΑ γλυκά glika
cakes, desserts

ΓΛΥΚΙΣΜΑ γλύκισμα glikisma
dessert

ΓΛΥΚΟ γλυκό gliko
sweet, dessert

ΓΛΥΚΟ ΒΥΣΣΙΝΟ
γλυκό βύσσινο gliko visino
candied cherries in syrup

ΓΛΥΚΟ ΚΑΡΥΔΑΚΙ ΦΡΕΣΚΟ
γλυκό καρυδάκι φρέσκο gliko
karithaki fresko dried fresh
green walnuts in syrup

ΓΛΥΚΟ ΜΑΣΤΙΧΑ
γλυκό μαστίχα gliko mastikha
vanilla-flavoured fudge

ΓΛΥΚΟ ΜΕΛΙΤΖΑΝΑΚΙ
γλυκό μελιτζανάκι gliko
melitzanaki dried small
aubergine/eggplant in syrup

ΓΛΥΚΟ ΝΕΡΑΝΤΖΑΚΙ γλυκό
νεραντζάκι gliko nerantzaki
dried bitter orange in syrup

ΓΛΥΚΟ ΣΥΚΟ γλυκό σύκο
gliko siko candied figs in syrup

ΓΛΥΚΟ ΣΥΚΟ ΦΡΕΣΚΟ
γλυκό σύκο φρέσκο gliko siko
fresko dried fig in syrup

ΓΛΥΚΟ ΤΡΙΑΝΤΑΦΥΛΛΟ
γλυκό τριαντάφυλλο gliko
triandafilo dried rose petals
in syrup

ΓΛΩΣΣΑ γλώσσα glosa
sole; tongue

ΓΛΩΣΣΕΣ ΤΗΓΑΝΗΤΕΣ
γλώσσες τηγανητές gloses
tiganites fried sole

ΓΟΥΡΟΥΝΟΠΟΥΛΟ ΣΤΟ ΦΟΥΡΝΟ ΜΕ ΠΑΤΑΤΕΣ
γουρουνόπουλο στο φούρνο
με πατάτες gooroonopoolo
sto foorno meh patates oven-
cooked pork with potatoes

ΓΡΑΒΙΕΡΑ γραβιέρα gravi-era
hard cheese like gruyère

ΓΡΑΝΙΤΑ γρανίτα granita
sorbet

ΓΡΑΝΙΤΑ ΛΕΜΟΝΙ
γρανίτα λεμόνι granita lemoni
lemon sorbet

ΓΡΑΝΙΤΑ ΜΠΑΝΑΝΑ
γρανίτα μπανάνα granita banana
banana sorbet

ΓΡΑΝΙΤΑ ΠΟΡΤΟΚΑΛΙ
γρανίτα πορτοκάλι granita
portokali orange sorbet

ΓΡΑΝΙΤΑ ΦΡΑΟΥΛΕΣ
γρανίτα φράουλες granita
fraooles strawberry sorbet

ΔΑΜΑΣΚΗΝΑ δαμάσκηνα
thamaskina prunes

ΔΑΜΑΣΚΗΝΟ δαμάσκηνο
thamaskino plum

ΔΙΠΛΕΣ δίπλες thiples pancakes

ΕΛΑΙΟΛΑΔΟ ελαιόλαδο
eleolatho olive oil

ΕΛΙΕΣ ελιές eli-es olives

> **Travel tip** When buying
> olives, look out for fat
> Kalamata or Amfissa ones
> – they're more expensive,
> but tastier. Locally gathered
> olives, especially the slightly
> shrivelled *throumbes* or fully
> ripened, ground-gathered
> *hamades*, often have a
> distinctive nutty taste, com-
> pensating for large kernels.

ΕΝΤΟΣΘΙΑ ΑΡΝΙΟΥ
ΛΑΔΟΡΙΓΑΝΗ εντόσθια
αρνιού λαδορίγανη endosthia
arnioo lathorigani lambs' intestines
cooked in lemon and oil

ΕΠΙΔΟΡΠΙΟ επιδόρπιο
epithorpio dessert

ΕΣΚΑΛΟΠ ΜΕ ΖΑΜΠΟΝ
ΚΑΙ ΣΑΛΤΣΑ ΝΤΟΜΑΤΑΣ
εσκαλόπ με ζαμπόν και σάλτσα
ντομάτας eskalop meh zabon keh
saltsa domatas escalope of veal
with ham and tomato sauce

ΖΑΜΠΟΝ ζαμπόν zabon ham

ΖΑΧΑΡΗ ζάχαρη zakhari sugar

ΖΕΛΕ ζελέ zeleh jelly

ΖΥΜΑΡΙΚΑ ζυμαρικά zimarika
pasta and rice

ΘΑΛΑΣΣΙΝΑ θαλασσινά
THalasina seafood

ΚΑΒΟΥΡΙΑ καβούρια
kavooria crab

ΚΑΚΑΒΙΑ κακαβιά kakavia
mixed fish soup

ΚΑΚΑΒΙΑ ΨΑΡΟΣΟΥΠΑ
κακαβιά ψαρόσουπα
kakavia psarosoopa fish soup

ΚΑΛΑΜΑΡΑΚΙΑ καλαμαράκια
kalamarakia baby squid

ΚΑΛΑΜΑΡΑΚΙΑ ΓΕΜΙΣΤΑ
καλαμαράκια γεμιστά
kalamarakia yemista
stuffed baby squid

ΚΑΛΑΜΑΡΑΚΙΑ ΤΗΓΑΝΗΤΑ
καλαμαράκια τηγανητά
kalamarakia tiganita
fried baby squid

ΚΑΛΑΜΑΡΙΑ καλαμάρια
kalamaria squid

ΚΑΝΑΠΕ καναπέ kanapeh
canapés

ΚΑΝΑΠΕ ΜΕ ΖΑΜΠΟΝ
καναπέ με ζαμπόν kanapeh meh
zabon ham canapés

ΚΑΝΑΠΕ ΜΕ ΚΡΕΑΣ ΨΗΤΟ
καναπέ με κρέας ψητό kanapeh
meh kreas psito meat canapés

ΚΑΝΑΠΕ ΜΕ ΜΑΥΡΟ
ΧΑΒΙΑΡΙ καναπέ με μαύρο
χαβιάρι kanapeh meh mavro
haviari black caviar canapés

ΚΑΝΑΠΕ ΜΕ
ΤΑΡΑΜΟΣΑΛΑΤΑ
καναπέ με ταραμοσαλάτα
kanapeh meh taramosalata
taramosalata canapés

ΚΑΝΕΛΛΑ κανέλλα kanela
cinnamon

**ΚΑΝΕΛΛΟΝΙΑ ΓΕΜΙΣΤΑ
κανελλόνια γεμιστά** kanelonia
yemista stuffed canelloni

ΚΑΝΤΑΪΦΙ κανταΐφι
kanda-ifi shredded and rolled
filo pastry in syrup

ΚΑΠΑΜΑΣ ΑΡΝΙ καπαμάς αρνί
kapamas arni lamb cooked in
spices and tomato sauce

ΚΑΠΝΙΣΤΟ καπνιστό
kapnisto smoked

ΚΑΠΠΑΡΗ κάππαρη
kapari caper

ΚΑΡΑΒΙΔΕΣ καραβίδες
karavithes king prawns;
crayfish

ΚΑΡΟΤΑ καρότα karota carrots

ΚΑΡΠΟΥΖΙ καρπούζι
karpoozi watermelon

ΚΑΡΥΔΙ καρύδι karithi nut

ΚΑΡΥΔΟΠΙΤΤΑ καρυδόπιττα
karithopita walnut cake; cake
with nuts and syrup

ΚΑΡΧΑΡΙΑΣ καρχαρίας
karkharias shark

ΚΑΣΕΡΙ κασέρι kaseri
Cheddar-type cheese

ΚΑΣΤΑΝΑ κάστανα kastana
chestnuts

**ΚΑΣΤΑΝΑ ΓΛΑΣΕ κάστανα
γλασέ** kastana glaseh glazed
chestnuts, marrons glacés

ΚΑΤΑΪΦΙ καταΐφι kata-ifi
shredded filo pastry with
honey and nuts

ΚΑΤΑΛΟΓΟΣ κατάλογος
katalogos menu

ΚΕΙΚ κέικ cake cake

**ΚΕΙΚ ΚΑΝΕΛΛΑΣ
κέικ κανέλλας** cake kanelas
cinammon cake

**ΚΕΙΚ ΜΕ ΑΜΥΓΔΑΛΑ κέικ
με αμύγδαλα** cake meh amigthala
almond cake

**ΚΕΙΚ ΜΕ ΚΑΡΥΔΙΑ ΚΑΙ
ΣΤΑΦΙΔΕΣ κέικ με καρύδια
και σταφίδες** cake meh karithia
keh stafithes nut and sultana
cake

**ΚΕΙΚ ΣΟΚΟΛΑΤΑΣ
κέικ σοκολάτας** cake sokolatas
chocolate cake

**ΚΕΙΚ ΦΡΟΥΤΩΝ κέικ
φρούτων** cake frooton fruit cake

ΚΕΡΑΣΙΑ κεράσια
kerasia cherries

ΚΕΦΑΛΟΤΥΡΙ κεφαλοτύρι
kefalotiri very salty, hard cheese

ΚΕΦΤΕΔΕΣ κεφτέδες
keftethes meatballs

**ΚΕΦΤΕΔΕΣ ΜΕ ΣΑΛΤΣΑ
κεφτέδες με σάλτσα**
keftethes meh saltsa
meatballs in tomato sauce

**ΚΕΦΤΕΔΕΣ ΣΤΟ ΦΟΥΡΝΟ
κεφτέδες στο φούρνο**
keftethes sto foorno
oven-cooked meatballs

**ΚΕΦΤΕΔΕΣ ΤΗΓΑΝΗΤΟΙ
κεφτέδες τηγανητοί**
keftethes tiganiti fried meatballs

ΚΙΜΑΣ κιμάς kimas
minced meat

ΚΛΕΦΤΙΚΟ κλέφτικο kleftiko
meat, potatoes and vegetables
cooked together in a pot or foil

ΚΟΚΚΙΝΙΣΤΟ κοκκινιστό
kokinisto in tomato sauce

ΚΟΚΟΡΕΤΣΙ κοκορέτσι kokoretsi
spit-roast rolled lamb offal

ΚΟΛΙΟΙ κολιοί koli-i mackerel

ΚΟΛΙΟΙ ΨΗΤΟΙ κολιοί ψητοί
koli-i psiti fried mackerel

ΚΟΛΟΚΥΘΑΚΙΑ κολοκυθάκια
kolokiТНakia courgettes/zucchini

**ΚΟΛΟΚΥΘΑΚΙΑ ΓΕΜΙΣΤΑ
ΜΕ ΚΙΜΑ κολοκυθάκια
γεμιστά με κιμά**
kolokiТНakia yemista meh kima
courgettes/zucchini stuffed
with minced meat

**ΚΟΛΟΚΥΘΑΚΙΑ ΓΕΜΙΣΤΑ
ΜΕ ΡΥΖΙ κολοκυθάκια
γεμιστά με ρύζι** kolokiТНakia
yemista meh rizi courgettes/
zucchini stuffed with rice

**ΚΟΛΟΚΥΘΑΚΙΑ ΓΙΑΧΝΙ
κολοκυθάκια γιαχνί** kolokiТНakia
yakhni courgettes/zucchini and
onions in a tomato sauce

**ΚΟΛΟΚΥΘΑΚΙΑ ΛΑΔΕΡΑ
κολοκυθάκια λαδερά**
kolokiТНakia lathera courgettes/
zucchini cooked in oil

**ΚΟΛΟΚΥΘΑΚΙΑ ΜΕ
ΚΡΕΑΣ κολοκυθάκια με
κρέας** kolokiТНakia meh kreas
courgette/zucchini and beef
stew

**ΚΟΛΟΚΥΘΑΚΙΑ ΜΕ
ΠΑΤΑΤΕΣ κολοκυθάκια με
πατάτες** kolokiТНakia meh patates
courgettes/zucchini with
potatoes

ΚΟΛΟΚΥΘΑΚΙΑ ΜΟΥΣΑΚΑΣ

κολοκυθάκια μουσακάς
kolokiТНakia moosakas
courgettes/zucchini with
minced meat and béchamel

**ΚΟΛΟΚΥΘΑΚΙΑ
ΠΑΠΟΥΤΣΑΚΙΑ
κολοκυθάκια παπουτσάκια**
kolokiТНakia papootsakia
courgettes/zucchini with
minced meat and onions

**ΚΟΛΟΚΥΘΑΚΙΑ ΤΗΓΑΝΗΤΑ
κολοκυθάκια τηγανητά**
kolokiТНakia tiganita fried
courgettes/zucchini

**ΚΟΛΟΚΥΘΟΚΕΦΤΕΔΕΣ
κολοκυθοκεφτέδες**
kolokiТНokeftethes fried
courgette/zucchini balls

**ΚΟΛΟΚΥΘΟΤΥΡΟΠΙΤΤΑ
κολοκυθοτυρόπιττα**
kolokiТНotiropita courgette/
zucchini and cheese pie

ΚΟΜΠΟΣΤΑ κομπόστα
kobosta fruit compote

ΚΟΤΑ κότα kota chicken

**ΚΟΤΑ ΒΡΑΣΤΗ
κότα βραστή** kota vrasti
boiled chicken

**ΚΟΤΑ ΨΗΤΗ ΣΤΟ ΦΟΥΡΝΟ
κότα ψητή στο φούρνο** kota psiti
sto foorno roast chicken

**ΚΟΤΑ ΨΗΤΗ ΤΗΣ
ΚΑΤΣΑΡΟΛΑΣ κότα ψητή
της κατσαρόλας** kota psiti tis
katsarolas chicken casserole

**ΚΟΤΑ ΨΗΤΗ ΤΗΣ ΣΟΥΒΛΑΣ
κότα ψητή της σούβλας** kota
psiti tis soovlas spit-roast
chicken

ΚΟΤΟΛΕΤΕΣ ΑΡΝΙΣΙΕΣ ΠΑΝΕ
κοτολέτες αρνίσιες πανέ
kotoletes arnisi-es paneh lamb
cutlets

ΚΟΤΟΛΕΤΕΣ ΜΟΣΧΑΡΙΣΙΕΣ
ΠΑΝΕ **κοτολέτες μοσχαρίσιες**
πανέ kotoletes moskharisi-es
paneh veal cutlets

ΚΟΤΟΠΙΤΤΑ κοτόπιττα
kotopita chicken pie

ΚΟΤΟΠΟΥΛΟ κοτόπουλο
kotopoolo chicken

ΚΟΤΟΠΟΥΛΟ ΓΙΟΥΒΕΤΣΙ
ΜΕ ΧΥΛΟΠΙΤΤΕΣ κοτόπουλο
γιουβέτσι με χυλοπίττες
kotopoolo yioovetsi meh hilopites
chicken with pasta

ΚΟΤΟΠΟΥΛΟ ΚΟΚΚΙΝΙΣΤΟ
κοτόπουλο κοκκινιστό
kotopoolo kokinisto chicken in
tomato sauce

ΚΟΤΟΠΟΥΛΟ ΜΕ ΜΠΑΜΙΕΣ
κοτόπουλο με μπάμιες
kotopoolo meh bami-es
chicken with okra

ΚΟΤΟΠΟΥΛΟ ΜΕ
ΜΠΙΖΕΛΙΑ κοτόπουλο με
μπιζέλια kotopoolo meh bizelia
chicken with peas

ΚΟΤΟΠΟΥΛΟ ΠΑΝΕ
κοτόπουλο πανέ kotopoolo
paneh breaded chicken

ΚΟΤΟΠΟΥΛΟ ΠΙΛΑΦΙ
κοτόπουλο πιλάφι
kotopoolo pilafi chicken pilaf

ΚΟΤΟΠΟΥΛΟ ΤΗΣ
ΣΟΥΒΛΑΣ κοτόπουλο της
σούβλας kotopoolo tis soovlas
spit-roast chicken

ΚΟΤΟΣΟΥΠΑ κοτόσουπα
kotosoopa chicken soup

ΚΟΥΚΙΑ ΛΑΔΕΡΑ
κουκιά λαδερά kookia lathera
broad beans in tomato sauce

ΚΟΥΝΕΛΙ κουνέλι kooneli rabbit

ΚΟΥΝΕΛΙ ΜΕ ΣΑΛΤΣΑ
κουνέλι με σάλτσα kooneli meh
saltsa rabbit with tomato sauce

ΚΟΥΝΕΛΙ ΣΤΙΦΑΔΟ κουνέλι
στιφάδο kooneli stifatho rabbit
with onions

ΚΟΥΝΟΥΠΙΔΙ κουνουπίδι
koonoopithi cauliflower

ΚΟΥΝΟΥΠΙΔΙ ΒΡΑΣΤΟ
ΣΑΛΑΤΑ κουνουπίδι βραστό
σαλάτα koonopithi vrasto salata
boiled cauliflower salad

ΚΟΥΡΑΜΠΙΕΔΕΣ κουραμπιέδες
koorabi-ethes Greek shortbread

ΚΟΥΡΑΜΠΙΕΔΕΣ
ΜΕ ΑΜΥΓΔΑΛΟ
κουραμπιέδες με αμύγδαλο
koorabi-ethes meh amigthalo
shortbread-type biscuits with
sesame seeds and icing sugar

ΚΡΑΚΕΡΣ ΑΛΜΥΡΑ κράκερς
αλμυρά krakers almira
salted crackers

ΚΡΑΣΑΤΟ κρασάτο krasato
cooked in wine sauce

ΚΡΕΑΣ κρέας kreas meat, usually
beef

ΚΡΕΑΣ ΜΕ ΑΝΤΙΔΙΑ
ΑΥΓΟΛΕΜΟΝΟ
κρέας με αντίδια αυγολέμονο
kreas meh antithia avgolemono
beef with endives in egg and
lemon sauce

ΚΡΕΑΣ ΜΕ ΦΑΣΟΛΙΑ ΞΕΡΑ
κρέας με φασόλια ξερά
kreas meh fasolia xera
beef with butter beans

ΚΡΕΑΤΙΚΑ κρεατικά
kreh-atika meat dishes

ΚΡΕΑΤΟΠΙΤΤΑ κρεατόπιττα
kreh-atopita minced meat in
filo pastry

ΚΡΕΜΑ κρέμα krema cream

ΚΡΕΜΑ ΚΑΡΑΜΕΛΕ
κρέμα καραμελέ krema
karameleh crème caramel

ΚΡΕΜΑ ΜΕ ΜΗΛΑ
κρέμα με μήλα krema meh mila
apples with cream

ΚΡΕΜΑ ΜΕ ΜΠΑΝΑΝΕΣ
κρέμα με μπανάνες
krema meh bananes
bananas with cream

ΚΡΕΜΜΥΔΑΚΙΑ ΦΡΕΣΚΑ
κρεμμυδάκια φρέσκα
kremithakia freska spring onions

ΚΡΕΜΜΥΔΙΑ κρεμμύδια
kremithia onions

ΚΡΕΜΜΥΔΟΣΟΥΠΑ
κρεμμυδόσουπα kremithosoopa
onion soup

ΚΡΕΠΑ κρέπα krepa pancake

ΚΡΟΚΕΤΕΣ κροκέτες
kroketes croquettes

ΚΡΟΚΕΤΕΣ ΑΠΟ ΚΡΕΑΣ
κροκέτες από κρέας
kroketes apo kreas meat
croquettes

ΚΡΟΚΕΤΕΣ ΜΕ ΑΥΓΑ ΚΑΙ
ΤΥΡΙ κροκέτες με αυγά και
τυρί kroketes meh avga keh tiri
egg and cheese croquettes

ΚΡΟΚΕΤΕΣ ΜΠΑΚΑΛΙΑΡΟΥ
κροκέτες μπακαλιάρου
kroketes bakaliaroo
cod croquettes

ΚΡΟΚΕΤΕΣ ΠΑΤΑΤΕΣ
κροκέτες πατάτες kroketes
patates potato croquettes

ΚΡΟΥΑΣΑΝ κρουασάν croissants
croissants

ΚΥΔΩΝΙΑ κυδώνια
kithonia quinces

ΚΥΔΩΝΟΠΑΣΤΟ κυδωνόπαστο
kithonopasto thick jelly made
from quince

ΚΥΝΗΓΙ κυνήγι kiniyi game

ΚΥΡΙΟ ΠΙΑΤΟ κύριο πιάτο
kirio piato main course

ΚΩΚ κωκ kok cake with cream
and chocolate topping

ΛΑΓΟΣ λαγός lagos hare

ΛΑΓΟΣ ΜΕ ΣΑΛΤΣΑ
λαγός με σάλτσα lagos meh
saltsa hare in tomato sauce

ΛΑΓΟΣ ΣΤΙΦΑΔΟ
λαγός στιφάδο lagos stifatho
hare and shallot stew

ΛΑΔΕΡΑ λαδερά lathera in olive
oil and tomato sauce

ΛΑΔΙ λάδι lathi oil

ΛΑΔΟΛΕΜΟΝΟ λαδολέμονο
latholemono olive oil and lemon
dressing

ΛΑΔΟΞΥΔΟ λαδόξυδο
lathoxitho oil and vinegar
salad dressing

ΛΑΖΑΝΙΑ λαζάνια lazania
lasagne

ΛΑΧΑΝΙΚΑ λαχανικά lakhanika
vegetables

ΛΑΧΑΝΙΚΑ ΜΙΚΤΑ
λαχανικά μικτά lakhanika mikta
vegetables

ΛΑΧΑΝΑΚΙΑ ΒΡΥΞΕΛΛΩΝ
λαχανάκια Βρυξελλών
lakhanakia vrixelon
Brussels sprouts

ΛΑΧΑΝΟ λάχανο lakhano
cabbage

ΛΑΧΑΝΟ ΚΟΚΚΙΝΟ
λάχανο κόκκινο lakhano kokino
red cabbage

**ΛΑΧΑΝΟ ΝΤΟΛΜΑΔΕΣ
ΑΥΓΟΛΕΜΟΝΟ** λάχανο
ντολμάδες αυγολέμονο lakhano
dolmathes avgolemono cabbage
leaves stuffed with rice in egg
and lemon sauce

ΛΑΧΑΝΟ ΝΤΟΛΜΑΔΕΣ
λάχανο ντολμάδες
lakhano dolmathes cabbage
leaves stuffed with minced
meat and rice

**ΛΑΧΑΝΟ ΝΤΟΛΜΑΔΕΣ ΜΕ
ΣΑΛΤΣΑ ΝΤΟΜΑΤΑΣ** λάχανο
ντολμάδες με σάλτσα ντομάτας
lakhano dolmathes meh saltsa
domatas vine leaves stuffed with
rice in tomato sauce

ΛΑΧΑΝΟΣΑΛΑΤΑ
λαχανοσαλάτα lakhanosalata
cabbage salad

ΛΕΜΟΝΙ λεμόνι lemoni lemon

ΛΙΘΡΙΝΙ λιθρίνι liTHrini
red snapper

ΛΙΘΡΙΝΙ ΨΗΤΟ λιθρίνι ψητό
liTHrini psito grilled red snapper

ΛΟΥΚΑΝΙΚΑ λουκάνικα
lookanika sausages

ΛΟΥΚΑΝΙΚΑ ΒΡΑΣΤΑ
λουκάνικα βραστά lookanika
vrasta boiled sausages

**ΛΟΥΚΑΝΙΚΑ ΚΑΠΝΙΣΤΑ
ΣΤΗ ΣΧΑΡΑ** λουκάνικα
καπνιστά στη σχάρα
lookanika kapnista sti skhara
grilled smoked sausages

ΛΟΥΚΑΝΙΚΑ ΤΗΓΑΝΗΤΑ
λουκάνικα τηγανητά
lookanika tiganita fried sausages

ΛΟΥΚΟΥΜΑΔΕΣ λουκουμάδες
lookoomathes doughnuts

ΛΟΥΚΟΥΜΙΑ λουκούμια
lookoomia Turkish delight

ΜΑΓΕΙΡΙΤΣΑ μαγειρίτσα
mayiritsa traditional Easter soup
made from lambs' intestines

ΜΑΓΙΑ μαγιά maya yeast

ΜΑΓΙΟΝΕΖΑ μαγιονέζα
mayoneza mayonnaise

ΜΑΪΝΤΑΝΟΣ μαϊντανός
maindanos parsley

ΜΑΚΑΡΟΝΑΚΙ ΚΟΦΤΟ
μακαρονάκι κοφτό
makaronaki kofto macaroni

ΜΑΚΑΡΟΝΙΑ μακαρόνια
makaronia pasta

ΜΑΚΑΡΟΝΙΑ ΜΕ ΚΙΜΑ
μακαρόνια με κιμά
makaronia meh kima
spaghetti bolognaise

**ΜΑΚΑΡΟΝΙΑ ΜΕ
ΦΡΕΣΚΟ ΒΟΥΤΥΡΟ ΚΑΙ
ΠΑΡΜΕΖΑΝΑ** μακαρόνια
με φρέσκο βούτυρο και
παρμεζάνα makaronia meh
fresko vootiro keh parmezana
spaghetti with butter and
parmesan cheese

**ΜΑΚΑΡΟΝΙΑ ΠΑΣΤΙΤΣΙΟ
ΜΕ ΚΙΜΑ** μακαρόνια
παστίτσιο με κιμά makaronia
pastitsio meh kima baked pasta
dish with minced meat and
béchamel

ΜΑΝΙΤΑΡΙΑ μανιτάρια manitaria
mushrooms

ΜΑΝΙΤΑΡΙΑ ΤΗΓΑΝΗΤΑ
μανιτάρια τηγανητά manitaria
tiganita fried mushrooms

ΜΑΝΟΥΡΙ μανούρι manoori
hard cheese

ΜΑΝΤΑΡΙΝΙ μανταρίνι
mandarini satsuma, tangerine

ΜΑΡΓΑΡΙΝΗ μαργαρίνη
margarini margarine

ΜΑΡΙΔΕΣ ΤΗΓΑΝΗΤΕΣ
μαρίδες τηγανητές marithes
tiganites small fried fish

ΜΑΡΜΕΛΑΔΑ μαρμελάδα
marmelatha jam, marmalade

ΜΑΡΜΕΛΑΔΑ ΒΕΡΥΚΟΚΚΑ
μαρμελάδα βερύκοκκα
marmelatha verikoka apricot jam

ΜΑΡΜΕΛΑΔΑ ΠΟΡΤΟΚΑΛΙ
μαρμελάδα πορτοκάλι
marmelatha portokali orange jam

ΜΑΡΜΕΛΑΔΑ ΡΟΔΑΚΙΝΑ
μαρμελάδα ροδάκινα
marmelatha pothakina peach jam

ΜΑΡΜΕΛΑΔΑ ΦΡΑΟΥΛΕΣ
μαρμελάδα φράουλες
marmelatha fraooles
strawberry jam

ΜΑΡΟΥΛΙ μαρούλι marooli lettuce

ΜΑΡΟΥΛΙΑ ΣΑΛΑΤΑ
μαρούλια σαλάτα
maroolia salata green salad

ΜΕ ΛΑΔΟΛΕΜΟΝΟ
με λαδολέμονο meh latholemono
with olive oil and lemon
dressing

ΜΕΛΙ μέλι meli honey

Travel tip The best honey
comes from the less for-
ested Greek islands, including
Limnos, Naxos, Kalymnos,
Fourni and Astypalea, plus
areas of the mainland. There's
no enforced quality control,
however, and adulteration
scams abound; much that is
touted as thyme honey isn't.
Always taste if possible – if
not, only buy a small jar.

ΜΕΛΙΤΖΑΝΕΣ μελιτζάνες
melidzanes aubergines/
eggplants

**ΜΕΛΙΤΖΑΝΕΣ
ΓΕΜΙΣΤΕΣ ΜΕ ΚΙΜΑ**
μελιτζάνες γεμιστές με κιμά
melitzanes yemistes meh kima
aubergines/eggplants stuffed
with minced meat

ΜΕΛΙΤΖΑΝΕΣ ΓΙΑΧΝΙ
μελιτζάνες γιαχνί melitzanes
yakhni aubergines/eggplants
with tomato and onions

**ΜΕΛΙΤΖΑΝΕΣ ΙΜΑΜ
ΜΠΑΪΛΝΤΙ** μελιτζάνες ιμάμ
μπαϊλντί melitzanes imam baildi
aubergines/eggplants with
garlic and tomato

ΜΕΛΙΤΖΑΝΕΣ ΜΟΥΣΑΚΑ
μελιτζάνες μουσακά melidzanes
moosaka layers of aubergine/
eggplant and minced meat
topped with béchamel

**ΜΕΛΙΤΖΑΝΕΣ
ΠΑΠΟΥΤΣΑΚΙΑ**
μελιτζάνες παπουτσάκια
melidzaness papootsakia
stuffed aubergines/eggplants

ΜΕΛΙΤΖΑΝΕΣ ΤΗΓΑΝΗΤΕΣ
μελιτζάνες τηγανητές
melitzanes tiganites fried
aubergines/eggplants

ΜΕΛΙΤΖΑΝΟΣΑΛΑΤΑ
μελιτζανοσαλάτα
melidzanosalata puréed
aubergine/eggplant dip

ΜΕΛΟΜΑΚΑΡΟΝΑ
μελομακάρονα melomakarona
sweet cakes with cinammon,
nuts and syrup

ΜΕΝΟΥ μενού menoo menu

ΜΕ ΣΑΛΤΣΑ με σάλτσα
meh saltsa with sauce, usually
tomato sauce

ΜΗΛΑ ΓΕΜΙΣΤΑ
μήλα γεμιστά mila yemista
stuffed apples with cinammon

ΜΗΛΟ μήλο milo apple

ΜΗΛΟΠΙΤΤΑ μηλόπιττα milopita
apple pie

μισοψημένο misopsimeno
medium (steak)

ΜΟΣΧΑΡΙ μοσχάρι
moskhari veal; tender beef

ΜΟΣΧΑΡΙ ΒΡΑΣΤΟ
μοσχάρι βραστό moskhari vrasto
veal stew

ΜΟΣΧΑΡΙ ΚΟΚΚΙΝΙΣΤΟ
μοσχάρι κοκκινιστό
moskhari kokinisto
veal in tomato sauce

ΜΟΣΧΑΡΙ ΜΕ ΑΡΑΚΑ
μοσχάρι με αρακά moskhari meh
araka veal with peas

ΜΟΣΧΑΡΙ ΜΕ ΚΡΙΘΑΡΑΚΙ
μοσχάρι με κριθαράκι
moskhari meh kriTHaraki
veal with pasta

**ΜΟΣΧΑΡΙ ΜΕ
ΜΕΛΙΤΖΑΝΕΣ** μοσχάρι
με μελιτζάνες moskhari
meh melitzanes veal with
aubergines/eggplants

ΜΟΣΧΑΡΙ ΜΕ ΜΠΑΜΙΕΣ
μοσχάρι με μπάμιες moskhari
meh bami-es veal with okra

ΜΟΣΧΑΡΙ ΜΕ ΠΑΤΑΤΕΣ
μοσχάρι με πατάτες moskhari
meh patates veal with potatoes

ΜΟΣΧΑΡΙ ΜΕ ΠΑΤΑΤΕΣ
ΣΤΟ ΦΟΥΡΝΟ μοσχάρι με
πατάτες στο φούρνο moskhari
meh patates sto foorno veal with
potatoes cooked in the oven

ΜΟΣΧΑΡΙ ΜΕ ΠΟΥΡΕ
μοσχάρι με πουρέ
moskhari meh pooreh
veal with mashed potatoes

ΜΟΣΧΑΡΙ ΜΕ ΦΑΣΟΛΑΚΙΑ
μοσχάρι με φασολάκια
moskhari meh fasolakia
veal and green beans

ΜΟΣΧΑΡΙ ΡΟΣΜΠΙΦ
μοσχάρι ροσμπίφ
moskhari rosbif roast beef

ΜΟΣΧΑΡΙΣΙΟΣ ΚΙΜΑΣ
μοσχαρίσιος κιμάς mos-
kharisios kimas minced meat

ΜΟΣΧΑΡΙ ΣΝΙΤΖΕΛ ΜΕ
ΠΑΤΑΤΕΣ ΤΗΓΑΝΗΤΕΣ
μοσχάρι σνίτζελ με πατάτες
τηγανητές moskhari schnitzel
meh patates tiganites
steak and chips/fries

ΜΟΣΧΑΡΙ ΣΝΙΤΖΕΛ ΜΕ
ΠΟΥΡΕ μοσχάρι σνίτζελ
με πουρέ moskhari schnitzel
meh patates pooreh steak with
mashed potatoes

ΜΟΣΧΑΡΙ ΨΗΤΟ μοσχάρι
ψητό moskhari psito veal pot roast

ΜΟΥΣΑΚΑΣ μουσακάς
moosakas moussaka – layers of
vegetables and minced meat
topped with béchamel sauce

ΜΟΥΣΑΚΑΣ ΠΑΤΑΤΕΣ
μουσακάς πατάτες moosakas
patates potatoes with minced
meat and béchamel

ΜΟΥΣΤΑΡΔΑ μουστάρδα
moostartha mustard

ΜΟΥΣΤΟΚΟΥΛΟΥΡΑ
μουστοκούλουρα
moostokooloora Greek biscuits

ΜΠΑΚΑΛΙΑΡΟΣ
μπακαλιάρος bakaliaros
cod; salt cod; haddock

ΜΠΑΚΑΛΙΑΡΟΣ ΚΡΟΚΕΤΕΣ
μπακαλιάρος κροκέτες
bakaliaros kroketes
haddock croquettes

ΜΠΑΚΑΛΙΑΡΟΣ ΠΛΑΚΙ
μπακαλιάρος πλακί
bakaliaros plaki salted cod
cooked in tomato sauce

ΜΠΑΚΑΛΙΑΡΟΣ
ΤΗΓΑΝΗΤΟΣ μπακαλιάρος
τηγανητός bakaliaros tiganitos
fried salted cod

ΜΠΑΚΛΑΒΑΔΕΣ μπακλαβάδες
baklavathes baklava – layers of
thin pastry with nuts and syrup

ΜΠΑΚΛΑΒΑΔΕΣ ΜΕ
ΚΑΡΥΔΙΑ μπακλαβάδες με
καρύδια baklavathes meh karithia
baklava – layers of thin pastry
with walnuts and syrup

ΜΠΑΚΛΑΒΑΣ μπακλαβάς
baklavas baklava – filo pastry
with nuts and syrup

ΜΠΑΜΙΕΣ μπάμιες
bami-es okra

ΜΠΑΜΙΕΣ ΛΑΔΕΡΕΣ
μπάμιες λαδερές bami-es
latheres okra in olive oil and
tomato sauce

ΜΠΑΝΑΝΑ μπανάνα
banana banana

ΜΠΑΡΜΠΟΥΝΙΑ μπαρμπούνια
barboonia red mullet

ΜΠΑΡΜΠΟΥΝΙΑ ΠΑΝΕ
μπαρμπούνια πανέ barboonia
paneh breaded red mullet

ΜΠΑΧΑΡΙΚΟ μπαχαρικό
bakhariko spice

ΜΠΕΖΕΔΕΣ μπεζέδες bezethes
meringues with cream

ΜΠΕΙΚΟΝ μπέικον bacon bacon

ΜΠΕΙΚΟΝ ΚΑΠΝΙΣΤΟ
μπέικον καπνιστό bacon
kapnisto smoked bacon

ΜΠΕΣΑΜΕΛ ΣΑΛΤΣΑ
μπεσαμέλ σάλτσα besamel
saltsa béchamel sauce

ΜΠΙΖΕΛΙΑ μπιζέλια bizelia peas

ΜΠΙΣΚΟΤΑ μπισκότα biskota
biscuits

ΜΠΙΣΚΟΤΑΚΙΑ ΑΛΜΥΡΑ
μπισκοτάκια αλμυρά biskotakia
almira savoury crackers

ΜΠΙΣΚΟΤΑ ΣΟΚΟΛΑΤΑΣ
μπισκότα σοκολάτας biskota
sokolatas chocolate biscuits

ΜΠΙΦΤΕΚΙ μπιφτέκι bifteki
hamburger; grilled meatballs

ΜΠΟΝ ΦΙΛΕ μπον φιλέ
bon fileh fillet steak

ΜΠΟΥΓΑΤΣΑ μπουγάτσα
boogatsa puff pastry with
various fillings

ΜΠΟΥΓΑΤΣΑ ΓΛΥΚΙΑ
μπουγάτσα γλυκιά boogatsa
glikia puff pastry with cream
and icing sugar

ΜΠΟΥΡΕΚΑΚΙΑ μπουρεκάκια
boorekakia cheese or minced
meat pies

ΜΠΟΥΡΕΚΙ μπουρέκι
booreki courgette, potato and
cheese pie

ΜΠΡΙΑΜΙ μπριάμι briami
ratatouille

**ΜΠΡΙΑΜΙ ΜΕ
ΚΟΛΟΚΥΘΑΚΙΑ**
μπριάμι με κολοκυθάκια briami
meh kolokiTHakia
courgettes/zucchini cooked
with potatoes in the oven

ΜΠΡΙΖΟΛΑ μπριζόλα
brizola chop; steak

ΜΠΡΙΖΟΛΑ ΜΟΣΧΑΡΙΣΙΑ
μπριζόλα μοσχαρίσια brizola
moskharisia beef steak

ΜΠΡΙΖΟΛΕΣ μπριζόλες
brizoles chops; steaks

**ΜΠΡΙΖΟΛΕΣ ΒΟΔΙΝΕΣ ΣΤΗ
ΣΧΑΡΑ** μπριζόλες βοδινές στη
σχάρα brizoles vothines sti skhara
grilled T-bone steak

ΜΠΡΙΖΟΛΕΣ ΣΤΟ ΤΗΓΑΝΙ
μπριζόλες στο τηγάνι brizoles
sto tigani fried T-bone steak

ΜΠΡΙΖΟΛΕΣ ΧΟΙΡΙΝΕΣ
μπριζόλες χοιρινές brizoles
khirines pork chops

**ΜΠΡΙΖΟΛΕΣ ΧΟΙΡΙΝΕΣ ΣΤΗ
ΣΧΑΡΑ** μπριζόλες χοιρινές
στη σχάρα brizoles khirines sti
skhara charcoal-grilled pork
chops

ΜΠΡΟΚΟΛΟ μπρόκολο
brokolo broccoli

ΜΥΑΛΑ μυαλά miala brains

ΜΥΑΛΑ ΠΑΝΕ μυαλά πανέ
miala paneh breaded cows'
brains

ΜΥΔΙΑ μύδια mithia mussels
ΜΥΔΙΑ ΤΗΓΑΝΗΤΑ
μύδια τηγανητά mithia tiganita
fried mussels

ΝΕΦΡΑ νεφρά nefra kidneys
ΝΕΦΡΑ ΨΗΤΑ/ΤΗΓΑΝΗΤΑ
νεφρά ψητά/τηγανητά nefra
psita/tiganita grilled/fried kidneys

ΝΤΟΛΜΑΔΑΚΙΑ ντολμαδάκια
dolmathakia vine leaves stuffed
with minced meat, rice and
herbs

ΝΤΟΛΜΑΔΕΣ ντολμάδες
dolmathes vine or cabbage
leaves stuffed with minced
meat and/or rice

ΝΤΟΛΜΑΔΕΣ
ΑΥΓΟΛΕΜΟΝΟ ΜΕ ΚΙΜΑ
ντολμάδες αυγολέμονο με
κιμά dolmathes avgolemono meh
kima vine leaves with rice and
minced meat in egg and lemon
sauce

ΝΤΟΛΜΑΔΕΣ ΓΙΑΛΑΝΤΖΙ
ντολμάδες γιαλαντζί
dolmathes yialantzi vine leaves
stuffed with rice

ΝΤΟΜΑΤΕΣ ντομάτες
domates tomatoes

ΝΤΟΜΑΤΕΣ ΓΕΜΙΣΤΕΣ
ΜΕ ΚΙΜΑ ντομάτες γεμιστές
με κιμά domates yemistes meh
kima stuffed tomatoes with
minced meat

ΝΤΟΜΑΤΕΣ ΓΕΜΙΣΤΕΣ ΜΕ
ΡΥΖΙ ντομάτες γεμιστές με
ρύζι domates yemistes meh rizi
tomatoes stuffed with rice

ΝΤΟΜΑΤΕΣ ΓΕΜΙΣΤΕΣ
ντομάτες γεμιστές domates
yemistes stuffed tomatoes

ΝΤΟΜΑΤΟΣΑΛΑΤΑ
ντοματοσαλάτα domatosalata
tomato salad

ΝΤΟΜΑΤΟΣΟΥΠΑ
ντοματόσουπα domatosoopa
tomato soup

ΝΤΟΝΑΤΣ ντόνατς
doughnuts doughnuts

ΞΗΡΟΙ ΚΑΡΠΟΙ ξηροί καρποί
xiri karpi nuts, dried fruit

ΞΙΦΙΑΣ ξιφίας xifias swordfish

ΞΥΔΙ ξύδι xithi vinegar

ΟΜΕΛΕΤΑ ομελέτα omeleta
omelette

ΟΜΕΛΕΤΑ ΛΟΥΚΑΝΙΚΑ
ομελέτα λουκάνικα omeleta
lookanika omelette with
sausages

ΟΡΕΚΤΙΚΑ ορεκτικά orektika
hors d'oeuvres, starters

ΟΣΤΡΑΚΟΕΙΔΗ οστρακοειδή
ostrako-ithi shellfish

ΠΑΓΩΤΟ παγωτό pagoto
ice cream

ΠΑΓΩΤΟ ΒΕΡΥΚΟΚΚΟ
παγωτό βερύκοκκο pagoto
verikoko apricot ice cream

ΠΑΓΩΤΟ ΚΟΚΤΑΙΗΛ
παγωτό κοκταίηλ pagoto cocktail
ice cream cocktail

ΠΑΓΩΤΟ ΚΡΕΜΑ
παγωτό κρέμα pagoto krema
vanilla ice cream

ΠΑΓΩΤΟ ΜΕ ΣΑΝΤΙΓΥ
παγωτό με σαντιγύ
pagoto meh sandiyi
ice cream with whipped cream

ΠΑΓΩΤΟ ΜΟΚΚΑ
παγωτό μόκκα pagoto moka
coffee-flavoured ice cream

ΠΑΓΩΤΟ ΜΠΑΝΑΝΑ
παγωτό μπανάνα pagoto banana
banana ice cream

ΠΑΓΩΤΟ ΠΑΡΦΑΙ
παγωτό παρφαί pagoto parfeh
ice cream parfait

ΠΑΓΩΤΟ ΠΡΑΛΙΝΑ
παγωτό πραλίνα pagoto pralina
praline ice cream

ΠΑΓΩΤΟ ΣΟΚΟΛΑΤΑ
παγωτό σοκολάτα pagoto
sokolata chocolate ice cream

ΠΑΓΩΤΟ ΦΡΑΟΥΛΑ
παγωτό φράουλα
pagoto fraoola strawberry
ice cream

ΠΑΓΩΤΟ ΦΥΣΤΙΚΙ
παγωτό φυστίκι pagoto fistiki
pistachio ice cream

ΠΑΞΙΜΑΔΙ παξιμάδι paximathi
dried, hard bread

ΠΑΝΤΖΑΡΙ παντζάρι pandzari
beetroot

ΠΑΠΙΑ πάπια papia duck

ΠΑΠΡΙΚΑ πάπρικα paprika
paprika

ΠΑΡΜΕΖΑΝΑ παρμεζάνα
parmezana parmesan

ΠΑΣΤΑ πάστα pasta cake

ΠΑΣΤΑ ΑΜΥΓΔΑΛΟΥ
πάστα αμυγδάλου pasta
amigthaloo almond gâteau

ΠΑΣΤΑ ΚΟΡΜΟΣ
πάστα κορμός pasta kormos
chocolate log

ΠΑΣΤΑ ΝΟΥΓΚΑΤΙΝΑ πάστα
νουγκατίνα pasta noogatin
cream gâteau

ΠΑΣΤΑ ΣΟΚΟΛΑΤΙΝΑ πάστα
σοκολατίνα pasta sokolatina
chocolate gâteau

ΠΑΣΤΑ ΦΡΑΟΥΛΑ
πάστα φράουλα pasta fraoola
strawberry gâteau

ΠΑΣΤΙΤΣΙΟ παστίτσιο
pastitsio macaroni cheese or
lasagne-type dish, with minced
meat and white sauce

ΠΑΣΤΙΤΣΙΟ ΛΑΖΑΝΙΑ
παστίτσιο λαζάνια pastitsio
lazania lasagne

ΠΑΣΤΙΤΣΙΟ ΜΑΚΑΡΟΝΙΑ
ΜΕ ΚΙΜΑ παστίτσιο
μακαρόνια με κιμά
pastitsio makaronia meh kima
baked pasta dish with minced
meat and béchamel

ΠΑΣΤΟ παστό pasto salted

ΠΑΤΑΤΕΣ πατάτες patates
potatoes

ΠΑΤΑΤΕΣ ΓΑΡΝΙΤΟΥΡΑ
πατάτες γαρνιτούρα
patates garnitoora potatoes

ΠΑΤΑΤΕΣ ΓΙΑΧΝΙ
πατάτες γιαχνί patates yakhni
potatoes cooked with onion
and tomato

ΠΑΤΑΤΕΣ ΚΑΙ
ΚΟΛΟΚΥΘΑΚΙΑ ΣΤΟ
ΦΟΥΡΝΟ πατάτες και
κολοκυθάκια στο φούρνο
patates keh kolokiTHakia sto

foorno potatoes, courgettes/
zucchini and tomatoes baked
in the oven

ΠΑΤΑΤΕΣ ΚΟΛΟΚΥΘΙΑ
ΜΟΥΣΑΚΑΣ πατάτες
κολοκύθια μουσακάς patates
kolokithia moosakas potatoes
with courgettes/zucchini,
minced meat and cheese sauce

ΠΑΤΑΤΕΣ ΠΟΥΡΕ
πατάτες πουρέ patates pooreh
mashed potatoes

ΠΑΤΑΤΕΣ ΡΙΓΑΝΑΤΕΣ
πατάτες ριγανάτες στο φούρνο
patates riganates sto foorno oven-
cooked potatoes with oregano

ΠΑΤΑΤΕΣ ΣΟΥΦΛΕ
πατάτες σουφλέ patates soofleh
potato soufflé

ΠΑΤΑΤΕΣ ΣΤΟ ΦΟΥΡΝΟ
ΡΙΓΑΝΑΤΕΣ πατάτες στο
φούρνο ριγανάτες patates sto
foorno riganates potatoes baked
in the oven with oregano,
lemon and olive oil

ΠΑΤΑΤΕΣ ΤΗΓΑΝΙΤΕΣ
πατάτες τηγανιτές patates
tiganites chips, French fries

ΠΑΤΑΤΕΣ ΤΣΙΠΣ
πατάτες τσιπς patates tsips
chips, French fries

ΠΑΤΑΤΟΣΑΛΑΤΑ
πατατοσαλάτα patatosalata
potato salad

ΠΑΤΖΑΡΙΑ πατζάρια patzaria
beetroot

ΠΑΤΣΑΣ πατσάς patsas tripe;
soup made from lambs'
intestines

ΠΑΤΣΑΣ ΣΟΥΠΑ
πατσάς σούπα
patsas soopa tripe soup

ΠΕΠΟΝΙ πεπόνι peponi melon

ΠΕΣΤΡΟΦΑ πέστροφα
pestrofa trout

ΠΕΣΤΡΟΦΑ ΨΗΤΗ
πέστροφα ψητή pestrofa psiti
grilled trout

ΠΗΧΤΗ πηχτή pikhti
potted meat

ΠΙΛΑΦΙ πιλάφι pilafi rice

ΠΙΛΑΦΙ ΜΕ ΓΑΡΙΔΕΣ πιλάφι
με γαρίδες pilafi meh garithes
shrimp pilaf

ΠΙΛΑΦΙ ΜΕ ΜΥΔΙΑ
πιλάφι με μύδια pilafi meh mithia
pilaf with mussels

ΠΙΛΑΦΙ ΜΕ ΣΑΛΤΣΑ
ΝΤΟΜΑΤΑ πιλάφι με σάλτσα
ντομάτα pilafi meh saltsa domata
pilaf with tomato sauce

ΠΙΛΑΦΙ ΤΑΣ-ΚΕΜΠΑΠ
πιλάφι τας-κεμπάπ pilafi tas
kebab rice with cubes of beef in
tomato sauce

ΠΙΠΕΡΙ πιπέρι piperi pepper
(spice)

ΠΙΠΕΡΙΕΣ πιπεριές piperi-es
peppers

ΠΙΠΕΡΙΕΣ ΓΕΜΙΣΤΕΣ ΜΕ
ΚΙΜΑ πιπεριές γεμιστές με
κιμά piperi-es yemistes meh kima
peppers stuffed with minced
meat

ΠΙΠΕΡΙΕΣ ΓΕΜΙΣΤΕΣ ΜΕ
ΡΥΖΙ πιπεριές γεμιστές με
ρύζι piperi-es yemistes meh rizi
peppers stuffed with rice

ΠΙΠΕΡΙΕΣ ΓΕΜΙΣΤΕΣ
πιπεριές γεμιστές piperi-es
yemistes stuffed peppers

ΠΙΠΕΡΙΕΣ ΚΟΚΚΙΝΕΣ
πιπεριές κόκκινες piperi-es
kokines red peppers

ΠΙΠΕΡΙΕΣ ΠΡΑΣΙΝΕΣ
πιπεριές πράσινες piperi-es
prasines green peppers

ΠΙΡΟΣΚΙ πιροσκί piroski minced
meat or sausage rolls

ΠΙΤΣΑ πίτσα pizza pizza

ΠΙΤΣΑ ΜΕ ΖΑΜΠΟΝ
πίτσα με ζαμπόν pizza meh
zabon ham pizza

ΠΙΤΣΑ ΜΕ ΜΑΝΙΤΑΡΙΑ
πίτσα με μανιτάρια pizza meh
manitaria mushroom pizza

ΠΙΤΣΑ ΜΕ ΝΤΟΜΑΤΑ ΤΥΡΙ
πίτσα με ντομάτα τυρί pizza
meh domata tiri cheese and
tomato pizza

ΠΙΤΣΑ ΣΠΕΣΙΑΛ
πίτσα σπέσιαλ pizza special
special pizza

ΠΙΤΤΑ πίττα pita pie

ΠΙΤΤΑ ΜΕ ΚΙΜΑ
πίττα με κιμά pita meh kima
minced meat pie

ΠΛΑΚΙ πλακί plaki baked in the
oven in a tomato sauce

πολύ ψημένο poli psimeno
overdone

ΠΟΡΤΟΚΑΛΙ πορτοκάλι
portokali orange

ΠΟΥΛΕΡΙΚΑ πουλερικά poulerika
poultry

ΠΟΥΤΙΓΚΑ πουτίγκα
pootiga pudding

ΠΟΥΤΙΓΚΑ ΜΕ ΑΝΑΝΑ
πουτίγκα με ανανά pootiga meh
anana pineapple pudding

ΠΟΥΤΙΓΚΑ ΜΕ ΚΑΡΥΔΙΑ
πουτίγκα με καρύδια pootiga
meh karithia walnut pudding

ΠΟΥΤΙΓΚΑ ΜΕ ΣΤΑΦΙΔΕΣ
πουτίγκα με σταφίδες pootiga
meh stafithes sultana pudding

ΠΡΑΣΑ πράσα prasa leeks

ΠΡΑΣΟΠΙΤΤΑ πρασόπιττα
prasopita leek pie

ΠΡΩΤΟ ΠΙΑΤΟ πρώτο πιάτο
proto piato starter

PABANI ραβανί ravani
very sweet sponge cake

ΡΑΒΙΟΛΙΑ ραβιόλια
raviolia ravioli

ΡΙΓΑΝΗ ρίγανη rigani oregano

ΡΟΔΑΚΙΝΟ ροδάκινο
rothakino peaches

ΡΟΣΜΠΙΦ ΑΡΝΙ ΜΟΣΧΑΡΙ
ροσμπίφ αρνί μοσχάρι
rozbif arni moskhari
roast beef, veal or lamb

ΡΥΖΙ ρύζι rizi rice

ΡΥΖΟΓΑΛΟ ρυζόγαλο
rizogalo rice pudding

ΡΩΣΙΚΗ ΣΑΛΑΤΑ
ρώσικη σαλάτα rosiki salata
Russian salad

ΣΑΛΑΜΙ σαλάμι salami salami

ΣΑΛΑΤΑ σαλάτα salata salad

ΣΑΛΑΤΑ ΑΜΠΕΛΟΦΑΣΟΥΛΑ
σαλάτα αμπελοφάσουλα salata
abelofasoola runner bean salad

ΣΑΛΑΤΑ ΚΟΥΝΟΥΠΙΔΙ ΒΡΑΣΤΟ σαλάτα κουνουπίδι βραστό salata koonoopithi vrasto boiled cauliflower salad

ΣΑΛΑΤΑ ΜΑΡΟΥΛΙΑ σαλάτα μαρούλια salata maroolia lettuce salad

ΣΑΛΑΤΑ ΝΤΟΜΑΤΕΣ ΚΑΙ ΑΓΓΟΥΡΙΑ σαλάτα ντομάτες και αγγούρια salata domates keh agooria tomato and cucumber salad

ΣΑΛΑΤΑ ΝΤΟΜΑΤΕΣ-ΠΙΠΕΡΙΕΣ σαλάτα ντομάτες-πιπεριές salata domates piperi-es tomato and green pepper salad

ΣΑΛΑΤΑ ΣΠΑΡΑΓΓΙΑ σαλάτα σπαράγγια salata sparagia asparagus salad

ΣΑΛΑΤΑ ΦΑΣΟΛΙΑ ΞΗΡΑ σαλάτα φασόλια ξηρά salata fasolia xira butter bean salad

ΣΑΛΑΤΑ ΧΟΡΤΑ ΒΡΑΣΜΕΝΑ σαλάτα χόρτα βρασμένα salata khorta vrasmena chicory salad

ΣΑΛΑΤΑ ΧΩΡΙΑΤΙΚΗ σαλάτα χωριάτικη salata khoriatiki Greek salad – tomatoes, cucumber, peppers, feta, olives and boiled eggs with olive oil and vinegar dressing

ΣΑΛΙΓΚΑΡΙΑ σαλιγκάρια saligaria snails

ΣΑΛΤΣΑ σάλτσα saltsa sauce

ΣΑΛΤΣΑ ΜΠΕΣΑΜΕΛ σάλτσα μπεσαμέλ saltsa besamel béchamel sauce

ΣΑΛΤΣΑ ΝΤΟΜΑΤΑ σάλτσα ντομάτα saltsa domata tomato sauce

ΣΑΜΑΛΙ σάμαλι samali semolina cake with honey

ΣΑΝΤΙΓΥ σαντιγύ sandiyi whipped cream

ΣΑΝΤΟΥΙΤΣ σάντουιτς sandwich sandwich

ΣΑΡΔΕΛΛΕΣ σαρδέλλες sartheles sardines

ΣΑΡΔΕΛΛΕΣ ΛΑΔΙΟΥ σαρδέλλες λαδιού sartheles lathioo sardines in oil

ΣΕΛΙΝΟ σέλινο selino celery

ΣΙΜΙΓΔΑΛΙ σιμιγδάλι simigthali semolina

ΣΙΡΟΠΙ σιρόπι siropi syrup

ΣΚΟΡΔΑΛΙΑ σκορδαλιά skorthalia thick garlic sauce

ΣΚΟΡΔΑΛΙΑ ΜΕ ΨΩΜΙ σκορδαλιά με ψωμί skorthalia meh psomi thick garlic sauce made with bread

ΣΚΟΡΔΟ σκόρδο skortho garlic

ΣΟΚΟΛΑΤΑΚΙΑ σοκολατάκια sokolatakia little chocolate cakes; milk chocolates

ΣΟΛΟΜΟΣ σολομός solomos salmon

ΣΟΛΟΜΟΣ ΚΑΠΝΙΣΤΟΣ σολομός καπνιστός solomos kapnistos smoked salmon

ΣΟΥΒΛΑΚΙΑ σουβλάκια soovlakia meat grilled on a skewer, served in pitta bread

ΣΟΥΒΛΑΚΙΑ ΑΠΟ ΚΡΕΑΣ ΑΡΝΙΣΙΟ σουβλάκια από κρέας αρνίσιο soovlakia apo kreas arnisio lamb souvlaki/ kebab

ΣΟΥΒΛΑΚΙΑ ΑΠΟ ΚΡΕΑΣ ΜΟΣΧΑΡΙΣΙΟ σουβλάκια από κρέας μοσχαρίσιο soovlakia apo kreas moskharisio veal souvlaki/kebab

ΣΟΥΒΛΑΚΙΑ ΑΠΟ ΚΡΕΑΣ ΧΟΙΡΙΝΟ σουβλάκια από κρέας χοιρινό soovlakia apo kreas khirino pork souvlaki/ kebab

ΣΟΥΒΛΑΚΙΑ ΝΤΟΝΕΡ ΜΕ ΠΙΤΤΑ σουβλάκια ντονέρ με πίττα soovlaki doner meh pita donner kebab with pitta bread

ΣΟΥΒΛΑΚΙ ΚΑΛΑΜΑΚΙ σουβλάκι καλαμάκι soovlaki kalamaki shish kebab

ΣΟΥΠΑ σούπα soopa soup

ΣΟΥΠΑ ΠΑΤΣΑΣ σούπα πατσάς soopa patsas tripe soup

ΣΟΥΠΑ ΡΕΒΥΘΙΑ σούπα ρεβύθια soopa reviTHia chickpea soup

ΣΟΥΠΑ ΤΡΑΧΑΝΑΣ σούπα τραχανάς soopa trakhanas milk broth with flour

ΣΟΥΠΑ ΦΑΚΕΣ σούπα φακές soopa fakes lentil soup

ΣΟΥΠΑ ΦΑΣΟΛΙΑ σούπα φασόλια soopa fasolia bean soup

ΣΟΥΠΑ ΨΑΡΙ σούπα ψάρι soopa psari fish soup

ΣΟΥΠΑ ΨΑΡΙ ΑΥΓΟΛΕΜΟΝΟ σούπα ψάρι αυγολέμονο soopa psari avgolemono fish soup with egg and lemon

ΣΟΥΠΕΣ σούπες soopes soups

ΣΟΥΠΙΕΣ σουπιές soopi-es cuttlefish

ΣΟΥΠΙΕΣ ΜΕ ΣΠΑΝΑΚΙ σουπιές με σπανάκι soopi-es meh spanaki cuttlefish and spinach stew

ΣΟΥΠΙΕΣ ΤΗΓΑΝΗΤΕΣ σουπιές τηγανητές soopi-es tiganites fried cuttlefish

ΣΟΥΣΑΜΙ σουσάμι soosami sesame

ΣΟΥΤΖΟΥΚΑΚΙΑ σουτζουκάκια sootzookakia spicy meatballs in red sauce

ΣΟΥΦΛΕ σουφλέ soofleh soufflé

ΣΠΑΓΓΕΤΟ ΜΕ ΦΡΕΣΚΟ ΒΟΥΤΥΡΟ ΚΑΙ ΠΑΡΜΕΖΑΝΑ σπαγγέτο με φρέσκο βούτυρο και παρμεζάνα spageto meh fresko vootiro keh parmezana spaghetti with butter and parmesan cheese

ΣΠΑΝΑΚΙ σπανάκι spanaki spinach

ΣΠΑΝΑΚΟΠΙΤΤΑ
σπανακόπιττα spanakopita
spinach (and sometimes feta)
in filo pastry

σπάνιος spanios rare (steak)

ΣΠΑΡΑΓΓΙΑ ΣΑΛΑΤΑ
σπαράγγια σαλάτα sparagia
salata asparagus salad

ΣΠΕΣΙΑΛΙΤΕ σπεσιαλιτέ
spesialiteh speciality

ΣΠΛΗΝΑΝΤΕΡΟ σπληνάντερο
splinandero intestines stuffed
with spleen

ΣΤΑΦΙΔΕΣ σταφίδες
stafithes dried fruit

ΣΤΑΦΙΔΟΨΩΜΟ σταφιδόψωμο
stafithopsomo bread with raisins

ΣΤΑΦΥΛΙΑ σταφύλια
stafilia grapes

ΣΤΙΦΑΔΟ στιφάδο stifatho
chopped meat with onions;
hare or rabbit stew with onions

ΣΤΟ ΦΟΥΡΝΟ στο φούρνο
sto foorno baked in the oven

ΣΤΡΕΙΔΙΑ στρείδια strithia
oysters

ΣΥΚΑ σύκα sika figs

ΣΥΚΩΤΑΚΙΑ συκωτάκια
sikotakia liver

ΣΥΚΩΤΑΚΙΑ ΜΑΡΙΝΑΤΑ
συκωτάκια μαρινάτα
sikotakia marinata liver cooked
in rosemary

ΣΥΚΩΤΑΚΙΑ ΠΙΛΑΦΙ
συκωτάκια πιλάφι sikotakia pilafi
liver pilaf

ΣΥΚΩΤΑΚΙΑ ΣΤΗ ΣΧΑΡΑ
συκωτάκια στη σχάρα sikotakia
sti skhara grilled liver

ΣΥΚΩΤΑΚΙΑ ΤΗΓΑΝΗΤΑ
συκωτάκια τηγανητά sikotakia
tiganita fried liver

ΣΥΚΩΤΙ ΨΗΤΟ συκώτι ψητό
sikoti psito charcoal-grilled liver

ΣΥΝΑΓΡΙΔΑ ΨΗΤΗ συναγρίδα
ψητή sinagritha psiti grilled sea
bream

ΣΦΥΡΙΔΑ ΒΡΑΣΤΗ
σφυρίδα βραστή sriritha vrasti
boiled pike

ΣΩΤΕ σωτέ soteh
lightly fried, sautéed

ΤΑΡΑΜΑΣ ταραμάς
taramas cod roe

ΤΑΡΑΜΟΚΕΦΤΕΔΕΣ
ταραμοκεφτέδες
taramokeftethes
roe pâté balls with spices

ΤΑΡΑΜΟΣΑΛΑΤΑ
ταραμοσαλάτα
taramosalata cod roe dip

ΤΑΡΤΑ τάρτα tarta tart

ΤΑΡΤΑ ΜΕ ΚΕΡΑΣΙΑ
τάρτα με κεράσια tarta meh
kerasia cherry tart

**ΤΑΡΤΑ ΜΕ ΚΡΕΜΑ ΚΑΙ
ΑΜΥΓΔΑΛΑ** τάρτα με κρέμα
και αμύγδαλα tarta meh krema
keh amigthala cream and
almond tart

**ΤΑΡΤΑ ΜΕ ΚΡΕΜΑ ΚΑΙ
ΚΑΡΥΔΙΑ** τάρτα με κρέμα και
καρύδια tarta meh krema keh
karithia walnut and cream tart

ΤΑΡΤΑ ΜΕ ΦΡΑΟΥΛΕΣ τάρτα
με φράουλες tarta meh fraooles
strawberry tart

ΤΑΡΤΑ ΜΗΛΟΥ τάρτα μήλου
tarta miloo apple tart

ΤΑΣ-ΚΕΜΠΑΠΙ τας-κεμπάπ
tas kebab spicy lamb cutlets

ΤΑΣ-ΚΕΜΠΑΠΙ ΠΙΛΑΦΙ
τας-κεμπάπ πιλάφι
tas kebab pilafi spicy lamb
cutlets pilaf

ΤΖΑΤΖΙΚΙ τζατζίκι
dzadziki yoghurt, cucumber
and garlic dip

ΤΗΓΑΝΗΤΟΣ τηγανητός
tiganitos fried

ΤΗΓΑΝΙΤΕΣ τηγανίτες
tiganites pancakes

ΤΗΣ ΚΑΤΣΑΡΟΛΑΣ
της κατσαρόλας
tis katsarolas casseroled

ΤΗΣ ΣΟΥΒΛΑΣ της σούβλας
tis soovlas roast on a spit

ΤΗΣ ΣΧΑΡΑΣ της σχάρας
tis skharas grilled over charcoal

ΤΟΝΝΟΣ τόννος tonos tuna

ΤΟΝΝΟΣΑΛΑΤΑ τοννοσαλάτα
tonosalata tuna salad

ΤΟΣΤ τοστ tost
toasted sandwich

ΤΟΣΤ ΚΛΑΜΠ τοστ κλαμπ
tost club toasted club sandwich

ΤΟΣΤ ΜΕ ΑΥΓΟ
τοστ με αυγό tost meh avgo
toasted egg sandwich

ΤΟΣΤ ΜΕ ΖΑΜΠΟΝ
τοστ με ζαμπόν tost meh zabon
toasted ham sandwich

ΤΟΣΤ ΜΕ ΚΟΤΟΠΟΥΛΟ
τοστ με κοτόπουλο
tost meh kotopoolo
toasted chicken sandwich

ΤΟΣΤ ΜΕ ΚΡΕΑΣ
τοστ με κρέας tost meh kreas
toasted meat sandwich

ΤΟΣΤ ΜΕ ΜΠΙΦΤΕΚΙ
τοστ με μπιφτέκι tost meh bifteki
toasted hamburger

ΤΟΣΤ ΜΕ ΤΥΡΙ
τοστ με τυρί tost meh tiri toasted
cheese sandwich

ΤΟΥ ΑΤΜΟΥ του ατμού
too atmoo steamed

ΤΟΥΡΣΙ τουρσί toorsi pickled

ΤΟΥΡΤΑ τούρτα toorta gâteau

ΤΟΥΡΤΑ ΑΜΥΓΔΑΛΟΥ
τούρτα αμυγδάλου toorta
amigthaloo almond gâteau

**ΤΟΥΡΤΑ ΚΡΕΜΑ ΜΕ
ΦΡΑΟΥΛΕΣ**
τούρτα κρέμα με φράουλες
toorta krema meh fraooles
strawberry cream gâteau

ΤΟΥΡΤΑ ΜΟΚΚΑ τούρτα
μόκκα toorta moka coffee gâteau

ΤΟΥΡΤΑ ΝΟΥΓΚΑΤΙΝΑ
τούρτα νουγκατίνα toorta
noogatina nougat gâteau

ΤΟΥΡΤΑ ΣΑΝΤΙΓΥ
τούρτα σαντιγύ toorta sandiyi
whipped cream gâteau

ΤΟΥΡΤΑ ΣΟΚΟΛΑΤΑΣ
τούρτα σοκολάτας toorta
sokolatas chocolate gâteau

ΤΡΟΥΦΑΚΙΑ τρουφάκια troofakia
small chocolate fudge cake

ΤΣΙΠΟΥΡΕΣ τσιπούρες tsipoores
sea bream

ΤΣΙΠΟΥΡΕΣ ΨΗΤΕΣ
τσιπούρες ψητές tsipoores psites
roast sea bream

ΤΣΙΠΣ τσιπς tsips
crisps, (US) potato chips

ΤΣΟΥΡΕΚΙ τσουρέκι
tsooreki light sponge

ΤΣΟΥΡΕΚΙΑ τσουρέκια tsoorekia
sweet bread with fresh butter
(Christmas/Easter dish)

ΤΥΡΙ τυρί tiri cheese

ΤΥΡΙΑ τυριά tiria cheese

ΤΥΡΟΠΙΤΤΑ τυρόπιττα tiropita
cheese and egg in filo pastry

ΤΥΡΟΠΙΤΤΑΚΙΑ τυροπιττάκια
tiropitakia small cheese pies

ΦΑΒΑ φάβα fava chick pea soup

ΦΑΚΕΣ φακές fakes lentil soup

ΦΑΣΟΛΑΔΑ φασολάδα
fasolatha bean soup with celery,
carrots and tomatoes

ΦΑΣΟΛΑΚΙΑ φασολάκια
fasolakia green beans

ΦΑΣΟΛΑΚΙΑ ΛΑΔΕΡΑ
φασολάκια λαδερά fasolakia
lathera green beans in olive oil
and tomato sauce

ΦΑΣΟΛΑΚΙΑ ΦΡΕΣΚΑ
ΓΙΑΧΝΙ φασολάκια φρέσκα
γιαχνί fasolakia freska yakhni
runner beans with onion and
tomato

ΦΑΣΟΛΑΚΙΑ ΦΡΕΣΚΑ
ΣΑΛΑΤΑ φασολάκια φρέσκα
σαλάτα fasolakia freska salata
runner bean salad

ΦΑΣΟΛΙΑ φασόλια fasolia
beans

ΦΑΣΟΛΙΑ ΓΙΓΑΝΤΕΣ
ΓΙΑΧΝΙ φασόλια γίγαντες
γιαχνί fasolia yigandes yakhni
butter beans with onion and
tomato

ΦΑΣΟΛΙΑ ΓΙΓΑΝΤΕΣ ΣΤΟ
ΦΟΥΡΝΟ φασόλια γίγαντες

στο **φούρνο** fasolia yigandes
sto foorno oven-cooked butter
beans

ΦΑΣΟΛΙΑ ΓΙΓΑΝΤΕΣ
φασόλια γίγαντες
fasolia yigandes large dried
beans in tomato sauce

ΦΑΣΟΛΙΑ ΣΟΥΠΑ **φασόλια**
σούπα fasolia soopa bean soup

ΦΕΤΑ **φέτα** feta feta cheese

ΦΙΛΕ ΜΙΝΙΟΝ **φιλέ μινιόν**
fileh minion thin fillet steak

ΦΙΛΕΤΟ **φιλέτο** fileto fillet steak

ΦΛΟΓΕΡΕΣ ΜΕ ΚΡΕΜΑ
φλογέρες με κρέμα
floyeres meh krema round
sweets filled with cream

ΦΟΝΤΑΝ **φοντάν** fondan sweets

ΦΟΝΤΑΝ ΑΜΥΓΔΑΛΟΥ
φοντάν αμυγδάλου fondan
amigthaloo almond sweets

ΦΟΝΤΑΝ ΑΠΟ ΚΑΡΥΔΑ
φοντάν από καρύδα fondan apo
karitha coconut sweets

ΦΟΝΤΑΝ ΑΠΟ ΚΑΡΥΔΙΑ
φοντάν από καρύδια
fondan apo karithia
walnut sweets

ΦΟΝΤΑΝ ΙΝΔΙΚΗΣ
ΚΑΡΥΔΑΣ **φοντάν ινδικής**
καρύδας fondan inthikis karithas
coconut sweets

ΦΟΝΤΑΝ ΠΟΡΤΟΚΑΛΙΟΥ
φοντάν πορτοκαλιού fondan
portokali-oo orange sweets

ΦΟΥΝΤΟΥΚΙΑ **φουντούκια**
foondookia hazelnuts

ΦΡΑΟΥΛΕΣ **φράουλες**
fra-ooles strawberries

ΦΡΑΟΥΛΕΣ ΜΕ ΣΑΝΤΙΓΥ
φράουλες με σαντιγύ fra-ooles
meh sandiyi strawberries with
whipped cream

ΦΡΙΚΑΣΕ ΑΡΝΙ **φρικασέ αρνί**
frikaseh arni lamb cooked in
lettuce with cream sauce

ΦΡΟΥΙ-ΓΚΛΑΣΕ **φρουί-γκλασέ**
frooi-glaseh dried assorted
fruits with sugar

ΦΡΟΥΤΑ **φρούτα** froota fruit

ΦΡΟΥΤΟΣΑΛΑΤΑ
φρουτοσαλάτα frootosalata
fruit salad

ΦΡΥΓΑΝΙΑ **φρυγανιά**
frigania toast

ΦΡΥΓΑΝΙΕΣ **φρυγανιές**
frigani-es French toast

ΦΥΛΛΟ ΠΙΤΤΑΣ **φύλλο πίττας**
filo pitas filo pastry

ΦΥΣΤΙΚΙΑ **φυστίκια**
fistikia peanuts

ΦΥΣΤΙΚΙΑ ΑΙΓΙΝΗΣ
φυστίκια Αιγίνης
fistikia Eyinis pistachios

ΧΑΒΙΑΡΙ **χαβιάρι** khaviari caviar

ΧΑΛΒΑΣ **χαλβάς** khalvas
halva, sweet made from
semolina, sesame seeds, nuts
and honey

ΧΑΜΠΟΥΡΓΚΕΡ **χάμπουργκερ**
khamburger hamburger

ΧΗΝΑ **χήνα** khina goose

ΧΟΙΡΙΝΟ **χοιρινό** khirino pork

ΧΟΙΡΙΝΟ ΜΕ ΣΕΛΙΝΟ
χοιρινό με σέλινο khirino
meh selino pork casserole
with celery

ΧΟΙΡΙΝΟ ΠΑΣΤΟ χοιρινό
παστό khirino pasto salted pork

ΧΟΙΡΙΝΟ ΣΟΥΒΛΑΣ
χοιρινό σούβλας khirino soovlas
pork on the spit

ΧΟΙΡΙΝΟ ΣΤΗ ΣΧΑΡΑ
χοιρινό στη σχάρα khirino sti
skhara grilled pork

**ΧΟΙΡΙΝΟ ΦΟΥΡΝΟΥ ΜΕ
ΠΑΤΑΤΕΣ** χοιρινό φούρνου
με πατάτες khirino foornoo meh
patates roast pork with potatoes

ΧΟΡΤΑ ΒΡΑΣΜΕΝΑ ΣΑΛΑΤΑ
χόρτα βρασμένα σαλάτα
khorta vrasmena salata
boiled chicory salad

ΧΟΡΤΑΡΙΚΑ χορταρικά
khortarika vegetables

ΧΟΡΤΟΣΟΥΠΑ χορτόσουπα
khortosoopa vegetable soup

ΧΤΑΠΟΔΑΚΙ ΞΥΔΑΤΟ
χταποδάκι ξυδάτο khtapothaki
xithato pickled octopus

ΧΤΑΠΟΔΙ χταπόδι
khtapothi octopus

ΧΤΑΠΟΔΙ ΒΡΑΣΤΟ
χταπόδι βραστό khtapothi vrasto
boiled octopus

ΧΤΑΠΟΔΙ ΚΡΑΣΑΤΟ χταπόδι
κρασάτο khtapothi krasato
octopus in wine

**ΧΤΑΠΟΔΙ ΜΕ
ΜΑΚΑΡΟΝΑΚΙ**
χταπόδι με μακαρονάκι
khtapothi meh makaronaki
octopus with macaroni

ΧΤΑΠΟΔΙ ΠΙΛΑΦΙ
χταπόδι πιλάφι khtapothi pilafi
octopus pilaf

ΧΤΑΠΟΔΙ ΣΤΙΦΑΔΟ
χταπόδι στιφάδο khtapothi
stifatho octopus with small
onions

ΧΥΛΟΠΙΤΕΣ χυλοπίτες khilopites
tagliatelle

**ΧΥΛΟΠΙΤΕΣ ΜΕ ΒΟΥΤΥΡΟ
ΚΑΙ ΤΥΡΙ** χυλοπίτες με
βούτυρο και τυρί khilopites meh
vootiro keh tiri tagliatelle with
butter and cheese

ΧΥΛΟΠΙΤΕΣ ΜΕ ΚΙΜΑ
χυλοπίτες με κιμά khilopites meh
kima tagliatelle with minced
meat sauce

**ΧΥΛΟΠΙΤΕΣ ΜΕ
ΚΟΤΟΠΟΥΛΟ**
χυλοπίτες με κοτόπουλο
khilopites meh kotopoolo
tagliatelle with chicken

ΧΩΡΙΑΤΙΚΗ ΣΑΛΑΤΑ
χωριάτικη σαλάτα khoriatiki
salata Greek salad – tomatoes,
cucumber, peppers, feta, olives
and boiled eggs with olive oil
and vinegar dressing

ΨΑΡΙ ψάρι psari fish

ΨΑΡΙ ΒΡΑΣΤΟ ΜΑΓΙΟΝΕΖΑ
ψάρι βραστό μαγιονέζα
psari vrasto mayoneza
steamed fish with mayonnaise

ΨΑΡΙΑ ψάρια psaria fish

**ΨΑΡΙΑ ΓΛΩΣΣΕΣ ΒΡΑΣΤΕΣ
ΜΕ ΑΥΓΟΛΕΜΟΝΟ**
ψάρια γλώσσες βραστές με
αυγολέμονο psaria gloses
vrastes meh avgolemono steamed
sole with oil and lemon

ΨΑΡΙΑ ΜΑΡΙΝΑΤΑ ψάρια
μαρινάτα psaria marinata
marinated fish

ΨΑΡΙΑ ΤΗΓΑΝΗΤΑ
ψάρια τηγανητά
psaria tiganita fried fish

ΨΑΡΙΑ ΨΗΤΑ ΣΤΗ ΣΧΑΡΑ
ψάρια ψητά στη σχάρα
psaria psita sti skhara
charcoal-grilled fish

ΨΑΡΟΣΟΥΠΑ ψαρόσουπα
psarosoopa fish soup

ΨΗΤΟ ψητό psito grilled over
charcoal; oven-roasted

ΨΗΤΟ ΣΤΗ ΣΧΑΡΑ ψητό στη
σχάρα psito sti skhara grilled

ΨΩΜΑΚΙ ψωμάκι psomaki roll

ΨΩΜΙ ψωμί psomi bread

ΨΩΜΙ ΑΣΠΡΟ ψωμί άσπρο
psomi aspro white bread

ΨΩΜΙ ΓΙΑ ΤΟΣΤ ψωμί γιά
τοστ psomi ya tost sliced bread

ΨΩΜΙ ΜΑΥΡΟ ψωμί μαύρο
psomi mavro brown bread

ΩΜΟΣ ωμός omos raw

Drink

Essential terms

beer i bira
bottle to bookali
brandy to koniak
coffee o kafes
cup: a cup of... ena flidzani...
fruit juice o khimos frooton
gin to tzin
   a gin and tonic
   ena tzin meh tonik
glass: a glass of... ena potiri...
milk to gala
mineral water
   to emfialomeno nero
orange juice i portokalatha

red wine to kokino krasi
rosé to rozeh
soda (water) i sotha
soft drink to anapsiktiko
sugar i zakhari
tea to tsa-i
tonic (water) to tonik
vodka i votka
water to nero
whisky to whisky
white wine to aspro krasi
wine to kras
wine list o katalogos ton krasion

another..., please
   ali mia..., parakalo

A– Ω

AΕΡΙΟΥΧΟ αεριούχο
aeriookho fizzy

ΑΛΚΟΟΛ αλκοόλ alko-ol
alcohol

ΑΝΑΝΑΣ ΧΥΜΟΣ
ανανάς χυμός ananas khimos
pineapple juice

ΑΝΑΨΥΚΤΙΚΟ αναψυκτικό
anapsiktiko soft drink

ΑΠΕΡΙΤΙΦ απεριτίφ
aperitif aperitif

ΑΣΠΡΟ ΚΡΑΣΙ άσπρο κρασί
aspro krasi white wine

ΒΟΤΚΑ βότκα votka vodka

ΒΥΣΣΙΝΑΔΑ βυσσινάδα
visinatha black cherry juice

ΓΑΛΑ γάλα gala milk

   ΓΑΛΑ ΚΑΚΑΟ γάλα κακάο
   gala kakao chocolate milk

ΓΑΛΛΙΚΟΣ ΚΑΦΕΣ
γαλλικός καφές galikos kafes
filter coffee; French coffee

ΓΛΥΚΟ ΚΡΑΣΙ γλυκό κρασί
gliko krasi sweet wine

ΕΛΛΗΝΙΚΟΣ ΚΑΦΕΣ
ελληνικός καφές
elinikos kafes Greek coffee

ΖΕΣΤΗ ΣΟΚΟΛΑΤΑ
ζεστή σοκολάτα
zesti sokolata hot chocolate

ΚΑΚΑΟ κακάο kakao cocoa

ΚΑΤΑΛΟΓΟΣ ΚΡΑΣΙΩΝ
κατάλογος κρασιών
katalogos krasion wine list

ΚΑΦΕΣ καφές kafes coffee

   ΚΑΦΕΣ ΜΕΤΡΙΟΣ
   καφές μέτριος kafes metrios
   medium-sweet Greek coffee

   ΚΑΦΕΣ ΒΑΡΥΣ ΓΛΥΚΟΣ
   καφές βαρύς γλυκός kafes varis
   glikos sweet Greek coffee

   ΚΑΦΕΣ ΜΕ ΓΑΛΑ
   καφές με γάλα kafes meh gala
   coffee with milk

ΚΟΚΑ ΚΟΛΑ κόκα κόλα
koka kola Coca-Cola

ΚΟΚΚΙΝΟ ΚΡΑΣΙ κόκκινο
κρασί kokino krasi red wine

ΚΟΚΤΕΗΛ κοκτέηλ
kokteil cocktail

ΚΟΝΙΑΚ κονιάκ koniak brandy

ΚΡΑΣΙ κρασί krasi wine

   ΚΡΑΣΙ ΑΣΠΡΟ κρασί άσπρο
   krasi aspro white wine

   ΚΡΑΣΙ ΚΟΚΚΙΝΟ
   κρασί κόκκινο krasi kokino
   red wine

   ΚΡΑΣΙ ΜΑΥΡΟΔΑΦΝΗ
   κρασί μαυροδάφνη krasi
   mavrothafni sweet red wine

   ΚΡΑΣΙ ΡΕΤΣΙΝΑ κρασί
   ρετσίνα krasi retsina retsina

   ΚΡΑΣΙ ΡΟΖΕ κρασί ροζέ
   krasi rozeh rosé wine

   ΚΡΑΣΙ ΤΟΥ ΜΑΓΑΖΙΟΥ
   κρασί του μαγαζιού krasi too
   magazi-oo house wine

ΛΕΜΟΝΑΔΑ **λεμονάδα**
lemonatha lemonade

ΛΙΚΕΡ **λικέρ** liker liqueur

ΜΕΤΑΛΛΙΚΟ ΝΕΡΟ
μεταλλικό νερό
metaliko nero mineral water

ΜΗΛΟΧΥΜΟΣ **μηλοχυμός**
milokhimos apple juice

ΜΠΥΡΑ **μπύρα** bira beer, lager

ΝΕΣΚΑΦΕ **νέσκαφέ** neskafeh
Nescafé, instant coffee

ΝΕΣΚΑΦΕ ΦΡΑΠΕ
νέσκαφέ φραπέ
neskafeh frapeh iced coffee

ΝΕΡΟ **νερό** nero water

ΝΤΟΜΑΤΑ ΧΥΜΟΣ
ντομάτα χυμός
domata khimos tomato juice

> **Travel tip** Ouzo, *tsipouro* and *tsikoudia* are simple spirits of up to 48 percent alcohol distilled from the grape-mash residue of wine-making, and usually flavoured with cinnamon, anise, pear or fennel. There are nearly thirty brands, but the best are reckoned to be from the islands of Lesvos and Samos, or Zitsa and Tyrnavos on the mainland.

ΟΥΖΟ **ούζο** oozo ouzo
ΟΥΙΣΚΥ **ουίσκυ** whisky, scotch

παγάκι παγάκι pagaki ice cube
ΠΑΓΟΣ **πάγος** pagos ice

ΠΟΡΤΟΚΑΛΑΔΑ **πορτοκαλάδα**
portokalatha orange juice

ΠΟΡΤΟΚΑΛΙ ΧΥΜΟΣ
πορτοκάλι χυμός portokali
khimos orange juice

ΠΟΤΑ **ποτά** pota drinks

ΡΑΚΗ **ρακή** raki strong spirit,
eau-de-vie

ΡΕΤΣΙΝΑ **ρετσίνα** retsina retsina

ΡΟΖΕ ΚΡΑΣΙ **ροζέ κρασί**
rozeh krasi rosé wine

ΡΟΥΜΙ **ρούμι** roomi rum

ΣΤΑΦΥΛΙ ΧΥΜΟΣ **σταφύλι**
χυμός stafili khimos grape juice

ΤΖΙΝ **τζιν** tzin gin

ΤΖΙΝ ΜΕ ΤΟΝΙΚ
τζιν με τόνικ
tzin meh tonik gin and tonic

ΤΣΑΙ **τσάι** tsa-i tea

ΤΣΑΙ ΜΕ ΛΕΜΟΝΙ
τσάι με λεμόνι
tsa-i meh lemoni lemon tea

ΤΣΙΠΟΥΡΟ **τσίπουρο**
tsipooro type of ouzo

ΦΡΑΠΕ **φραπέ** frapeh iced coffee

ΧΥΜΟΣ **χυμός** khimos juice
ΧΩΡΙΣ ΚΑΦΕΪΝΗ
χωρίς καφεΐ΄νη
khoris kafeini decaffeinated

Picture credits

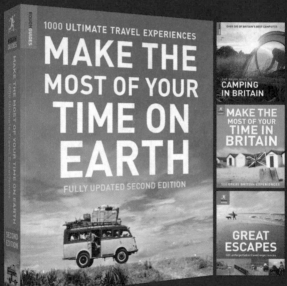